THE DYNAMIC FAMILY

(A Study in the Development of Growth Within
the Family, the Treatment of Family Disorders,
and the Training of Family Therapists)

by

Shirley Gehrke Luthman, L.C.S.W.

with

Martin Kirschenbaum, Ph.D.

SCIENCE AND BEHAVIOR BOOKS, INC.
Palo Alto, California

Library of Congress Card Number 74-84560

ISBN *0-8314-0037-4*

DEDICATED

To each other with respect and affection

and

To Virginia Satir, the Master Teacher

CONTENTS

Contents

FOREWORD

Much has happened since something called family therapy made its little-heralded debut in the middle fifties. At that time there began to emerge the germ of the idea that a person's symptom had something to do with the family from which he came—the nuclear family—and also with the family to which he currently belonged. This idea was largely born out of the despair of therapists struggling how to ameliorate the plight of an individual labeled "schizophrenic" in a context of secrecy and isolation.

As with all new ideas, this one was met with fear and resistance on the part of many in the helping professions and excited interest and promise from a few others. Some therapists began to question the then-used methods of interpreting symptomology. And once a doubt translates itself into some deeper observations, new factors emerge, and new ways to look further are invented. In point of historical fact, this is precisely what began to happen. What developed was the use of the family as a treatment unit in which there was an identified patient or symptom-bearer.

In 1964, I wrote one of the first books in this new field, *Conjoint Family Therapy*, which encompassed the theory and practice of family therapy as it existed then, as far as I knew.

Today—exactly ten years later—Shirley Luthman and Martin Kirschenbaum have written this book which has built extensively on previous concepts and practices of family therapy. I have learned much from reading their book. Things have been clarified and new areas for exploration have been pointed out to me. I do believe that we "stand on the shoulders" of those who have gone before us.

Their book is not historical, but is a lively presentation of how and what they do today, and how they think about what they do.

Both of them are outstanding former students of mine. I have watch-ed them struggle through their trepidations to the point where they finally dared to start an institute of their own. I have watched them challenge, struggle, and be creative as they came to grips with treat-ing families, always evolving, and ultimately developing a first-rate training program.

To use the metaphor of an iceberg in the sense of "seeable to the unseeable" (but feelable) Shirley and Marty shed much light on the mysteries and facets that exist together with the processes that oper-ate within the family. I particularly appreciate their further defining and differentiating family systems in relation to the kinds of symp-toms these systems present. They have refined and defined very clearly and specifically what a really functioning pair is all about. They have stated these refinements and definitions in relationship to co-therapy, but I think their findings could serve as model for any pair.

I am delighted and excited about what the authors have put to-gether. They have done what I had hoped for—built and expanded on what they got from me. Their writing shows a maturity which allows them to be inclusive of all those things that fit, without mak-ing a case against those which do not fit. In this way, their writing reflects the congruence with which they treat and teach. It is clear that they have approached themselves as people who have been evol-ving, are still evolving, and who will continue to evolve.

Shirley and Marty's book opens a large window through which to view the "iceberg" of family functioning. As a result, you, the reader, will most likely have an evolving experience of your own, which will open even more windows and thus show new directions for you.

Virginia Satir

PREFACE

We want to pay tribute to our mentors and teachers—Virginia Satir, Don Jackson, Gregory Bateson, Jay Haley, and Frederick Perls. Some of the concepts discussed in this book were originally developed by these creative genuises. In the process of exploring their concepts in our own work, we have further developed their ideas about the growth model, communication and interaction processes, and responsibility for one's own manifestations in words and behavior. Thus, we present to you in this book the culmination of their stimulus combined with our unique experience, expression of ourselves, and our ideas. The resulting sum is therefore similar but different from all its parts as it is the essence of both of us as influenced by all of them.

In addition, we are presenting many concepts which we believe originate with us as outgrowths of our male-female combination in teaching, therapy and administrative teamwork. Our concepts about change, therapists' use of self, male-female co-therapy, the training of family therapists, and most important, integrative theory and therapy, are the result of eight years of intensive work with each other.

We are presenting this book at a time when many things are coming together for us, resulting in a time of flowering and fruition. We have just finished a tour of Europe, teaching family therapy in Holland and Sweden. Shirley has published her own book, *Intimacy*, and Martin has received a grant through FTI and Marin Open House to further his research and training interests in the relationship of drug usage and family dynamics. This book is the natural outpouring of that fruition. It is written as an expression of us, in the same way that we teach. We hope you will use it as a base for developing your own exploration, experimentation and creativity.

Preface

The actual writing of this book, except for Chapter 16, was done by Mrs. Luthman who took a six month sabbatical from the Institute for that purpose, while Dr. Kirschenbaum administered the Institute alone. The book was done with the collaboration and full approval of Dr. Kirschenbaum. Chapter 16 is a reprint of an article written by Mrs. Luthman and Dr. Kirschenbaum for the journal Family Process *in 1968.*

All of the material presented in this book belongs to both Dr. Kirschenbaum and Mrs. Luthman and has been presented by them in their teaching and lecture tours in the United States, Canada, and Europe. This book is a culmination of their eight years of research, exploration, and development in their chosen field.

PART I

BASIC INTERACTIONAL THEORY

Chapter 1

FOUNDATION:
THE GROWTH MODEL

The concept of the Growth Model is the basis for all therapies as we practice them. The Growth Model theory implies that each individual, in order to function relatively symptom-free, must feel that he is growing, producing and creating in ways that are fitting to him. In addition, it implies that families must have ways for individual members to express their differentness without that expression resulting in a loss of self-esteem. For the individuals within the family unit to achieve their maximum growth potential, families must also have ways to maintain the stability of the family unit; and, at the same time, adapt to the continually changing growth needs of individual members.

This concept is a dynamic one—the individual and the family are seen in motion. Thus, when the therapist looks at either, the most important thing for him to understand is how the current state, intraphysically and interactionally, relates to where the client has been and where he wants to go. For example, a family—consisting of mother, father, John aged ten, Dan aged 12 and Sarah aged 14—comes into treatment because John is failing in school and shows a lack of interest in friends, preferring to sit in his room and read most of the time. After a certain number of family sessions, he suddenly begins to flare up into some rebellious behavior at home and get into a couple of fights with other boys at school. At the same time, Sarah, who has been the family's fair-haired child in terms of being a star pupil and community leader, begins to show some signs of depression. The family members, of course, become concerned that treatment has

3

resulted in their getting worse instead of better and they want to leave treatment. However, when the therapist teaches the family to look at themselves in terms of the flow of their own growth pattern, alternative ideas begin to occur to them. They see John as beginning to come out of his withdrawal and express feelings, even though the feelings may be coming out in a way that is not acceptable to the family or the community. So, the other family members begin to appreciate the positive growth aspects of John's behavior while at the same time helping him to learn how to channel his expression into more acceptable patterns. The very fact that they can separate his expression of feeling (always positive) from the way in which it comes out (sometimes destructive) is so validating to him that it makes it possible for him to more easily gain control of his manner of expression and be willing to modify it. Thus the baby (feeling) does not get thrown out with the bath water (destructive behavior).

Sarah's depression may be a reaction (notice the flow pattern) to John's improvement in that she lost her role in the family as the star, since John is also beginning to shine. She needs help from family members to understand that the change may hold advantages for her as there is now room for her to come out with the parts of herself that aren't so grown up or proper. It has been a strain for her to always present such a perfect image and she has lost some of her childhood in trying to maintain that image. Now, family members are more understanding and willing to see each one in the family as a whole person. Expressions of anger, hurt, jealousy, pettiness, sadness and pain are seen as part of being human, and therefore vital to her growth process, rather than an indication of lack of respect, love, or appreciation for the family. Now, she has room to open up these parts of herself without fear of losing appreciation for her other attributes which family members enjoy and praise.

The family no longer operates by the rule that you are either all good or all bad. With that rule, if you do one wrong thing or have one bad mood, your image and all the goodies connected with that image can be lost. Now the family focus is on each member growing in his ability to know and express himself; and, on developing ways for each member to do that without a loss to himself or intrusion on others. With the growth model and the concept of flow, emphasis is always on the stimulus, action, and reaction as they ripple around and through the family system as in a stream into which something new has been added. Thus, new or different behavior is looked at in terms of how it relates to changes and the on-going moving flow of life in the family both internally in individuals and externally in the daily life situations, adjustments and trauma the family faces. This is an extremely different view from that of looking at different behavior in the light of how it fits or doesn't fit a rigid structure of how this particular family has always behaved externally and should continue to behave in order to preserve the family name.

THEORY OF POSITIVE INTENT

The growth model is based on the assumption that in every piece of behavior, no matter how destructive that behavior appears, there is some kernel of an intent to grow. The individual may have learned in his life experience that he has to fight, grab, bully or even kill to grow; or, he may live with distortions that growth means outcome—money, possessions, or power. However, the desire to expand, to develop himself and to experience life is instinctive and innate. That desire can be trampled on, brutalized, put under unbelievable pressure, and, it may be twisted into destructive pathways, but never destroyed. Even suicides, often at the same moment they are destroying themselves, also leave a message in words or behavior that says, "save me, maybe there is another way." The theory of positive intent involves finding that pure kernel of growth intent, labeling the growth process, nourishing it and enabling the individual to find ways of expressing the specific growth process that are self-enhancing, not self-destructive.

For example, a wife may be feeling very hurt, but in her life experience a person was seen as weak and either depreciated or ignored if he expressed hurt. Therefore, when she is hurt she comes out swinging. Her husband says or does something that hurts her feelings; so, instead of letting him know she is hurt, she starts attacking him verbally—calling him names, telling him he is a bastard and doesn't appreciate her. That way of expressing her feelings not only does not bring her any comfort; it repulses her husband and depreciates him. The positive intent is that she hopes for understanding and appreciation of her feelings. However, her life experience has taught her that no one understands and appreciates her feelings. Therefore, she operates on her expectations rather than her hopes—her behavior telegraphs that she doesn't expect understanding even though she may be asking for it. If someone broke through the chip on her shoulder and gave her appreciation she would not trust it and would disqualify it in some way.

We remember a session with a couple in which the wife complained bitterly that the husband was no longer sexually interested in her, did not find her attractive, and didn't care about her anymore. The very next week in their interview with us, she said he had been chasing her around the house all week—she couldn't understand it—"the bastard is just trying to make me pregnant!" The first step for this woman is to become aware that she really does want appreciation and understanding—that that is the underlying hope in all her expressions. Then, she needs to see how she defeats that hope by expressing herself in such a way that she drives away the very response she wants. The next and most important step is for her to recognize that she doesn't defeat herself because she is bad, sick, stupid or crazy: but, because she has never learned how to appreciate, honor, and express her own positive intent or to assume that it exists in others. In her origin family, if she hurt someone, that person assumed she meant to hurt and was being deliberately mean. There was no room for error; the fact that someone could do something hurtful even though he had no intention of doing so. Therefore, she operates the same way with her husband. With her, he has no opportunity to differentiate between the times he may really want to hurt her feelings and the times when that is the furthest thing from his mind; he knows she is hurting and he is in a mood to be genuinely helpful and considerate.

The husband, in this instance, may have come from a family in which people handled his hurt feelings by turning away from him with the mistaken idea that they would be intruding if they recognized he was hurt. So, he learned that you handle your own feelings and don't "burden" anyone else. When his wife blows up at him, he may at times even be able to see past the external angry behavior and recognize she is hurt. However, he thinks he is helping her by ignoring her behavior and letting her "rave on," just tuning her out. His positive intent really may be to help her, to give her room to get control of herself; but, the way he expresses it may look to her like he doesn't care, isn't interested in her, and can't be bothered, which confirms her original expectations that no one will understand or appreciate her feelings. She may then give up and go into a depression or busy herself with daily activity to get away from her feelings. Either way, things smooth over and confirm the husband's expectations that nothing he can do is going to make any difference anyway. He learned that in his growing up experience when no matter what he did, he was still ignored. Again, the first step for him is to recognize his positive intent to help his wife at times, to become aware of his expectation that he is ineffective at doing it; and, most important to understand that that expectation is a distortion based on his family's difficulty in hearing him, not an inability on his part to express himself effectively.

Once a family understands positive intent, each member of the family has a broader view of behavior. For example, an adolescent boy shoplifts something from the dime store and gets caught. The parents discipline him by withdrawing his allowance or taking away the car or whatever their rules are. However, *in addition*, they give him the message that such behavior isn't like him; therefore, he must be trying to say something by this behavior that he felt he couldn't say some other way, and they might explore with him what that could be. The validating message is, you are not a bad boy. If you do something that is destructive, you must have some reason for it. Let's understand that reason so you can find a way to express yourself that isn't hurtful to you or to us. Understanding and looking for positive intent doesn't mean you deny the reality that there are times when people are deliberately hurtful, or that children sometimes get into trouble just for the hell of it or because they want to experiment with danger. It does mean giving each family member a chance before automatically assuming negative intent and attacking back as though that assumption were true. If each family member trusts that others in the family see him basically as a caring person who doesn't really want to hurt, he knows that his occasional lapses will be disciplined, but understood as the exception rather than the rule. He will, over time, respond to that trust by learning how to trust and respect himself based on others' trust of him as a basically good person. When he learns to trust and respect himself, then the rules he makes for his own behavior will come out of his own self-respect, and not out of fear or any attempt to manipulate others.

SIMULTANEOUS DEVELOPMENT

The natural emotional growth of the human organism takes place on two levels at the same time. These levels are the development of self-esteem and the ability to make relationships with others that are satisfying and enhancing. The qualities that an individual must learn in order to develop and build a solid sense of self worth are:

Authenticity. This is the ability of the individual to be real. He has a sense of who he is as a person based on a willingness to be honest with himself about his thoughts, feelings and actions without dumping judgements, criticisms, recriminations and comparisons on his head. His acceptance of himself in this way produces a sense of:

Integrity. Integrity involves the ability to set values and codes of behavior for yourself based on what fits you and not on how someone else does or doesn't behave or respond. For example, I treat you with dignity regardless of whether or not you respect yourself or me because depreciating you is the same as depreciating me since we are all part of the ebb and flow of the human system. It is not possible to treat anyone else in a depreciating, brutalizing, or otherwise destructive manner without badly damaging one's own self-esteem, even though that result might not be immediately evident. Whether we like it or not we are all connected to each other. To paraphrase a statement from the Bible, "As you do to others, you do to yourself."

Authenticity and integrity generate:

Courage. The ability to take risks in trying new things, in exposing vulnerable feeling states for learning purposes, and to grow and experiment in relating and new ways of behaving with unfamiliar parts of self.

Spontaneity. The individual is able to risk responding with his innermost feelings without "editing"—wondering what another person will think and modifying his expression to some program he thinks others expect him to perform.

Responsibility. Ownership of one's behavior, thoughts, feelings, and mood states in relationship to others. For example, if I make a mistake I can acknowledge it and express regret without depreciating myself or blaming someone else. If I am feeling and behaving childishly by my own standards, I can own that at times there is a childish part of me that comes out. Others don't have to like it or even tolerate it, but neither do I have to pretend it doesn't exist or isn't a part of me. I am not bad, sick, stupid, or crazy because I sometimes express both feelings and behavior that I don't like or approve of; I am just human. That is not an excuse, it is a recognition that my growth is an on-going, flowing process, and I will impede that process less if I recognize the parts of myself that I don't like, but don't chastise myself for them. The process of owning and accepting those parts, without punishing myself, will automatically promote growth.

Commitment. The ability to pin oneself down. This requires the willingness to be honest about one's limitations. For example, I may promise to do something and find that in the process I have over-estimated my abilities and cannot do what I promised. If I honor my commitment, then I have to let others involved in the con-tract know about my limitations and inability to complete my agree-ment. This requires that I be able to commit myself to new ideas and ways of behaving, accepting the risk that I am going into unknown territory and therefore may lose or fail. It is important that I see loss or failure as an indication of my limits rather than an invalidation of my worth; otherwise, I will weasel out of my commitment with ex-cuses, denial, or withdrawal, which is the same as no commitment at all. The willingness to make commitments and follow through, not necessarily in terms of the promised outcome, but in the process of letting others involved in my commitment know where I am, pro-duces a character structure in me which has:

Congruency. Words, behavior, actions, feeling tones, voice qual-ity, body expression all produce the same messages—"I know where I stand and I'll make it equally clear to you where I stand—you can count on it!"

Explosion (vs. implosion). The person whose self-esteem level is appropriate will be able to let go with a sense of abandon (not the same as loss of control) into areas of expression such as joy, grief, anger, and sexuality. He can experience himself as a feeling organism suffused with joy, sadness, outrage, or intense pleasure. He trusts that his sense of who he is will never desert him no matter how suffused he is with feeling. His ability to thus allow himself to be an open channel through which such aliveness can flow, unblocked, further enhances his sense of himself and his knowledge about himself and others.

The ability of the individual to connect in a meaningful way with others is the other level of development which occurs simultaneously in the natural growth process. The stepping-stones in this achieve-ment which are learned or not learned or badly distorted in the family structure are:

1. The experience of differentness as growth-producing. We must learn to see other individuals who happen to think, feel and act dif-ferently from us as providing us with opportunities for learning new things and relating in new ways rather than as a source of threat or depreciation.

2. The experience of separateness as wholeness, not isolation. Each person must be able to experience himself as a whole person when he is alone and when he is with others, and to develop his own natural

flow back and forth between those two experiences. If he does not have this sense of wholeness, he feels a loss of himself when he is alone or with others—never completely satisfied or replete. When alone, he feels lost and anxious; when with others, he feels fuzzy about who he is and tends to imitate or define himself around what he thinks others expect.

3. Assertion must be seen as vital to survival and growth, regardless of the outcome of the assertive action. The act of expressing genuine, deep feeling, in a way that you see as fitting to who you are as a person, will produce growth in the individual regardless of the response or lack of response of the other person involved in the exchange. Each time a person expresses himself in this way, he puts another notch in his self-esteem and he opens up new areas of feeling within himself which he didn't know about before. If he receives a positive response from the other person, that further enhances his own growth, but it is icing on the cake. The main issue in terms of his growth is his ability to express who he is and risk whatever the outcome is. Once each individual understands this concept, he is much more willing to expose his feelings because when his values are attached to his evolving growth rather than some fixed outcome, he realizes he cannot lose.

4. The ability to respect and accept the executive of another individual—his freedom to be in charge and make his own choices for himself. We must be able to recognize that others, even children, are really in charge of themselves. We cannot force them to think, feel or behave in our ways or to accept our values. In families, we can give each other choices based on an understanding of each person's rights, feelings and limitations—i.e., if you live here, you have to do so-and-so because otherwise I will feel intruded on or used and I won't let you live here—but we cannot think, feel, or act for someone else. We cannot get inside the head of the smallest child or a person we have known for thirty years and really know what is going on inside that head without confirmation or expression from that other person.

5. The ability to hear and empathize with another's feelings without loss of self. It is important for an individual to be able to hear the pain or joy or concern of someone important to him without translating it in terms of what he (the listener) has done wrong, how he has failed, or why he isn't appreciated. Each individual in the family needs room occasionally to come out with his complaints or his upset feelings without getting offers of solutions, defensive responses,

or withdrawal. .... s is a sympathetic ear. He can ask for more help if he wants it. If he is really directing his complaints to the listener in a devious way, he will learn to come out much more directly in the future if the listener doesn't bite.

6. The ability to accept the uniqueness of other individuals without question. Each person in the family is unique. Just because they are all related is no reason each should be anything at all like the others. Therefore, each must learn to accept the other's expression of how he feels without putting him on the witness stand about why he feels the way he does. Feelings are seldom logical and the "why" approach usually carries the implication that the other person should not feel that way, and, if he really cared about everyone else in the family, he *wouldn't* feel that way!

7. Taking full responsibility for choices, current internal states, determination of what behavior fits self and yet recognizing the rights and feelings of others in the family. No one is totally responsible for anyone else. Even in a family structure, very small children make choices for themselves and must learn early that they do take responsibility in certain areas on a consistently expanding basis. Three-year-olds can say "I took the candy because I wanted it," rather than "I took the candy because you yelled at me yesterday," if there is room in the family for people to deliberately disobey the rules or make mistakes without getting labeled bad, sick, stupid, or crazy.

8. The recognition that death is not synonomous with the lack of environmental support. When a child is very young, he feels that he will die if his family is in some way broken up or destroyed. That is an appropriate feeling in a young child. However, it is the task of the family to teach him, over time, that his survival is connected to himself and to his own growth. If he learns that, then when he is of age, he can leave his family and see its members as friends with whom he can share, rather than seeing them as Santa Clauses, judges, or gods. Then, he will look for a spouse who is a friend and lover, not an eternal parent.

It is the responsibility of the family unit to provide the nurturing, structure, and room for all of its members to grow in the development of self-esteem and their ability to relate to each other and to others outside the family. This means the family must develop processes for correcting its learning distortions and for adapting to the constant change generated by its constantly growing members. In addition, family members need processes for coping with the everyday traumas and demands imposed by the outside world and the realities of living without allowing such traumas to totally block the growth of the family and all its members. Tall order, hm? No wonder the development of family therapy has occurred!

In summary, the major aspects of the growth model theory are:

Concept of the family as a dynamic system, always in flux based on evolution of individuals in the family, development of interactional ability with each other and others outside of the family; and, the stresses, demands and changes imposed from the outside.

View of the individual as an energy system whose goal is aliveness which is dependent on the individual's ability to grow and create and produce in ways that are fitting to him and acceptable to his group.

All behavior is looked at to determine the growth intent in relation to past history of the individual and the family, how it relates to the current family state and the individual's growth needs, and what it means in relation to the hopes of the individual and his family members for their futures.

Chapter 2

INTERACTIONAL FRAMEWORK

The term "Family Therapy" is really a misnomer. When we speak of family therapy, we're really talking about interactional theory and therapy. The interactional framework is basic to any type of group therapy—couple, unrelated individuals in a group, married couple group therapy, family group and multiple family groups. There are distinctive aspects to therapy with each of these different types of groups. Here, we're presenting the interactional framework basic to them all with emphasis on the family group. The family is different from a group of unrelated individuals because it has a history and because members live with the assumption that destruction of the group would mean a serious internal loss, perhaps even threatening their emotional survival. Therefore, family therapy is one of the most difficult forms of therapy because any outside intervention (i.e., therapy) perceived by family members as a threat to the survival of the unit will mean an immediate exit from therapy or a closing of the ranks in the family against the therapist. Therapists wanting to learn family therapy must then be prepared to lose clients at a much greater ratio than when learning individual therapy. Such quick departures on the part of clients may be very bruising to the ego of the therapist, especially one who is already skilled as an individual therapist and not used to such losses. However, we don't know any other way to learn, as family therapy requires that the therapist risk using himself in an active way which automatically produces a threat to the family's way of operating. Families usually come to a therapist wanting a reduction of their pain without any disturbance whatsoever of the way they operate, which they think is necessary to their survival as a unit.

Therapists who have had extensive training in individual therapy, especially with a Freudian base, must realize that family or interactional therapy is not built on nor does it extend from that base. They must temporarily set aside what they have learned and start anew as neophytes to learn the interactional framework. When they have mastered that, they can then combine and integrate their understanding of individual psychodynamics with interactional and communication processes. However, one is not built on the other. Becoming such a neophyte is very difficult for those who feel they have developed considerable expertise from years of education and clinical experience in another form of therapy. However, our own experience is that on-going growth on our part requires the continued willingness to relinquish our thrones in favor of new worlds to experience and understand. The trip is often painful, but the view and the sensation are worth it.

We break the interactional framework down into seven major concepts:

System. We define system as the complex of patterns of behavior and ways of functioning with one another which family members believe necessary in order for the family to survive and perform its tasks. The more practical definition of system, as used by researchers in family therapy, is a unit of at least three people so that there can always be an observer. Mother can watch father and daughter interact, father can watch mother and daughter, or daughter can observe father and mother.

The system can be open or closed. Families who come for therapy usually have closed systems and the goal of the therapist is to make them aware of this, the price they are paying for such closure, how to open the system, and the pros and cons of that choice. An open system is one which has room for different ideas and is constantly open to alternative ways of looking at the external world. It accepts that its members are constantly changing and growing so that what fit yesterday may not fit today. In a closed system, members see change as a threat, difference as a lack of love or respect, and have fixed assumptions about how other family members think, feel and behave, which are not subject to question. In a closed system, for example, family members make comments like, "What he's saying is not what he really feels—*I* know what he really feels," "You don't like asparagus, do you, dear?—you've never liked asparagus," "I don't trust you; I've never been able to rely on you," "If I say what I feel, he'll hit me," "If I say what I feel, she'll leave me," "No one here cares about me or my feelings," "She enjoys hurting me."

The nature of the system—whether it is closed or open, and how it operates—is determined by its rules, patterns of behavior, and homeostasis. By rules, we mean those tacitly understood ways of operating, never written down or voiced, which each family member follows, often not even aware he is observing a rule. For example, a family may have a rule that no one criticises mother. The therapist can become aware of that rule by watching the family's patterns of behavior as they interact. Someone in the family says something that could be interpreted as critical of mother and someone else interrupts. Another time, someone else makes a similar comment or complaint and two of the younger children get into a fight. A third time it looks as though the rule may be breeched and someone changes the subject.

These shifts in the interaction may seem totally unrelated to what is being discussed, but when the therapist sees a pattern emerge at least three times, he can be sure a family rule is involved. These rules and the patterns of behavior which define and support the rules maintain the homeostasis of the family unit. The homeostasis is the balance mechanism of the family which maintains the *status quo* and keeps the boat from rocking. The homeostasis mechanism is observable in many different aspects of the family's operation—the cooperation of all family members in preventing criticism of mother as discussed above, the fact that a family with a delinquent member usually also has a "goodie-two-shoes" member, the victim has a victimizer (and those roles may be reversed, but operate simultaneously), the acting-out child has a brother or sister who is withdrawn or has psychosomatic problems, the emotional wife has a stoic husband, the controlling, aggressive husband has a little-girl wife. A husband or wife frequently expresses the feelings of his spouse without even being aware that the feelings belong to the spouse and not to him. For example, the wife may blow up at the husband's mother for something she is saying or doing to the husband and he sits back and lets his wife speak and feel for him. Children may take on the pain of the parents and behave in such a way as to draw attention to themselves and away from the parent's pain. The internal rationale in all the homeostatic behavior is to preserve the stability of the family unit at any cost.

Symptom. In the interactional framework, a symptom is considered an indication that growth is being inhibited in some area of the individual's expression of himself, in the way in which family members are able to share feelings, express individuality, or work out problems, or in the ability of family members to make room for themselves and at the same time maintain the functioning of the family unit. The symptom may be expressed by one member of the family—an underachieving child, a delinquent child, a suicidal parent or child, a schizophrenic parent or child, an alcoholic parent, drug addiction or psychosomatic expression, depression or acting-out by anyone in the family. When the symptom appears to be carried by one family member, the therapist looks at what the symptom means in terms of that person's own growth pattern and what it reflects about the family system as a whole. For example, a child who becomes delinquent at the age of fourteen may be reacting to a loss in his own growth pattern—perhaps he had rheumatic fever for two years and lost out considerably in his social development resulting in a depression when he reaches adolescence with all the pressures that that entails. He handles the depression with acting-out behavior, which may be destructive for him and the family, but is still healthier and easier to work with than a withdrawal symptom expressed by a child who has given up. His symptom may also be expressive of, and complicated by, pain in the family which has nothing to do with him. His father may be having difficulty at work and feels deep frustration, despair, and helplessness which he is not expressing. His mother may be reacting to this with panic which she is not expressing. Everyone in the family is thus walking on eggshells, and this particular child is acting out the family's anger, frustration, and fear, as well as his own. As far as we can determine, there does not seem to be any reliable criteria for why one particular child in a family becomes the symptom-bearer for the whole family. We have noticed that the oldest child of the same sex most frequently expresses the pain of the parent who is not handling or expressing his or her feelings. Also, if there are two daughters in the family, one will sometimes express one side of the mother's personality and the second will express the other side. One daughter may appear very controlling and verbal—the other may be soft and sensitive. The mother is indirect and unclear in expressing either of these sides of herself and the girls are expressing these parts of her at the loss of the opportunity to discover and develop all parts of their own personalities. Thus the homeostasis is maintained, but at what cost! The payoff is that the mother doesn't have to risk coming out straight with her feelings and the daughters get direct or tacit approval for playing their roles. However, everyone loses in the area of her own personal growth and expression of uniqueness.

Sometimes the symptom may be the family interaction itself, rather than the behavior of one particular member. The rule in the family may be that no one gets pinned down. If it looks as though someone may get into a painful, embarrassing, or tension-producing feeling, something happens to interrupt that expression. The interaction resembles a hot potato being thrown around from person to person. Often, this interaction is so rapid and subtle that the therapist gets thoroughly lost or else caught up in it. Families will go into a joke routine in which everyone joins in, they may get into a family fight, they may all talk at once, or they may not talk at all, so that there is no interaction. The family may have a rule that everyone is reasonable and nice and they really cannot understand why they are in the therapist's office. They have been pushed to come by school people who call because every once in a while one of the children does something bizarre like setting a fire in the washroom, insulting a teacher, or taking off his clothes in the play yard. Family members always have very reasonable explanations for all these escapades which don't seem to have any particular pattern to them except they keep occurring, as though the family needs periodic safety valves.

Some families have multiple symptomatology. It has been our experience that when this is the case, the breakdown in the growth processes of the family unit and the individuals within it—is severe, even though all the symptoms may not appear to be severe if taken individually.

As you can see, this view of symptomatology is quite different from the psychoanalytic theory of symptomatology in terms of individual psychodynamics. This does not mean that we ignore or depreciate knowledge of individual psychodynamics. On the contrary, we think that extensive knowledge and experience in individual psychodynamics and therapy is necessary in order to do family therapy. Family therapy is a method which is useful for many people who would not come for individual therapy. They are not aware of interpersonal problems—they are only aware that something is breaking down in the family unit or in what they perceive as their ability to perform the necessary tasks of mothering, fathering, or growing within the system. The task of the therapist is to use that method as an immediately effective way of getting to the individuals in the family so that each can begin to look at himself and take responsibility for his own growth. Then the method may be used to enable family members to handle new ways of looking and new ways of being as individuals with assistance from the therapist to integrate their knowledge back into the family system.

For example, a family may come into therapy because the oldest child is taking drugs. When the therapist explores the family system, he may discover that this symptom expresses the lack of nurturance in the family. Everyone is concerned about one another and trying very hard, but no one feels he is getting anything back. Each person feels unappreciated and isolated. As the focus is shifted off the drug symptom and onto the sense of isolation in the family, it becomes evident that mother is sending out strong messages to everyone in the family to stay away from her feelings, and in this way she has controlled the whole family. Everyone is afraid to express feelings at all, so each person has operated as a self-contained unit. However, as therapy progresses, everyone in the family except mother begins to use the opportunity to come out with some of the feelings that have been building up to the point of explosion. As this happens, mother's withdrawal, lack of affect, and denial system become increasingly pronounced and rigid, enabling the therapist to recognize that he is dealing with a potentially psychotic internal system. That knowledge and awareness will determine how he handles the family at that point. He will not push further, thus triggering a psychotic episode. He may stop therapy at that point, indicating he feels he has gone as far as he can go without upsetting the family balance to the point that it might be destructive. He may indicate very clearly what he observes—that mother has become more and more withdrawn and left out as other family members come out with their feelings—and talk with all of the family members about how they want to handle this. In doing so, he takes decision-making off the right-wrong, good-bad framework, and explains in terms of the growth model that each person has a different rhythm of growth and cannot be pushed beyond that rhythm at any time without damage. Therefore, other people aren't bad because they want to open up their feelings, and mother isn't bad because she doesn't want to. They are simply at different places in terms of their growth and their needs. This way the children don't have to feel responsible for mother. They can understand that their feelings are basically okay, but may not be acceptable to her at this point in time. She, perhaps, can then understand that when people in the family come out with feelings, they are not doing something deliberately to her but are expressing where they are in their own growth processes quite separate from her.

The term "symptom," as it is used in interactional therapy, again is a misnomer. Part of our difficulty is that we do not have a complete language to express interactional concepts as yet. In origin, symptom is a medical term implying sickness. When we use it interactionally, we mean a barrier in the way to growth–an indication that some change is occurring in the individual or family, and the system is having difficulty adjusting or adapting to such change, or a symptom may be a signal that some new growth spurt is about to take place. Quite often in therapy, a family may have broken its negative patterns of connecting and appear to be moving along well when suddenly an exacerbation of an old symptom will appear. Instead of being a resurgence of the old problems in the family, this is often the signal that a major change is about to take place and everyone is afraid and erecting a last stand against change. If the therapist recognizes and labels this signal aspect of the symptom with the family, its members can then open up their fears about change and not waste energy being obsessed about whether or not they have really made progress. Thus, they are introduced to the concept that change is always difficult even though it may be greatly desired and there must be room in the family for people to express and appreciate their ambivalence without being seen as undermining the family's growth.

Content versus Process. Process has to do with the way in which a family comes to a decision or outcome. Content has to do with what they are deciding. For example, a family is talking about whether or not Joan should wash the dishes. This has come up many times and never been resolved. If the therapist looks at what happens when the family tries to solve this problem—who says and does what and how does it fit with what he really feels, how are his words and behavior interpreted by other family members, and where does the process break down in terms of repetitive or withdrawal patterns—he may see a variety of distortions. Mother and father may both agree verbally that Joan must do the dishes. However, Joan doesn't do the dishes and no one does or says anything. When this pattern is labeled openly, then the therapist may deal with what blocks action. In one instance, parents may be unable to "impose" their wills on anyone because they came from overly strict families in which they felt intruded upon. They don't want their children to have the kind of resentment toward them that they experience toward their parents. On the other hand, they may have come from overly permissive families and never learned ways of setting limits and giving choices so that they feel helpless in dealing with their children. Intrapsychic conflicts are then exposed, in terms of parents' self-esteem and origin family interactional experience, and translated into interactional terms within the current family system.

Another process pattern may be that mother and father discuss Joan's doing the dishes and differ on a solution. Mother then says, "You never agree with me and are always against me." Father says, "Nothing I ever do is right." They are then suddenly talking about whether or not they love each other and the issue about Joan and the dishes is totally forgotten and unresolved so that she never gets a clear message from either parent. Then intrapsychic conflicts get exposed in examining how come whether or not the parents love each other gets tied up with setting rules for the children.

Still another process follows the scapegoat mold. Parents look as though they are going to have a conflict over whether Joan does the dishes, and another child has a temper tantrum, starts a fight with a brother or sister, or does something that draws attention away from the issue and possible conflict between the parents.

The goal of the therapist is to get the family off of issues and into their process. With some families, it is important to do this in the first session; otherwise they will probably not stay in therapy. Some families have such destructive ways of interacting and communicating that if the therapist does not intervene to shift them off these patterns, they see his inactivity as support of their negative patterns and feel too hopeless and frightened to continue. With other families, the therapist must lay considerable groundwork before moving into process. These are families that have operated with very rigid repressive patterns of interaction and are afraid of feelings. The therapist must then start with the concrete—what is wrong and how each person sees the picture—and gradually teach family members that feelings can be safe and enable them to get into their process slowly.

There are many techniques for moving into process which we will discuss in detail in a later chapter. However, here we just want to mention that these techniques fall into three general categories:

Discrepancy Analysis. The therapist may observe discrepancies between the way the father in the family looks and the things he says. His words may be placating; his expression is stern and angry looking. When the therapist labels this difference, it may encourage the father to look at what he is really feeling and what is getting in the way of his saying it clearly instead of covering his annoyance with obsequious behavior. There may be a verbal discrepancy. Someone may say one thing one time and contradict himself two sentences or an hour later. The tone may be discrepant—the words and body behavior may be saying "I want to help you," and the tone may sound harsh and angry so that the receiver of the message "I want to help you" hears it as, "I want to control you."

Non-verbal Behavior. The therapist may observe that every time the parents in the family start to get close or to talk about their feelings, the children get fidgety. We video-tape many of our family sessions in our training program at the Institute, and we have one particular tape which is a classic example of this process. The father is beginning to talk about his angry feelings toward his first wife, and his three children ages 5, 6, and 8 go through what looks like a ballet on the film as father talks. They stretch, move around him, cut off his view, climb on him, constantly moving in synchronized patterns. When the therapist pointed this out to the family, the children were able to verbalize that they were afraid of another divorce if people in the family, especially father, began to get angry. There had been a rule in the family that no one showed anger. The symptomatology on the part of the children that brought the family into treatment was that the 5-year-old was cutting up her stepmother's dresses and urinating in the garbage can. So, the symptom was congruent with the non-verbal pattern of the children's behavior: an expression of the fear and subsequent repression of anger in the family.

The Therapist's Internal Experience. This is the source of what we feel are our most valuable therapeutic assets—imagery, fantasy, physical sensations, and mood states. For example, the family members may be talking with one another quite reasonably and realistically about their problems and appear to be doing a good job of it. However, the therapist is feeling very sad inside. When he checks his internal state, he realizes he did not feel that way prior to the interview, so, he may say as much to the family—"You seem to be talking very reasonably with each other, but I have strong feelings of sadness inside. Am I picking that up from any of you?" Family members may deny this, but usually will not. Someone in the family may break into tears and start to come out with hurt feelings. Then it becomes apparent that the family has had a rule that no one could show sad feelings, because that was an indication that others had failed and their feelings would be hurt. So, family members protect each other from their feelings and maintain a placid, reasonable exterior, and their pain is coming out indirectly—maybe in a drinking problem or an underachieving child, or psychosomatic symptomatology. In another situation, the therapist may feel a pain in his neck and when he expresses this symptom, someone in the family may relate to a feeling he has that he hasn't been expressing. Once in an interview, the parents were talking about the boat they were building together, and the therapist discovered she was tuning out and experiencing sexual fantasies. She offered that information to the couple, and the man looked stunned and then responded that he had been very concerned for months about his sexual relationship with his wife, but had been unable to talk about it before.

In another session, a man was talking about his relationship with his father and the therapist interrupted to say that as the man was talking, he (the therapist) had a mental image of a small forlorn boy sitting alone at the top of some stairs. The man began to cry, saying that was his image of himself because he felt so alone as a child and wanted warmth and contact from his father that he never received.

Dr. Frederick Perls used to say that most of us operate on ten percent of our potential because we only use our thought processes. Our experience has more than confirmed that observation and we believe that the most effective therapy is based on a blend of the observable interaction, communication, and individual intrapsychic data, with the therapist's internal subjective manifestations of his experience with the family and its members.

Pathology versus Health. This concept involves the relationship between the balance of tendencies to health and illness in individual family members, and parallel tendencies of the family group to maintain emotional health in its members or to induce in them special forms of disturbance. This idea is comparable to the concept in individual therapies regarding the assessment of ego strengths and weaknesses. It is different, however, in that it includes an assessment not only of individual strengths and weaknesses, but also of the ability of others in the family group to tolerate and cope with the strengths and weaknesses of others. For example, some families operate as though it is impossible for one family member to be well unless another is sick. We have an interview on tape which Don Jackson did with a family whose 17-year-old son had been in and out of mental hospitals for five years. Don kept focusing the family on the question of what would they have to give up if their son stayed well. The family fought this question at first, but as Don persevered, the young, supposedly schizophrenic son, began to make more and more sense. Finally, toward the end of the interview, he told Dr. Jackson that he thought other family members needed for him to be sick so that they would have something to focus on and so they could feel well.

In some families, assertion of differences by family members is perceived as threatening and disrespectful. The tacit rule is, "If you love me, you will not differ with me openly and you will think and feel the way I think and feel." On the other hand, a family with an open system committed to growth looks upon assertion as positive even if it sometimes comes out in unacceptable ways. Differentness is considered exciting and interesting rather than threatening.

In still other families, individuals are unable to give to each other when the other feels strong and sure. They can only give when others feel weak and sick. Thus, the message in the family is that if you are strong and take responsibility for yourself, you don't get anything. The only way to get taken care of is to be weak, helpless, or ill.

Therapeutic Role. The unit of the family interview consists of the entire group of persons that constitutes a psychic entity—the nuclear family (father, mother, and children), and all others under the same roof. In addition, significant persons outside the home may also be included if they influence family functioning on a consistent basis. The therapist enters the family as an active participant, catalyst, and facilitator. The dilemma of the therapist is that the family wants a decrease in pain without change in the family's basic patterns of operation perceived by family members as necessary to their survival. For example, parents want a child to stop stealing. However, they do not want to look at the fact that father works days, mother works nights and they meet only at mealtime, as isolation defends against family conflict. Or, parents complain that a child will not communicate his feelings within the family. They want the child to change in this respect, but they do not want to look at the part they have played in teaching the child such reticence. They do not react spontaneously within the family; they maintain rigid controls on the ways their feelings are expressed; they operate as though they must appear god-like and unflustered to their children.

The aim of the therapist is to help the family achieve a clearer definition of the real conflict. The issue is not who does the dishes, but whether or not each loves the other.

The second aim of the therapist is to open up interpersonal conflicts. How does the task of doing the dishes get to be a love issue in the family? What is going on in the family that causes members to feel unloved and unappreciated? These conflicts are then brought overtly into the current flow of the family interaction with the therapist openly labeling the family's previously tacit out-of-awareness rule "If you love me, you'll think like I do, and do what I want."

The therapist should then aim to lift concealed intrapsychic conflict to a level of intrapersonal relations where it can be coped with more effectively. The therapist explores the history basis for the dishes becoming a love issue, as we discussed earlier in the paragraph on content and process. The parents explore, in front of their own children, the processes they learned in their origin families with their parents that are destructive or inadequate in dealing with their current family.

His next goal should be to neutralize scapegoating and irrational prejudices involved in displaced conflict so that the conflict can be attached to its original source. Parents may be excessively punitive toward a misbehaving child, expressing anger or coldness far out of proportion to the stimulus. With exploration, parents reveal they came from families in which they were expected to behave like little adults almost from birth with no room for mistakes or play or rebellion. They carry much resentment and sadness inside because they bought that package and have kept their noses to the grindstone all their lives. When their children do not buy the same package, they do not see that they have given their children something they never got from their parents—the strength to fight for their own ways. They see their own wasted and empty years, and are enraged.

Next the therapist's goal is to reduce the pain in conflict by reinterpreting and labeling the expression of feeling. Many times when family members realize that the way in which they express themselves may not fit what they are really feeling inside, they can afford to look and explore without immediately jumping to the defensive position. For example, a wife who is expressing anger to her husband in a blaming, depreciating way may really be feeling very hurt. When she sees there is a discrepancy between what she feels and the way she is expressing it, she realizes she doesn't have to change herself—just the ways of expressing herself that she has learned which don't fit her and don't work for her. At the same time, when her husband really sees and hears the hurt behind the attack behavior, he may be more willing to hear and respond to her and to think twice the next time before he immediately leaps into battle or withdraws. Everyone in the family begins to look beyond and behind the external expression, to look at the broader range of communication within the group. That new way of looking gives everyone more room for error, more chance to be understood because if the real message is missed on one level, it might be picked up on another. So, anger may really be hurt, attack and withdrawal may be fear, and suspicion and control behavior may really be masking a concern and a desire for approval.

The therapist should offer hope. If hurtful behavior can be perceived on the basis of the real message underneath, then family members can look at hurtful behavior without so much pain and loss. If a wife can consider that her husband may really have a positive intent to help her when he is doing something hurtful like trying to control her, then change becomes a possibility. He can change his behavior without feeling that he is bad, only that the previous behavior didn't work. She can let him know how the way he expresses himself affects her in a hurtful way.

Communication Evaluation. A family's ability to use communication as a tool for growth is indicated by its members being able to listen and hear one another, their ability to question or comment on what they hear, and their ability to use what they hear and what they comment to make outcomes that fit. The more difficulty a family has in accepting change and differentness, the more difficult it may be for each member to hear the others. Therefore, when the therapist is evaluating that aspect of interaction which is communication, he looks for the following:*

1. Clarity of speech.

2. Topic change. Do transactions get completed or is the exchange tangential, interruptive, unrelated?

3. The ratio of agreement to disagreement. Are family members able to disagree with one another without being assaultive, and can differing opinions be heard as contributions and not attack? Does the family have a rule that everyone must be nice and agreeable so that people must use devious means to get their real wishes across?

4. Intensity. Can family members communicate anger, tenderness, affection, sexuality, sadness, and other feelings with appropriate intensity or do such expressions occur in a monotone, in a measured cadence, or always reasonable? On the other hand, the communication may always be of such intensity that there never seem to be any gradations. The therapist looks for the communication flow or lack of flow between various levels of intensity.

5. Relationship implication. Are comments made in a friendly or attacking manner? Mother may say the same words to two children.

---

* J. Riskin and E. E. Faunce, "An Evaluative Review of Family Interaction Reserach, *Family Process, 11,* 4 (December 1972).

The message to one implies a warm camaraderie and to the other an armed truce.

6. Speaking order. Who speaks to whom, who is left out, who speaks for whom?

7. Commitment. Can family members pin themselves down to respond to each other's demands with yes, no, or clear messages about what they will and won't do?

8. Ratio of commitment to agreement. Do family members agree to do things and then not do them? Or, do family members follow through on what they promise?

9. Sequential patterns. Mother talks to Father and the children interrupt. Father talks and no one listens. Mother talks and everyone in the family listens and responds except Father. Oldest son starts to talk and conversation ends with lecture by Mother or Father.

Model Analysis. If it is evident that family members are operating in incongruent ways in terms of roles within the family, then an understanding of the family's functioning involves a knowledge of adult family members' perceptions about roles in their origin families. A therapist who is treating a family with a mother, father and two children, really has six clients because he is also involved with the "ghosts" which are the perceptions the mother and father carry over from their own parents without even being aware they are operating out of their parents' framework, not their own. What worked for their parents may not work for them and yet they may be using the same processes even though they don't fit because they haven't developed ways of operating that fit their own uniqueness.

In observing the family, it may be evident that the children are really in control, that no one is in charge, that mother is operating as a little girl and the oldest daughter is taking on the role of wife and mother in the family. The father may appear to be the authority, judge, and boss in the family, yet in reality Mother controls behind the scenes. Everyone knows this, but no one mentions it. They preserve the facade, but this results in a feeling of confusion about roles for all family members. Family members have rigid expectations about what males and females should be like which do not fit the reality so they maintain the facade of what they think should be and express the reality in devious ways. All are depreciated by this farce but are too afraid to risk being who they really are because each person's sense of himself or herself as male or female is unclear and no one wants to risk being embarrassed, feeling inadequate, or behaving inappropriately according to someone else's standards.

Chapter 3

PROCESS AND PROCESSES

We discussed process briefly in the preceding chapter. However, accurate diagnosis of the family's use of content and the resultant process is the crux of interactional therapy, so we thought the concept deserved elaboration in a chapter all its own.

To understand process is to accept the human organism as an energy system which connects in an ebb-and-flow pattern with the energy systems of other people and with the universe around us, all of which is made up of energy systems. Any energy system is healthiest and most radiant when it is connected to growth, change, and constant expansion, which is geared to its own unique growth rhythm. Unfortunately, much of our education from the cradle on is geared to the search for security, external manifestations of success, and stability—all the exact opposite of change and growth. There is no security in security—only death. The organism must learn ways of thinking, being, and operating which support its natural inclination toward growth and change; otherwise, it will stagnate out of fear or ignorance, and symptomatology will develop.

In family therapy, the concept of process requires that the therapist look at the family system and its individual members as being constantly in flux. Each individual is in the past, present, and future at the same time. Therefore something may occur in the family system which reveals a block that some individual in the family cannot seem to get past. For example, mother has been complaining for years that father never comes out with his feelings and is always stoical. With therapy, he suddenly burst forth in one session with some pain he has been holding in all his life. His wife, even though she is now getting what she has always wanted from him, is now immobilized and unable to respond. The therapist encourages her not to judge herself or to doubt that she really wants her husband's feelings. Instead he asks her to consider that although she really does want to share feelings with her husband, there is something she has learned about doing so that is frightening to her. Then the therapy process moves into her past in terms of what she learned about intimacy and the sharing of feelings in her growing up experience that might be getting in her way now to respond to her husband. She remembers her parents fighting and herself cowering in a corner in her room, terrified that they would hurt each other and someone would leave. The therapist asks her to be that little girl in the corner of her room, to relive that experience and let herself feel the terror without forcing it or running from it. She closes her eyes and lets herself get into it with the support of the therapist and her family. The therapist takes in consideration at the same time the flow of feeling in the family system at this moment and, if the family is uneasy, explains what is happening with mother. "She is carrying around some unfinished business in the form of feelings she was never able to allow herself to feel and complete as a child. Now these feelings are getting in the way of her relating to you husband and to you the children in the family. We need to make room for her to feel her feelings so she can lay them to rest and go on about her business. So, let yourselves feel with her or just feel your own feelings, but don't rescue her; this is something she has to do for herself." With this support, the mother sinks deeper into her experience and great sobs come from her. Her face grimaces like that of a small child in pain, her body is curled almost into a fetal position, and her sobs come in great gasps like an infant crying. The therapist comments on this and encourages her to be whatever age she feels—to be congruent with the feeling. As she lets go, there is a sense of great release and relief. It is now safe for her to feel and do what she had to deny and repress as a child because there was no one there at that time to take care of her feelings. The therapist and her family give her plenty of room to experience her feeling with the therapist periodically supporting her by telling her what is happening, and why, and not to fight it or analyze it but just to let the feeling have its course. When subsided, she opens her eyes. The therapist then brings her back to the present situation with her family and asks her to tell them what she wants from them. She wants to know what they are feeling. The therapist encourages them to be honest with her. One child says he is afraid; he has never seen her do this. Another child is pleased that she would share such a deep experience and feeling with the family. Her husband says her feelings triggered some of his own as he remembered his own experience of fear and loneliness when his parents fought. His parents did divorce and maybe he has connected that loss with the expression of feeling, so it has always been hard for him to risk saying what he feels. The therapist then pulls together the past and present and at the same time makes a bridge for the future. He says that perhaps part of their old connection with each other is that they each married someone who was afraid to come out with feelings because each of them had lived in a family that was unable to handle feelings constructively. However, the price they have paid for that protection is isolation and a lack of contact, which has become too painful for them. Now, they have grown to a place in their development where they want to change, but they are afraid because they don't know how to share feelings in a constructive way. That is not something one is born knowing— it has to be learned. Since they did not learn in their origin families, they must learn now, and the therapist will assist them in finding ways to begin to share how they feel that fit for them and work for them. At this point, the therapist—always conscious of the dynamic flow of the system—will ask all the family members to share with one another their feelings about undertaking this new task. They are encouraged to express their ambivalence and see that expression as a gift because it keeps the door to contact open. They are informed that each time someone holds back a feeling, even though he is doing it with the best of intentions, he automatically puts up a barrier between himself and the rest of the family. Therefore, the goal of the family has to shift from everything being smooth and unruffled to everyone being in contact. Then they must learn ways of staying in contact that don't intrude on anyone or result in a loss of self-esteem. At this point, family members may have a very meaningful experience in sharing their deepest feelings of helplessness, uncertainty and fears for the future. The therapist, aware of the natural flow of process, knows that such intense contact can often trigger a delayed panic reaction after the therapy session is over and prepares the family for this so that their growth flow can make room for this natural reaction. "You have had a taste of what communication can be like for you in this family. However, every family has its own rhythm for how it grows and develops as a system. You may find that you want to pull back from each other and each to be in your own separate place for a while. If that happens, don't see it as a rejection or depreciation of what happened today—see it as each person's way of reacting to a new experience and give each other room to assimilate and savor the experience, each in his own way. You may find that fights may develop over nothing, and you may feel discouraged that that should happen after such a lovely experience. Consider that while each of you has enjoyed this experience today, it is new and may therefore be somewhat frightening. So, you may fall back into an old familiar fight pattern as a reaction to your fear. Don't let that throw you if it happens. Just consider it part of the process and gradually you'll learn ways to handle your fear of new situations that are not so destructive to you. On the other hand, you may not have a reaction at all. You may come next week with expectations and the readiness to go deeper. I want you to know that any way you go is all right with me. I do not have a program for you. It is obvious to me that you are moving (the goal in process) and that is all that is important. The speed, depth, and way in which you move is connected to your own natural growth rhythm which we must all get acquainted with and trust as that is the best way for you to go."

You can see by this example how the therapist stays in tune with the flow of the family system and the flow of each individual within the family system, as well as the flow between past, present, and future. Thus the direction of the therapy follows the salient pattern of the flow from the interaction between husband and wife to the interaction between the wife and her parents to her internal experience in the current situation of the interview—the internal reactions of other family members about themselves and their own history—to the family's fears about change and a clearer understanding about what change will mean to them and what it will cost them—to a beginning awareness of how the therapy really works, what they can expect, and what the goals really are in terms of growth and an understanding of their own natural rhythms. Therefore, the therapist may have a sense of where he and the family need to go in the treatment plan, but he must be prepared to shift if the major energy thrust of the system goes in a different direction. For example, husband and wife may be getting into an important exchange of feelings for the first time in a session. The therapist may be very interested in this because he has been working with them toward this goal for several sessions. However, the children keep interrupting and interfering with this interaction. A neophyte family therapist could get very annoyed with the children for interrupting and show his annoyance by giving them an order to stop, by trying to ignore them, or by excluding them from the session. An experienced family therapist, who understands the value of process, would see this as an indication that the system is not yet ready for this kind of intimacy and must be prepared for it before the parents can go ahead. Otherwise, whatever would be accomplished in that exchange would be sabotaged or undermined in future family interactions. Therefore, the therapist may ask the parents how they feel about what the children are doing. The parents may say they are annoyed. Then it is important to understand why they don't express their annoyance. What is going on that they don't make room in their family for their intimacy to flourish? Unless the parents are willing to do this, they will not sustain what they learn in the session. The parents' own fears about intimacy may find expression through the children. If that is so, then the parents need room to express their ambivalence to each other and to other family members. The therapist encourages them to share these feelings and let a decision evolve rather than force themselves in a direction for which they are not ready.

The therapist may then explore with the children what they are feeling about their parents' interaction. With encouragement from the therapist, the children may reveal they are feeling left out. The therapist may then explain that the parents are learning something new for them. At first, the children may feel left out because the parents have not behaved in this way before. However, if the children will give them room, they will find that they will get much more from their parents if the parents learn to give to each other in this way. Children don't always understand the words of the therapist, but they usually get the message.

DEFINITION OF THERAPY PROCESSES

It is very important to distinguish between process and process*es*. Process is the dynamic energy flow within the individual, with the interaction between two people, or with the interactional flow of the entire family system as described in detail above.

Process*es* are the way of thinking, looking, being, and behaving which family members follow and use in their expression of themselves and their interactions with one another. We will go into detail in Chapter Twelve about the many different negative and growth processes we have seen in working with families. However, at this point we'll use an example in order to define the term and differentiate it from process.

The Jones Family comes in for therapy because their 14-year-old son is stealing hubcaps, and was picked up by the police, who didn't hold him, but did encourage the family to seek treatment. They also have a 16-year-old daughter who is mystified by her brother's behavior, as she is a model student and her parents' fair-haired girl. As the therapist observes the family's interaction with him and with each other, he sees that their process is blocked. The energy in the system is being used to hold in so that the family system feels dead and heavy. No one touches anyone and no one looks at another person when he is talking to that person. The boy's head and body posture is down and contained, the father looks rigid and swelled up like a toad, and the daughter has eyes that look bright and alive but her body posture is rigid and controlled. The therapist would use these observations to get deeper into the process of what is really going on in this family. As he labels his observations about the way in which the system is operating, family members may get away from their rigidity and their focus on the boy as the family's only problem. Then feelings may come out and the process open wider and clearer. It becomes apparent that father is feeling very sad and helpless, but that does not come out in the family. What comes out instead is an occasional anger outburst when he hits his son, stoicism, or a pained lecture about how his disrespectful son doesn't appreciate all he tries to do for him and will end up in jail. When the process moves to explore why the father expresses his hurt and helplessness in such incongruent ways, then the processes emerge. These are: Men do not express sadness or helplessness. If they do, it is a sign they are failures, weak, and unreliable. They must take care of their feelings themselves and protect the family from knowing they are at all upset in order to maintain their authority and the stability of the family system. Children must do as they are told if it is reasonable and for their own good, and they must not express their differences or anger about it. If something you are asked to do is reasonable and for your own good, you should not feel angry or unhappy about it. If you do, you are disrespectful and don't love your parents. Parents should present a united front and give the same message to a child regardless of how they feel. That is one of the processes. The *process* that evolves, however, is that both parents say the same thing, but mother sabotages by not following through or giving in later when the father isn't around. That behavior reveals another of the processes. Mother does not disagree openly with father because he is head of the house and disagreeing with him would be disrespectful and destructive to the family unit.

Processes, then, are the ways of thinking, seeing, being, and doing which family members believe they have to follow in order to grow and survive as a family unit. Process is the flow apparent with the expression of these processes in terms of whether or not they keep the system open, healthy, and growing, or cause discrepancies between internal states and external facades which produce breakdowns and blockage in the energy flow of the system with resultant symptomatology.

Chapter 4

COMMUNICATION ANALYSIS

Communication is part of the interactional framework, but we're breaking it down into more detail here for purposes of learning.

Communication—as we define its real meaning—is an interaction between two people who encounter each other and attempt to make meaning out of the encounter that is relevant to both of them. There is much interaction that is meaningless. For purposes of definition we do not consider such meaningless interaction as communication. It is game-playing, manipulation, or play acting, but not communication as we define it here. Communication provides an opportunity for change. If I communicate my inner feeling and experience which is unique and you do the same, then each of us must grow by the experience. Since I am different from you, you have to develop new ways of looking to understand me. Since your life experience is different from mine, I have the opportunity to learn new ways of coping, as your life problems and adjustments have been different from mine. Whenever two people communicate who they are from the inside, a growth experience results for both. When two people play games—their talk and interaction has nothing to do with who they are or what they are feeling inside—only repetition, disorganization, or ennui are the result. Communication is an opportunity for reinforcement and expansion. When I communicate to you, I look at you and my eyes see you as a person separate from me who does not think, feel, behave, or look at things the same way that I do. I express my feelings based on who I am and not on what I think you want me to be. I hear what you say as a statement about who you are and how you see the world and not as a judgement about me. Therefore, your expression of yourself may confirm my own feelings; it may offer me a new dimension I hadn't been aware of before, or, it may not be useful to me at all. However, in communication there is always the opportunity for expansion of one's own inner world.

Communication lays the base for real connection between two people. If we can share our deepest feelings with each other—our demands, hopes, dreams and limitations—without either of us feeling a loss of self-esteem or of our own separate identity in the process, then we have the base for developing a consistently growing and mutually enhancing relationship.

COMMUNICATION IS MULTI-LEVEL

Communication occurs on many different levels at the same time. We once took a brief course from Dr. Albert Scheflin who had done considerable research in communication. He illustrated that a person could give out seven different messages at once by the way in which he talked, looked, and held his body. The words gave one message, the tone another, the eyes, mouth, right arm, left arm, and stance all gave different messages. Neither of us have ever been able to emulate his acting ability in this respect, but we can vouch for its effectiveness in thoroughly confusing the receiver.

The levels of communication include:

Content. This is the information being discussed, the tangible, concrete issue or day's experience the family is relating. There may be many areas of confusion in the information alone. People can shift times. They start talking about something that happened yesterday and before you know what has happened the reference point has shifted to a similar situation that occurred ten years ago. Or, people can have totally different pictures of the same experience and get bogged down in who is right rather than what each person's picture of the incident was and how such discrepancies occur.

Relationship Messages. The way in which a person says "How are you?" conveys a message about the relationship. If the tone, words, and manner are distant and perfunctory, it may be congruent with a relationship which is the same, or it may imply unresolved conflict in a relationship which is normally intimate as in a marriage or with a good friend. In a family system, the way in which a father reprimands each of his children may seem to him exactly the same. He may be totally unaware that the relationship implied by the words, tone, and manner of his message is quite different with each child. It then becomes important for the therapist to make room for the children to share with him their differing perceptions of how he conveys his message to each of them and the meaning each child makes of the message for himself.

Verbal and Non-Verbal—Double Messages. The most common breakdown in communication in families occurs in this area. A mother may be offering to help a child and consistently gets rebuffed by the child. When the therapist explores this discrepancy between her intent and the outcome with the family, the children in the family reveal that her offers to help seem very aggressive and pushy to them so that they feel there isn't any room for them, that she is trying to take over. When the mother gets this same message from all the children, she has to consider that either she is trying to take over in some way she is not aware of, or the way in which she offers help has to be changed to match her intent more clearly. If only one child feels intruded on and the others experience her helpfulness as helpfulness, then she can consider that each person in the family is different and what works with one may not work with another. She can open herself up to learning alternate ways of expressing herself that fit her, but also fit different members of her family. After all, we do not live in a vacuum. What good is it if we feel totally free and clear in expressing who we are, but no one can hear us because of the way we do it? There is no one right way. There are many ways, and in the area of intimacy, we are concerned about what works, not what is right.

A wife may be saying she wants to hear her husband's feelings and to be close to him, yet she turns away from him every time he starts to come out with his feelings and she has difficulty looking at him. The husband may be talking about a problem that is serious to him and smiling at the same time. The whole family may be laughing and joking even though they are in the therapist's office to talk about separation and divorce.

Double messages occur frequently in most communication. It is difficult to be clear and congruent all the time and no one is perfect in this respect no matter how knowledgeable and practiced. Problems occur when senders are totally unaware that they are giving double messages and will not take comments from receivers about this without feeling attacked and depreciated. Families must have processes for letting each other know when mixed messages are being delivered and for seeing such information as helpful and growth-producing, not depreciative or disrespectful.

Meta-Messages. A meta-message is a message about a message, an atmospheric phenomenon. For example, you walk into a room in which a meeting is being held and immediately you feel depressed and heavy; feelings you did not have before you entered the room. That's a message about what is going on in the meeting which is not communicated by any words or body movements. Such a meta-message is very important for a therapist to heed. He may walk into his waiting room to meet a new couple who are coming into therapy with him. Immediately upon shaking hands with the couple, he perceives meta-messages. He senses a withdrawn, suspicious quality on the part of the husband and an over-anxious attempt at pleasantry on the part of the wife. That observation may be the appropriate basis on which to start the interview unless something more salient immediately emerges, as that will get the couple very quickly into their process.

A meta-message also designates the context in which a message is given. For example, a "May I help you?" is immediately understood by the receiver if the sender is a clerk in a store and is saying this phrase from behind a counter. If the same message were sent by some stranger on the street, the receiver wouldn't know what was meant and would be at a loss as to how to respond. In other words, the context in which the message is given clarifies the meaning of the message.

Overt-Covert Messages. This is a type of double message in which the overt manifestations of words and body seem to be giving a congruent message. It looks as though everyone in the family is being clear and congruent and effectively dealing with their problems. However, over time, nothing changes, nothing gets resolved, and nothing at all happens. The therapist then explores this phenomenon with the family on the basis that there must be something going on that is not being opened up and is sabotaging the family's progress. Father then reveals that he has been having an affair for three years with a next door neighbor and everyone in the family reveals that he knew about the affair, but it has never before been openly discussed or even mentioned in the family. All family members have been in tacit agreement to maintain a united front of denial with regard to father's double life.

Another type of overt-covert situation occurs when family members are in tacit agreement to protect one member of the family who is psychotic. The psychotic processes of that family member are not immediately apparent to the therapist because family members operate in such ways to make that member look good and to subtly divert pressure from that member. However, again, nothing changes in the family and the delinquent child they came about gets worse and worse. As the therapist opens this up and begins to put pressure on each family member about hiding something, cracks begin to appear in the family defense armor. Perhaps the psychotic one is Mother, and she begins to get bizarre in her punishment of the delinquent child, instead of reasonable and righteous which is the defense she has used in the past to cover her internal disorder. Other family members begin to complain about her sometimes erratic behavior and the covert family system begins to open up. It becomes apparent that underneath this superficially stable, intelligent, well-functioning family lie tremendous feelings of pain and terror covered by elaborate defense systems developed by each individual in the family and by the family system itself.

TECHNIQUES BY WHICH MESSAGES ARE CONVEYED

It is impossible not to communicate. We think psychoanalysts have lived with an illusion that it is possible to maintain total objectivity by having a patient lie on a couch facing away from the therapist. The patient perceives all kinds of messages from the way the therapist breathes, rattles his papers, moves in his chair, and from the slightest nuance of change in any of his usual patterns. The patient's assumptions about what is being communicated to him may not be accurate, but the therapist is certainly not a nonentity who doesn't reveal himself. In turn, family members live with illusions if they assume they aren't communicating just because they aren't talking or aren't saying what they feel.

One of the initial concepts that families who come for therapy need to understand is that the message sent is not always the message received. Many major arguments in marriages occur in situations such as the husband upstairs in the bathroom shaving and the wife downstairs in the kitchen cooking—maximum opportunity for misunderstanding. Or, they are both in bed at night talking with the lights out. They can't see each other so major avenues for clarifying communication are cut off. Or, they are talking on the telephone, again not able to see each other, touch, or pick up meta-messages more clearly.

Dysfunctional families (those whose processes for solving their problems are not working and who have come for help to learn new ones) need to develop techniques for checking out what they are perceiving from each other. They must learn not to assume that just because they have lived together a long time they automatically know what meaning the other is communicating. That particular dogma is the mark of a closed system!

What some families consider communication is really consistent disqualification which serves the purpose of keeping real feelings covert and the family system un-threatened. They talk for each other; they assume what other family members are thinking or feeling without checking it out; they interrupt; they change the subject; they laugh or cry inappropriately, and they cut each other off or depreciate each other in a hundred other devious and subtle ways.

Another technique for conveying messages is the double-bind. The double-bind theory was developed by Gregory Bateson in his research into schizophrenic families. It also operates in families in which there is no psychotic member, but its consistent use often provokes psychotic-like behavior in the moment from whichever family member happens to be on the receiving end. We see the double-bind technique in this way: A parent is telling a child to go in two directions at once. The parent may be saying overtly "Come and sit on my lap," but when the child obeys, he feels a subtle message that says "Don't touch," or "Don't get too close." It may be a body message, a facial expression or a meta-message. The second component of the double-bind technique is that the receiver feels dependent for his survival on the sender of the double message. Otherwise, he could simply confront the sender with his duplicity or walk away. Next, there is no room to comment on the bind without provoking attack or abandonment. For example, a 17-year-old son is constantly admonished by his parents to "grow up and be a man." In the next breath, a parent is telling him to wear his galoshes when he goes out and which girls he can date. When he comments on the inconsistency of these messages, his mother bursts into tears and his father reprimands him for upsetting his mother and not being a respectful son. Or, perhaps they both get very cold and don't speak to him for several days. With these three components, the receiver has the choice to try to go in both directions at the same time or to act a little crazy so he isn't responsible for his choice. When he acts a little crazy, he becomes the victimizer instead of the victim because other family members feel responsible for his "sickness" and therefore are unable to make reasonable demands on him or to have realistic expectations from him. Such families may double-bind each other in this way to the point where they are chained in this seesaw victim-victimizer pattern forever.

Another technique for conveying messages in the family involves the use of coalitions. Mother and daughter may have a tacit agreement that daughter protects mother from father. She intercedes when it looks as though the parents are not working things out and explains to father what mother is feeling. She argues with father in mother's place. She may also listen to father's problems and provide warmth and sympathy. She is the mediator through whom the parents send their messages to each other. Her mediation serves the purpose of keeping the parents at a distance from each other because they are obviously afraid of intimacy. In return, she gets a great deal of approval from both parents for her role and feels she is important in holding the family together. She is building her personality structure around rescuing her family—a potential therapist! (We'll cover the nuances of that remark in a later chapter.)

Each family may use any or all of these techniques at one time or another. However, a family may have an overall, pervasive communication pattern which is consistent and inherent to the family structure. The pattern may be one of uproar. Interviews with families like this can be exhausting. They can go into violent discussions, threats, screaming, and yelling sessions with everyone talking at once, and they can turn it off and on at will. As a result, no one ever gets anything in the family—not even a hearing. Another family may be very reasonable, polite, and considerate in their conversation. After a few sessions of this, the therapist may become aware of a splitting headache and realize that his body is telling him what it is costing this family to maintain this pattern constantly at the expense of their real feelings. Another overall pattern may be one of silence and quick closure. Family members do not talk much and when they do, someone offers an idea or a solution and that's the end of that. The therapist begins to feel it is his responsibility to get something going and develop interaction in the family. He is picking up the message members of the system are sending to each other and the outside world: "It's your responsibility to save me and give me life." They may not be aware of this, but their communication pattern reveals that infantile plea.

All of the above techniques produce and maintain closed systems. The first step the therapist must take in working with a family is to teach them the concept of feedback and establish a contract with them that they will allow feedback among themselves and to and from the therapist. Feedback is vital to an open system. The degree to which a family is dysfunctional is directly related to the degree to which feedback is disallowed or unknown. Feedback is a process by which family members can comment on how they perceive the way in which a message is sent and on their feelings in response to the message. The feedback is heard as an attempt to understand and keep the flow of communication open, and not as an attack.

TYPES OF COMMUNICATION SYSTEMS

The uproar pattern of communication tends to develop an *Uproar* family system characterized by an infantile quality. Frequently family members will respond to the therapist only when he takes a firm stand with them about what he will and won't allow in his office, or when he touches them physically. They are like wounded animals in their behavior and the meta-message they present. They have negative contact only which has a quality of energy and aliveness, but it is out of control. They are very afraid of intimacy because they have never had any positive experience in that area. Their life experience has led them to expect loss or attack if they reveal their vulnerable, deep feelings of fear and inadequacy and yearnings. They each have a defensive, protective posture like armies meeting each other with their shields up in front, comforted by the noise of attack—at least someone is there; they are not alone on the battlefield.

The reasonable pattern of communication usually designates a *Repressive* family system. This system has a judgmental structure as its base. Everyone operates according to what he has heard, read, or been taught is right or wrong, good or bad. Everyone attempts to match himself to this external image which appears to have been gleaned from an old-fashioned ladies' magazine or TV show idea of what an all-American family should be like. The system is characterized by the expression of psychosomatic symptomatology or withdrawn behavior on the part of its members. It has a quality of dullness even though members may be very industrious. The therapist frequently has trouble staying awake and his body may respond with numerous aches and pains during the sessions as he picks up all the repressed anger. Often the repressed rage is murderous.

The stoical, wrap-up pattern of communication is often characteristic of a *Depressed* family system. The meta-message in this family is heaviness and deadness. The therapist feels as though the family is one huge vacuum cleaner and he is being sucked dry of all his energy and life as he sits there with them. They project a message of hopelessness, helplessness, and guilt as though it is his fault they are in trouble and he should do something. They may not say this directly, but the therapist feels the message very strongly and can easily get seduced into doing all their work for them. The symptomatology is usually a suicide attempt, or other self-destructive behavior like alcoholism or heroin addiction.

In the *Schizophrenic* family system, the communication pattern is disorganized and totally unclear. The therapist can spend an hour or ten hours with this family, and at the end not have the faintest idea what they are talking about. In this context, we do not mean that any family members are actually psychotic or schizophrenic, but the system is, in that nothing is ever clear. No one ever knows where he or she stands. Decisions never get made until people are backed against a wall and then they react impulsively like children striking out, so that the action has no real meaning. Affect is usually unclear. When it is clear, then the actions don't match the feelings. People do not back up their feelings with action and when they do act, it is out of panic or frustration and not a clear assertion of a demand or limit.

There is a type of uproar communication that produces a *Placater-Blamer* family system in which someone is always under attack and someone is always trying to make peace. The nature of the system is that this is the only way people know how to make contact. When they are not in this pattern, there is no contact or interaction at all. They are polarized between an attitude of distance and depression and this placater-blamer form of communication. They expect others to take responsibility for them and make them happy. They have a scapegoat structure to keep them from having to look at themselves and feel overwhelmed with sadness, depression and anger. These families are generally made up of people who have been severely deprived and never opened up and worked through their feelings about their deprivation.

Chapter 5

CONCEPT OF BASIC DYADIC INTERACTIONAL UNIT

In order to clarify the concept of interaction, we'll take a two-person (dyadic) interaction here and examine it step by step as though it were occurring in a slow-motion film. First of all, the dyad interactional ingredients for each person include:

Internal Perceptors. These are the eyes, ears, nose, and skin. Each individual absorbs data from the other person by means of seeing, hearing, smelling, and touching, out of which he attempts to make meaning.

External Manifestors. These include language, facial expressions, voice tone, body tonus, and dress. These are the avenues through which each individual expresses his own uniqueness and responds to stimulus from the other.

Let's imagine Person 1 and Person 2 (husband and wife) sitting and facing each other at the breakfast table. Wife sends the message to husband, "Let's go to a movie tonite." Now, the interaction between them may break down right at this point. Her words are an invitation, but her tone is sullen. Husband notes the discrepancy but doesn't comment on it directly. He assumes that she is still annoyed at something that happened the night before and is sending him the message that she wants to go to a movie, but knows he's too much of a tightwad to take her. He responds as though his internal assumption were true: "You're never satisfied!" She then is outraged because on her insides she feels she has made a simple, conciliatory request and he hit below the belt. She says, "You bastard, you don't appreciate anything I do!" And they are off and running.

For purposes of exploration, we consider the above example as a complete unit of interaction—stimulus (message sent), feedback (reaction and reply), and response (outcome of original message: the dye is cast). Now, when a message is sent, it is screened by the receptor through his current condition. If the husband has a cold and is running a fever, he either may not hear at all or may have a much stronger tendency to receive the message inaccurately or negatively. Many couples don't make room for these differences in mood or body states. They assume that if the other person doesn't hear or hears inaccurately that he does it deliberately with malice and they don't allow for the reality that no one is always in perfect condition to hear. The receptor also screens the message through his expectations, based on his history in this relationship and in his origin family. In the example, the husband expected a hostile greeting from his wife at breakfast because of the fight they had had the night before which had gone unresolved. Therefore, when he picked up a somewhat negative tone in her feedback to him, he concluded that his expectations were accurate and acted on that conclusion. Many arguments begin when couples don't have check-out techniques for determining whether or not their assumptions are correct when they get double messages. Without even being aware of what he is doing, each person carries on a private dialogue inside of himself almost as though the other person wasn't there. He makes an assumption based on the stimulus of the other's words or behavior; goes through several explanations inside himself and concludes what the message means, then he acts on his conclusion as though it were a reality.

The husband's negative expectations may also come from his own origin family experience. He may have had a mother who was very critical and demanding of him. He may have hope that his wife could be understanding and appreciative toward him, but his expectation based on his experience with his mother is that she will not be. His tendency is to act on the expectation rather than the hope so that he is quick to interpret the slightest unclear nuance in his wife's communication as a negative message toward him. The message may also be screened through self-preoccupations. He may be worried about a transaction he has to complete at work that day and be so absorbed that any message from anyone is an intrusion.

Now, on the other side of the interaction, the wife's internal state during her delivery of her request was that she did recall the fight the night before and wanted to make amends, so she sent out an invitation. However, without her being aware of it, her invitation was sabotaged by her expectations so that her words expressed an invitation, but her tone expressed her feeling that he really didn't want to be with her and wasn't going to respond. She has a father who was withholding and punitive with her, so while she hopes her husband wants to give to her, she expects that he does not. Or, she also may be preoccupied and her words express what she wants to do with him, but her tone expresses her feeling that it's going to be a rough day with the children. She's giving him two messages which are unrelated to each other and he's receiving them as though they are both directed at him. The problem is that each of them operates in a defensive posture with the other, so there is no room for error or lack of clarity. Without such room, the system remains closed and each uses the interaction to constantly confirm what they have always known: men don't appreciate you and women are never satisfied.

When the wife replies back to her husband (response), that response is screened through her rules for reporting herself. These are different from the family system rules we discussed earlier. Rules for reporting have to do with the individual's learned experience about how he has to manifest himself to avoid attack or abandonment. For example, the wife may have learned in her original family that if she expressed angry feelings, she got clobbered or ignored. So, if she is hurt or angered by her husband's response, she doesn't strike back. Instead, she bursts into tears. She may have married a man who operates similarly to her father in the feeling area, and he reinforces her original expectations by his withdrawal behavior when she gets upset. The husband, on the other hand, has learned that you don't criticize women. If you do, then they don't give to you—don't take care of the house, the meals, or respond sexually. So, instead of coming out directly with his anger, he looks pained or walks away. The individual's rules for reporting are out of his awareness. He doesn't realize that he operates by such a rigid pattern for expressing who he is, and it is evident to the therapist only by the discrepancies.

There are many other distortion possibilities in the context of interaction. Either party may have a receptor difficulty. He or she may be hard of hearing, not see well, be in pain or handicapped in some other way. Also, a couple may have coded negative expressions. For example, in the husband's experience, every time the wife calls him "darling", it means she wants something from him. So he doesn't hear that word as a love message; he flinches instead, waiting for the string. The word "movie" may be coded for him, because every time they have gone to a movie in the past month, they have had a fight.

So, the request is heard as an invitation to another fight rather than a chance to be together. In addition, she may be getting messages from his dress and his body as he sits at the breakfast table. He may be slouched over his coffee, unshaven and bleary-eyed. One part of her is inviting him to be with her; another part is registering disgust at his appearance and manner. Both messages are coming through, but not clearly and separately. When the love message and disgust message get lumped together—obviously one cancels out the other, and nothing constructive gets across. The husband may look at the wife as she comes down to breakfast and see that she's wearing a housecoat he hates. He interprets that as a direct insult because he operates by the rule that if she loved him, she would do what he asks and wear what pleases him. So, he's angry even before she opens her mouth.

When the therapist is working with any dyadic interaction in a family, he has to follow the flow very closely to see where the interaction breaks down and what may be getting in the way. His first step, then, is to get the two parties to face each other and look at each other. Then they have maximum opportunity for use of all their preceptors and manifestors so there is maximum opportunity for contact. The sequence the therapist then follows is:

Stimulus. How congruent is the message Person 1 is sending? Do the words, body, tone, and mannerisms match and do the therapist's insides register a clear message?

Reception. How ready is Person 2 to hear? Is he looking at Person 1? Does his posture look open and interested, or does he appear closed and turned off?

Sensation. Does the emotional reaction of Person 2 appear congruent with the message he is receiving? For example, when Person 1 sends a clear, congruent love message, does Person 2 recoil as though he is being attacked or does he respond in kind or with a clear message about not being in a receiving mood for a love message?

Perception. If Person 2 receives a clear love message as an attack, then there is a breakdown in his perceptual apparatus in this area. What has he learned either in this relationship or previous relationships that produced this barrier to receiving the affection he says he wants?

Cognition. What is the meaning Person 2 makes out of certain words, gestures, body tonus, voice tone, and facial expressions when conveyed by Person 1? Does that meaning fit with the message Person 1 was intending to convey? If not, where did the breakdown occur? Was Person 1 delivering double or unclear messages? Was

Person 2 distorting the messages he received, or were both of these processes happening?

Rules for Reporting. Does Person 2 appear to be editing (exploring possible replies inside himself) or is he able to respond spontaneously? Does he give clear feedback about how he interprets the message and how he feels in response to it, or does he reply with what he thinks (reasons, defenses, judgements rather than feelings), or what he guesses the other person wants to hear? If his feedback stays on a head level and doesn't say anything about where he is inside, then how did he learn not to come out with his feelings?

Feedback. Is Person 2 able to hold his ground and stay with himself and his own feelings in the face of any kind of a message from Person 1? Or, does he respond as though Person 1 is in charge of him, a judge over him, a parent, or a threat to him in some way?

Response. Can Person 1 respond spontaneously or does the interaction drop like a stone at this point? Do his rules for reporting allow him to respond to some feelings and not to others? Can he stay in contact with his partner or does he look away and give body avoidance messages? Does he respond to both the verbal and non-verbal messages of his partner or just to one level? For example, a husband may only hear his wife's criticism and respond to that, but not respond to her non-verbal expressions of pain or fear. On the other hand, a child may ignore a parent's words which are pleading with him and pay attention only to the parent's body messages, which are threatening.

Interaction can break down at any or all of these points, so the job of the therapist is difficult in this framework. The interaction may occur very rapidly; the breakdowns may be subtle and fleeting to the observer; and, the therapist must not only keep his eye on all these things, but also on how the rest of the family is responding to this interaction between two of its members.

PART II

TREATMENT CONCEPTS
AND TECHNIQUES

Chapter 6

THERAPIST'S USE OF SELF

The most difficult aspect of family therapy is that the therapist is operating on many different levels simultaneously. This principle of simultaneity may seem overwhelming as we discuss it here. However, we would like to say to beginning family therapists that the ability to operate on all of these levels at the same time does develop with time and experience. The problem is that the beginning therapist must be prepared to lose families without being harsh with himself. He may be operating very well on one or more levels, but miss another important one which will lose him the family in treatment. It is simply impossible to become proficient enough in all of these levels all at once. Therefore, the beginning family therapist does not have the means to flow freely with the family's energy and process. At this point, we would like to enumerate the major simultaneous levels of operation.

First, the therapist must be in and out of the family system at the same time. The therapist operates best by taking enough physical distance from the family so that he can see the entire family within his area of vision. He watches the family's interaction and communication patterns. In addition, he tunes into his own experience of sitting in with the family system. For example, a therapist is interviewing a family with both parents and five children. He is sitting between the two parents. The interaction of the family members seems to be moving fairly freely verbally, but they are getting nowhere. The therapist looks at their patterns and considers the possibility that they may be masking the real problem by trying to cover too much ground. So, he asks them to take a specific incident that occurred recently and go into it in detail in terms of what each person's picture was, what each said and felt. They begin to do this and all seem to be involved but, again, the feeling tone of the session has the quality of spinning wheels or bogging down. The therapist then momentarily checks out of the system and into his insides. He picks up a heavy feeling, a chaotic feeling, and he is also aware that he feels more and more constricted as he sits between the two parents. He offers all of this information to the family; thus intervening back into the system in an attempt to shake it up because all the data indicates that the family is not dealing with the real issues. The family responds to the therapist's observations with confusion (on the part of the parents) and nods of understanding from the children.

The therapist then asks each child in turn to change places with him, sit between the parents, and communicate his feelings about this experience. Each child communicates either by his words or his physical behavior that this is an uncomfortable place to be. The therapist then offers to the parents that six people including himself are picking up something that is transpiring between them. He then asks what each of them is experiencing. He checks in with his own insides and realizes he is much relieved and the heaviness has vanished. This data is validated by the system as the physical behavior and energy level in the family is much less constricted. Therefore, he knows he is in paydirt. He then asks the parents to face each other and begin to explore what might be going on between them.

As the parents take the physical positions facing each other and looking at each other directly, the tension again builds. The therapist is aware of his hands perspiring; he checks out the other family members and they are fidgeting, withdrawing, or interrupting in some way. He uses this data to again move back into the system to keep it open, offers his observation, and wonders if they are frightened or worried. Two of the children say that they are but are unable to clarify the reasons for their feelings. Both parents confirm that they are very tense. The therapist asks them to describe their tension to each other. As you can see, the therapist is constantly moving into the system with interventions designed to break all the rules and trigger crises in the system in order to develop movement. At the same time, he keeps checking back into his own internal system for data about the family since they are so well defended and therefore unrevealing in their external image. When he gets data from his internal processes that is incongruent or discrepant with the family's image, he looks for behavior or communication patterns that would support or deny his internal data. When he gets supportive behavior, he puts pressure on the family to further explore along whatever pathway produces that anxiety.

In this particular family, it came out over time that everyone in the family was operating as though he or she had many secrets from the others. The parents were involved in husband-and-wife-swapping encounters which they thought the children didn't know about. The husband and wife each had had brief, periodic affairs which each thought were unknown to the other. The children often lied to their parents and thought they were getting away with it. What emerged as these things came out was that all of these things were known by all family members, but never discussed, as though they were all in a conspiracy of pretense. The result was a build-up of tremendous rage and frustration which was producing a fear and distance in the family.

In another instance, the therapist who is working with a judgmental family will suddenly find himself in an argument with the father in the family about who is right. If the part of himself that is outside the system is operating, he will become aware that he has been caught by the system and can offer this to the family: "Look, here I am doing the same thing you do to each other. I'm arguing about who is right or wrong instead of sharing my feelings and dealing with yours. That's a statement to me about how strong your system is and how difficult it must be for each of you to break out of that framework, even though it isn't working for you any longer."

The therapist must also be aware of his own body posture, his tone, and his energy level in comparison with the system; otherwise, if he is the same as the system, he will support and reinforce its negative processes. For example, the family appears very depressed and heavy. The therapist finds himself working hard to put energy into the system and he feels increasingly heavy and depressed. If he allows this to continue, he will become angry and withdraw or attack the family, or he will feel guilty because nothing is happening, and work even harder. If, on the other hand, he is able to step out of the system, he can observe what is happening to him as a message about the system. Then he can say to the family "As I work with you, I find my voice getting lower and lower, my posture sinking, and my gut feeling depressed as though it is my fault you aren't producing or moving or getting what you want. I wonder if that is the message you perceive from each other?" He then throws his data back into the system which is a clear message that he can maintain his boundaries and therefore help them in a way that leaves him intact and them responsible for their own choices. That is something they are not able to do with each other. So, he is operating in opposition to the negative processes in the family system, and at the same time is modeling a positive process for opening and exploring because he is using himself to observe and comment without criticising or depreciating any of them.

Secondly, the therapist is constantly checking back and forth between his own inferences in terms of assessment and treatment direction with the salient processes emerging in the family's interactional flow. For example, as he is interviewing a family in a first session, he observes that the interaction is limited. Family members do not touch each other or look at each other when they talk. Their body postures are stiff and rigid; the dress of all the family members is noticeably discrepant with the one member whom all others identify as the patient or the disturbed one in the family. Verbally, the focus is on this member, the son, and on his use of drugs. The underlying message is that the family would be fine if he were not around and he would be fine if he had never known about drugs. The father lectures as though he were on a soapbox when he talks, usually looking at the ceiling or out at some unknown audience. The mother is passive in her behavior, does not speak unless drawn out and then responds in a tiny, little girl voice. The daughter lectures like the father, appears more the wife in the family than the mother does. The family sits in such a way that the son seems to be outside the system.

The therapist notes all these factors and begins to make inferences in his head about possible meanings and directions, that may go something like this: There seems to be a role dysfunction between mother and daughter in that daughter appears more the adult. That coupled with the mother's passive behavior and her little girl voice suggests that the mother doesn't have much to give as an adult woman; and the family, including the husband, is not getting any nurturing from her even though she may perform as a very capable homemaker. That suggests a serious breakdown between the parents in terms of giving and receiving which seems validated by the husband's stiffness, deadness, and the total feeling of asexuality which the family projects. The therapist further infers this has been a long-standing problem in view of the rigidity of the roles and the family's defense system, so he cannot push the marital relationship prematurely. Therefore, perhaps the best direction to go is to open up the communication between the father and son. The son is the one most discrepant with the system and therefore perhaps most available to change, and the father is so desperate about loss of control over his son that he might be amenable to some change. The therapist decides he must move slowly because the family is obviously very frightened and could panic and become overwhelmed easily. He is about to proceed in this direction when suddenly the wife lashes out at her husband, "I'm sick of your preaching and your judgments about how everyone should be—I don't blame Jimmy for getting out—if it weren't for the children I would kill myself!"

At this point, the evolving process is making it clear that the therapist has to shift both in his inference process and his treatment direction. That doesn't mean that his previous inferences were incorrect, necessarily; it does mean that the mother is in crisis, that crisis is the most salient factor in the family's current energy flow and, therefore, it has to be dealt with immediately. If the therapist does not deal with this crisis, but proceeds with his previous inferences, the family will assume he is not able to handle them and will not trust him. In order to build trust, the therapist always has to go where the energy, the aliveness, the feeling in the system is. Again that is discrepant with the dysfunctional system which is dysfunctional because family members are afraid of their aliveness (intensity), and do not know how to handle it without hurting themselves or others. It is the therapist's job to teach them how to handle their energy in ways that promote growth and do not result in internal loss or damage.

The therapist's inference level shifts. The mother feels pushed beyond her support system; she is potentially suicidal. The message in her words, behavior, tone, and body position, is congruent—panic and desperation. The therapist acknowledges that she is obviously in terrible pain, and asks that she share more of this pain with the family. He asks family members to listen without feeling as though they are responsible, but just hear and stay in touch with their own feelings so that they can share them. As the mother opens up more, the therapist may move in one of two directions depending on where the energy is. If it appears that the wife is wanting support and release of feelings with her family, he will move in an interactional direction, helping her to come out with her feelings in a way that doesn't blame, dump, or depreciate others, and enabling others in the family to learn how to hear and respond with their own feelings. If, on the other hand, her panic and rage seem to be out of control, he infers that it is vital to give her some release or she may suffer a serious depression or make a suicide attempt. Therefore, he moves in the direction of a physical release through Gestalt techniques like beating a chair and screaming. This would be supported with much explanation, encouragement, and understanding offered to her and the rest of the family so that they can tolerate and allow this shift. When she is relieved, the therapist would then integrate this change into the system by getting everyone else's reaction, both to her and within themselves, and then teaching them to look at this explosion in a growth framework while at the same time supporting how frightened all of them must be. However, even though they are fearful of change, they are faced with the reality that their old ways of operating are killing them as evidenced by the son's symptom and the mother's feelings expressed in the session. Therefore, in order to live and grow, they have to change. Thus it is clear to them what their choices are, but there *are* choices. The family is still in charge of what it does. The therapist does not take over. He then explains that he will assist the family in learning new ways of operating that fit them better and are not destructive, but it will take time. He may discuss with the family members what safety valves they will need in the meantime to give them temporary relief while they are learning new ways. His inference level tells him that the family members are very child-like, need a lot of support and structuring about what has happened to prevent a crisis during the week. There may be one anyway, no matter how much support they get, so the therapist is preparing for that by opening up that this can happen and it isn't terrible. It just means that families have different learning patterns, and so it is important to explore how can we handle a crisis if it does occur, with minimal upset to the system.

The important point is that the therapist does make inferences continually as a way of cataloguing and assimilating all the data constantly in front of him, but he must be prepared to shift instantly if the flow of energy in the family system moves to a new or different level.

Third, the therapist must be aware of communication patterns among the family members, between himself and the family as a whole, and between himself and each family member. He may observe that, although family members say father is the boss in the family, mother seems to be the spokesman. Mother and father often don't speak to each other directly; they speak through the oldest son, who translates to each what the other one means. This is discrepant with the family members' insistence that they all communicate easily with each other except for the daughter whom they see as the family "problem." All family members, except for the daughter, communicate with the therapist with a deferent manner as though he is a judge or some superior being. Yet, they do not accept any feedback that he offers them. They are quick to defend, explain, or give reasons why what he offers isn't so, and they don't allow themselves any room to assimilate and consider what he says. It is as though they are so couched for defense that they don't even hear him. No one is open to any feedback that suggests change as they see feedback as criticism and attack. The father in the family is wary even of supportive, empathetic comments from the therapist. The mother is more amenable to warmth from the therapist, but the children quickly interfere if it looks as though the therapist and the mother may be developing a positive connection.

In this instance, the communication patterns on all these levels seem to give a congruent message—the family members are all feeling emotionally hungry and depleted. Everyone wants but no one feels he is getting anything. People in the family do not listen, cannot accept feedback and are not yet ready for a therapy contract. Their beginning sessions would be geared toward a slow, supportive explanation of what is involved in therapy and what their alternatives are separate from therapy so that they can make a decision about what they want. The therapist would handle this preparation phase with recognition of their immediate sense of helplessness and emotional drain. The family may or may not be at a point where they can actually move into therapy, but it will be a therapeutic experience for them to be clearly confronted in a non-judgmental way with the real issues they are facing and their possible choices about these issues. That process alone is discrepant with their own way of dealing with each other which is critical and demanding.

In another family, there might be considerable discrepancy among the communication patterns which would require a very different way of handling the family system. When these family members talk to each other their words may express denial of their feelings, but when they talk to the therapist, the feelings may begin to emerge. The therapist could then use that phenomenon to explore with family members what they experience with him that they would like to have with each other so that they could share and communicate.

In still another situation, there may be coalitions. Father can communicate with daughter and mother, but not with son. If he can also communicate with a male therapist, then the therapist might assume there is a learning gap in his experience in the area of fathering, due to an absent or unknown father, and explore that possibility with him. If he cannot communicate with the therapist, but is withholding and distant, the therapist might assume there are some feelings of hurt and rage connected with his father which are in the way and explore his boyhood relationship with his dad in terms of what he got that he didn't want or what he wanted that he didn't get.

Fourth, we think that the most important area of observation for the therapist has to do with body and behavioral clues. There are numerous simultaneous levels of observation around this data. We think the most important are:

1. The congruency of the body messages of each member of the family with his words, tone, and quality of expression. The father's whole organism may express a congruent message of rigidity and containment. Or, his body message may express rigidity but be discrepant with his voice and facial expression which indicate that he is close to tears. The therapist notes the father's congruency or discrepancy of expression and also observes the reaction of each of the other family members to this expression from father.

2. The therapist's own body posture is important as a way of assessing the family system. The therapist may be slumping in an increasingly depressed position as he works with the family. He may be sitting with arms and legs crossed—a possible statement that either he or the family or both are trying to go in two directions at once. The point is, it is helpful if the therapist can be aware of his own body posture on the level of what it may express about the family with whom he is working as well as the level of what it means in relation to his own personal circumstances at the moment.

3. The therapist must be aware of the discrepancy of body movement to the family system. For example, a family may be discussing its situation very reasonably, but there are constant body movements that seem to just ripple through the system from one family member to another.

4. Body movements may occur in patterns. Each time the communication gets to a feeling level between the parents, the youngest son starts kicking the table. Or, every time father starts to become angry, the children begin stretching and yawning. The therapist then codes these patterns for intervention at an appropriate point.

Fifth, the most important tools the therapist has are his own internal manifestations as they relate to all these other levels we've been describing. If his internal experience of the interview is different from all the other data he is observing and he is fairly sure his re-action is not related to something going on in his own life; then, the most effective way to proceed is on the basis of that internal data. The beginning therapist will usually not do this because he doesn't feel he has educated himself enough to his internal manifestations to be sure of them. So, he will try all other directions first, but will usually end up back with his internal experience. This is all right because it takes time and experience for the therapist to test out his resources in this respect until he feels they are finely tuned and balanced. However, once he is more sure of himself in this area, he will save himself and the family considerable treatment time. The therapist may learn via checking out his internal manifestations with the family that when he feels tension in his stomach, he is picking up fear. When he feels a pain through his neck and shoulders, he is perceiving anger. When he becomes sleepy, even though he has had sufficient sleep, he is experiencing rage. Everyone is different in terms of how his body reacts to subliminal feeling messages, and each person must learn to read his own clues. However, if the thera-pist takes the trouble to learn about himself in this way, he will never be at a loss for an alternative way to proceed in a therapy session. When all else fails, this mechanism is always reliable.

In addition to all of the above, the therapist also operates as an observer, a camera, a sex and communication model, and he deter-mines the degree of intimacy to which the family will go with one another and with him. As an observer, it is important for the thera-pist to learn how to look and see without interpretation, just for registration, and to teach the family to do the same. Many of us have not learned just how to simply observe. For example, a therapist may ask a couple to sit facing each other, look at each other and say what they see. The wife looks at the husband and instead of saying, "His eyes are blue—his skin is tan and smooth." She will say, "He looks angry at me." That is an interpretation, not an observation.

Many times in the process of training family therapists at the Institute, we will ask a therapist just to observe a family and tell us what he sees. We often get comments like, "They are frightened of each other and the therapy situation," when the observable data is that family members do not look at each other or the therapist—they look down at the floor. The body postures of family members appear tight and closed with legs crossed, arms folded and shoulders hunched. Frequently, we will turn off the sound in a video tape of a family and teach people to just comment on what they observe happening without interpretation or judgement. Learning how to observe is a basic step in becoming a family therapist and a basic step in developing intimacy in a family.

The therapist operates as a camera in that he captures data from communication patterns, interactional processes and other observable phenomena for development into his internal picture of how the family operates. What are the negative processes they use for relating? How do these processes occur, and what results do they produce that are destructive to the family? He uses his eyes and ears to perceive what happens when family members try to reach each other and what breaks down in their attempts to make contact. He mirrors their behavior as though he were actually taking a picture of it. He may express this by imitating the family communication patterns, by getting involved in the system and commenting on what that is like for him, or by sharing his picture of how he, as an outsider, sees the family operating.

The therapist is a model of sexuality in terms of the way he communicates himself or herself to the family and the way in which he or she responds to the family. If a male-female co-therapy team is operating, then this factor becomes even more important because the therapy itself depends on their ability to communicate clearly and constructively with each other. Family members get confronted with all their mythology about male and female roles. They learn that feelings are not male or female, that they are just feelings. Men and women both can be tender, powerful, sensitive, petty, warm, considerate, overbearing, and there are no feelings peculiar to one sex and not the other. In addition, they learn that ways of expressing feelings are not distinctly male or female. Men and women both can cry, rage, get hysterical, have temper tantrums, express helplessness or power, and it has nothing to do with whether they are male or female, strong or weak. Having feelings and learning how to express them in ways appropriate to one's own unique nature is just part of being human.

If the female therapist sees the husband's expression of anger at her (the therapist) as a desire to make contact, or his ability to express tears as a strength, she models for the wife a new way of perceiving as well as a different way of responding to her husband. If the male therapist hears the wife's criticism of him without having to defend himself or convince her otherwise, but can respond to her non-verbal behavior which is expressing pain, he models for the husband. He shows him how to be in charge of himself and not use his wife as judge as well as how to respond to more than one level of communication.

The degree of intimacy that a family will pursue in its growth in therapy is determined by the degree of intimacy with which the therapist is comfortable. The family tests this out in terms of their relationship with him (the therapist), and their relationships with each other. In the beginning phases of treatment, family members will test out whether the therapist is in charge of himself. Can he do with them what he is asking them to do with each other—be honest and open about his feelings in ways that are not judgmental or depreciating? Sometimes a family will produce an uproar situation and it is important that the therapist be able to take charge of himself and the situation by setting his own boundaries in terms of the conditions he requires for working. He must do this in a way that leaves the family in charge of themselves so that they do not feel as though the therapist is treating them like infants.

Sometimes families feel very grateful to a therapist and want to love him by asking personal questions, expressing thanks and appreciation, or touching him. If the therapist has difficulty receiving affection from people, he may block such expression with interpretations that the family is being seductive with him to avoid something in their process, or with curt responses, or by simply not acknowledging what the family is doing and shifting to their interaction. What the therapist needs to understand is that he is not just tearing down old processes that are destructive to the family; he is also helping them build new ones that will enhance their experience with each other. Allowing them to give to him is a way of teaching them how to do this with each other. In some families parents can give to their children, but they do not know how to allow the children to give to them. Many people have difficulty receiving and the therapist can be an important model in this respect by learning how to genuinely enjoy a family's ability to give to him.

In our teaching of therapists, we have become aware that many people have difficulty when working with couples who have gone beyond their problem areas and are moving into deepening their intimacy with each other. It is not infrequent that a couple will be in a beautiful flow of interaction and the therapist will interrupt with an interpretation, completely oblivious that he has just cut off the very process he has spent months trying to develop with this couple. When we brought this to the therapist's attention and explored with him what might be going on, we find that the couple's deepening intimacy has triggered feelings of loneliness or dissatisfaction on the part of the therapist, or, that the couple is going into a depth the therapist has not experienced and does not know how to handle. Our experience has been that therapists who are skilled in techniques and processes can help people develop and express all kinds of feelings that the therapist himself may not be in touch with within himself. However, when it comes to building a relationship, we find that the therapist cannot take people where he has not been. This doesn't mean that he should stop working in these areas; it simply means that he must be aware of his current stage of growth and thus aware when the family he is working with has gone beyond him. This is not in any way a criticism of the therapist. We are all in varying stages of growth all the time and usually the kinds of clients we work best with will change as we develop, and we will find ourselves working with different types of problems and relationships at different stages of our own growth.

Chapter 7

INTERVENTION TECHNIQUES (INTERACTIONAL LEVEL)

Now we will begin to discuss techniques for intervention into the family system as they relate to different aspects of the system: the interactional framework as a whole, which is the system level; the individual in the family in terms of intrapsychic conflict, which is the individual growth level; the dyadic level—usually the parental or marital relationship, which is the relationship of one individual to another; and the process level in terms of making covert conflicts overt and conscious, which is the feeling flow and action in all of the previous three areas.

In the first aspect of the family system listed—the interactional framework as a whole—the following are effective intervention techniques.

Discrepancy in the interaction of the family unit. Here we're talking about system comments—discrepancies in the way the whole family system operates. The words may be joking while the meta-message is sadness. The words say everything is all right, but the body messages express anxiety and tension. The words and tones are angry, but the facial expressions on different family members often reveal impending tears. The family's words, behavior, and expression appear light and clinical while the subject material they are talking about must obviously be very loaded. These discrepancies are system interactions in that they show up in the whole system all at once or ripple through the system showing in different family members at different times. They indicate a total family defense structure as differentiated from an individual defense structure. The purpose of the defense is to keep the family system intact in the face of threat. The discrepancies indicate that the threat is too great and that the defense is crumbling. The family needs to understand this fact as a step in realizing that while change may produce further crisis, it will also offer an opportunity for new growth and stability. The discrepancies in their system indicate they cannot maintain their status quo or go back, so they have no choice but to go forward. Many families refuse to face that reality on their own and may have to be confronted with the evidence of their own behavior many times before they will begin to move.

Homeostatic patterns. The therapist notices that each time mother and father begin to talk directly to each other and make some kind of contact, the children interfere in some way. He intervenes with that observation, pointing out the instances in which this has happened (observable data), questions what the children are concerned about, and checks with the parents about whether the children are picking up any messages from them which invite interference. This intervention accomplishes two major steps: it takes blame off the children and offers an opportunity to explore their behavior from the energy flow concept, and it encourages each member of the family to take responsibility for looking at his own feelings and their effect on the whole family system without self-flagellation. The desire to see and understand barriers in the way to their growth becomes the major issue, rather than attempts to place blame and judgements.

Non-verbal clues. The therapist notices that the two-year-old in the family moves around from family member to family member giving and getting much affection—fondling, sitting on laps, patting, kisses. He seems to be the only one in the family able to do this as other family members do not touch or even sit near each other, but seem quite distant. The therapist could simply make that observation, or if his clinical judgement allowed, he might go further and question whether this particular child was expressing what everyone else in the family wanted but was unable to go after. The family members may deny that there is any meaning to these non-verbal clues, and the therapist does not need to push his observation further. However, if he comments on the family's non-verbal behavior consistently—just as observations without forcing any opinion—the family may become aware of its body messages to the point that it is difficult to brush them away as coincidences. Thus, the therapist is modeling new ways of looking and new ways of handling the family's additional resources. As you can see, we consider good therapy a process of education on many levels in addition to the head level, which is the only level which most of what we usually call education in our culture occurs.

Discrepancy between hopes and expectations. Family members very often talk about their hopes for themselves, each other, and the family as a whole. However, they are usually not aware that they do not give these hopes a chance to develop. In our classes, we often tell a joke about a man who had a flat tire on his auto at 3:00 a.m. on an old country road. He sees a house on the hill nearby and decides to wake them up and see if they can loan him a jack to change his tire. As he is going up the hill, he's talking to himself about how upset they will be when he wakes them up at this hour. By the time he gets to the house, he is in such a state that when he knocks and someone answers the door, he says, "Keep your damn old jack, I don't need it anyway!" People operate very often, not on what they want, but on the basis of what they expect. Then, when they get just what they expect, they can confirm their old, familiar ways about how the world will never change. That assumption may keep them in an unhappy state of being, but it is a familiar state and they have developed many processes over the years for fighting and defending themselves so they could handle unhappy states. If they began to operate according to their hopes, then they would be in unfamiliar territory and have to learn new ways of dealing with success, getting what they want, and the intensity of pleasure. We have been amazed to find that people would often rather be unhappy than have to go into unfamiliar territory where they would be neophytes and feel like awkward adolescents. That is not just true of the people we see in therapy. It seems to be true of most of us—people everywhere. We seem to have some sort of rule against being awkward, uncool, and vulnerable to error. We operate as though we expect all of our errors to have been made before we were twelve. We fail to accept that continued growth requires a willingness to go into areas in which we are not expert or even knowledgeable at all.

Our experience has been that people's hopes are seldom unreal; they are usually within the realm of possibility. However, the hopes may be based on something inside of themselves which is intangible and therefore not respected or appreciated by their owners, in this concrete-oriented world. The expectations, on the other hand, are based on very concrete repeated experiences. Therefore, people will usually govern their behavior according to the expectations: "You don't really want to give to me, do you?" The speaker is not aware that he is setting himself up to stay in the same place, to get the expected results. People deliberately make choices to maintain the *status quo* rather than risk getting hurt in new, unfamiliar ways. Again, the teaching point is that once people are aware that they are really controlling their environment and are not just helpless victims, that knowledge has to produce some kind of growth and change within them, visible or not.

Therapist exposure. System comments, such as the ones we've been discussing, are most important in beginning sessions as it is necessary to upset and break through a destructive family system in order to promote any change and growth in its individual members. When all else fails, very often the therapist's ability to use himself becomes the lever which tilts the family toward change. In this way he is saying to them, "I am not afraid of who I am, or of who you are." The therapist may reveal himself in many ways, depending on what his experience of himself, and himself with the family, is at the moment. For example, he may offer to the family, "I don't feel like being here right now. I don't know what it is, but I feel like being distant from you." The family could take offense at this remark, and offer an opportunity for the therapist to explore what made them assume he meant that as a criticism. Or, they might offer that they often feel the same way when they are together which provides another opening into their process. They may not respond at all and the therapist could deal with that according to his reaction. "Well, I feel that in this family you could set a bomb off at the dinner table and no one would flinch. What does it take to get a response out of you?"

The therapist might offer family members some of his own experience either in his own therapy or with the kind of problem they are having in terms of his feelings about having been in a similar situation. There is a fine line here in two respects. First of all, the therapist needs to feel comfortable enough with the information he is sharing that he doesn't suddenly unload on the family members and they become *his* therapists. Secondly, he must offer personal material only if he really feels it at the moment, not because it makes a good gambit, or it comes across as patronizing. An example would be, "The first time I went to a therapy session, I had many mixed feelings. I felt angry, relieved, ashamed, and confused, I wonder if you feel any of those things, or if you have other feelings about being here?"

The therapist may feel like crying at some particularly poignant moment or interaction in the family situation. Such expression is not harmful to the therapy; it is only an indication that the therapist is human. Even if it gets out of hand, indicating that some unresolved problem on the part of the therapist has been triggered, he can let the family know that something of his own is getting in the way and end the session to give himself time to deal with his own feelings. Good therapists do not have to be cool; they only have to be in charge of themselves enough to be honest about where they are inside and determine what is appropriate to deal with in the session and what needs to be dealt with elsewhere.

Content vehicle. Some families have such a nebulous process that the therapist needs to pin them down to a particular vehicle—money, sex, religion, rules for the children, or anything else that all of them will agree to talk about. The therapist may have to work hard to keep them focused on whatever issue they choose; however, his doing so will be reassuring to them. Since they have so little structure of their own, structuring from the outside reduces their anxiety. When left on their own, their anxiety level gets so high, it is impossible to tell what is really going on. Focusing them on a vehicle gives the therapist a chance to see how each one expresses himself, how they talk to each other and whether or not they are able to follow through on an interaction with the assistance of outside support. If they are not, then family therapy may not be the treatment of choice. We'll go into that in more detail in a later chapter.

Another type of family may be very structured, but be so afraid of feelings that it is impossible to move into their process early in treatment without scaring them off. In these families, getting them to focus on a concrete issue is also reassuring because it is familiar territory. As they do this, the therapist may get right into their structure and begin to teach them new ways of perceiving that will gradually open up the way for them to come out with their feelings. For example, they may be discussing an issue which involves the discipline of the children. The therapist says to them, "You have a very clear picture of how you want your children to behave and you're clear in stating to them your rules and their choices. I wonder if there is room in your picture, without upsetting anything, for you and the children to separate how you feel from what you do?" With this statement, the therapist acknowledges the validity and importance of their already existing structure, but offers the possibility of expanding that structure to include some new ways of looking and behaving. This may lay the groundwork for all of them, at a later time, to allow themselves to acknowledge their occasional rage at each other which they have had to repress up to now because it didn't fit their "reasonable" image.

Context. Some families can talk about a particular vehicle and not get in touch with how they really felt in that situation. With these families, it can be very helpful to get them to define the context of the interaction in great detail. This means describing the room in which the interaction occurred, where each person in the family was at the time, how the room looked, and perhaps even what people were wearing. Sometimes, it is necessary to act the situation out in the therapy session—set the room up so that they really are having a meal at the table as in the home situation and have them pretend to be eating or whatever else they were doing. As they get into an actual gestalt of the experience, they can often get more in touch with what they were experiencing on a feeling level. Also, important details may come out that they previously hadn't mentioned, or had glossed over.

Analysing constituent parts of one family interaction. Don't make the mistake of assuming that any subject or interaction is too unimportant or ridiculous to use as an issue or to go into great detail about. The processes families use for small issues are the same as for major issues and often easier to analyze because they aren't so clouded over with many other issues or past experiences as is more loaded material. We have had sessions in which the whole family talked about toilet paper for a full hour—who bought what kind, why she didn't buy another kind, how everyone in the family felt about this, and what made them handle their feelings the way they did. We had to take each interaction apart step by step to find out how each person felt, how they expressed what they felt, what were the discrepancies between their feelings and actions, how did those discrepancies occur, what did other family members make of those discrepancies, and what was the outcome.

Positive Double-Bind. This maneuver is so important in understanding change that later on we have a whole chapter devoted to it. Here, we will just state briefly that this technique involves putting the client in such a spot that any direction he decides to go in will produce some kind of growth. One of the best examples of this is in an interview Virginia Satir did at Esalen with a family in which the father was growing progressively blind. Virginia asked him if he had learned Braille or made use of other assistance that would be important to him when he became totally blind. He proceeded to tell her with great pride that, even with his blindness, he was as good a man as anyone else and could even take his car engine apart and put it back together again. Virginia then asked him something like this, "How does it come about that the possible adding of new knowledge and skills to your repertoire would make you feel less in some way?" In the most supportive way possible, the man was confronted with the reality of his choice. If he admitted that adding new knowledge did make him feel less, he would be forced to look at the absurdity of that reaction and doubt would emerge. If he said that it didn't make him feel less, then Virginia had given to him a way he could learn new skills without feeling as though he had lost something.

Another validating case for this point is the one Dr. Don Jackson handled with the 17-year-old boy whose family made him feel he "had to" be schizophrenic.

The positive double-bind technique makes the obvious explicit; it expands the awareness with alternative thoughts, ideas and new ways of perceiving, and it demolishes the individual's image of himself as a helpless victim in exchange for the picture of himself making choices that produce readily foreseeable results. When confronted with any of these, the individual has to grow even if it is only in the direction of tightening the defense structure. That process also promotes growth because as the defense structure tightens consciously, the individual becomes increasingly aware of what that structure is doing for him and what it is costing him. That knowledge brings the day of choice closer.

The patterning structure of therapy and the therapy contract. The therapist is living with an erroneous assumption if he thinks that everyone who comes into his office is ready for therapy. Even people who are coming voluntarily with no pressure from schools, physicians, or probation facilities may simply want a palliative to reduce their pain without their having to change anything. The first few sessions may be focused on what the family wants for itself in this experience; how the therapist works, what his expectations are, and whether or not they (the family and the therapist) like each other, fit with each other, and can arrive at mutually-agreed-upon goals. We often tell families that no matter how well qualified the therapist or well motivated the family, their therapy will not work well unless the therapist and the family like each other. That doesn't mean they have to be always pleasant and agreeable, but a mutual respect and appreciation are important. In order to proceed with therapy, family members must be willing to accept and give feedback to each other and the therapist; to allow time and space for mistakes and experimentation with new ways of behaving, and to take responsibility for the decision to be in the therapy situation.

Now, some people will insist that they are there because of someone else, either another member of the family or a community agency which is insisting they get help. The therapist must hold to the reality that that may be so, but a part of that person wants to be here or he or she would find a way out. If the therapist holds to that premise, most people will respond eventually—even recalcitrant children. However, if they don't, then the therapy becomes a waste of everyone's time because the client insists he is being done to and therefore nothing that happens has anything to do with him.

With regard to feedback, family members don't have to agree with everything said by the therapist or others in the family. It is only important that each be willing to accept that every person may have a different picture of any event and needs room to share his particular view so that an overall total picture of the family's process can be clarified. The therapist asks that family members hear him, assimilate his feedback, and *then* throw out what doesn't fit and use what does Family members must understand that no one changes overnight. For example, if people in the family have not been used to expressing anger, first attempts to do so will sometimes come out in odd or destructive ways. They need room to be able to experiment, get feedback from other family members and the therapist about how they are coming across so that they can develop ways of expressing that fit them and are understood by other family members. During this process, other family members can get annoyed or hurt or upset and can certainly express it. What's important is that no one makes a decision, based on this one expression, to end the therapy or the marriage, or to close off further growth.

The therapist must be willing to accept feedback from the family about how they see him. Virginia Satir once said, "If a family member says, 'you look like a pig', the first thing you do is go get a picture of a pig. Then, you stand in front of a mirror and compare. If you don't look like a pig, then you can explore with the family what that impression is all about. If you do look like a pig, then you've learned something about yourself." I think the point is well made. The therapist lets the family know that it is in a discovery process together and everyone is going to learn something. We've learned professionally and personally from every family we have treated.

Process therapy does not have a beginning, middle, and an end.

We let families know that we look at them in terms of the phase of growth they are in individually and as a family unit. We try to ascertain what is breaking down at this particular stage in their ability to adapt to changes and continue their growth. We then try to make obvious the destructive processes they are using that are blocking their growth, help them understand why and how they learned those processes, and what these processes do for them as well as what they cost. With that knowledge, they can then decide whether they want to let go of old ways and move into the frightening, unknown territory of learning new processes that will encourage an open system and growth. They also need to understand what such new learning will do for them and what it will cost. Growth is often painful. We can guarantee people that if they opt for a growth direction, they will feel more and more alive, but we cannot guarantee that their marriage or family will survive in the same way. Growth sometimes leads into unpredictable, sweeping changes in the individuals and families involved. If they do choose to go into a growth direction, they may do so because they want the excitement of continued growth no matter what the cost, or because their current situation is so painful that they feel they have no choice. Either way, we then teach them new processes for maximizing their individual growth, developing relationships with each other that allow for deepening intimacy and at the same time greater freedom, and for maintaining an open system in the family unit. Once they feel secure with these new processes, they are on their own. They may return at a later time because they have reached a new stage of growth and need some additional processes to deal with that stage, or because they have run aground against a new barrier. Therefore, the therapy follows the growth flow.

This may mean for some families that they are in therapy for three months, then they take three to six months to progress on their own and return at a later time for two or three more months of therapy. Another family may stay in therapy a year and return two years later for one or two sessions because they are at a new stage of development and want some feedback. Still another family may come in once every two weeks or once a month rather than once a week because it fits their process better. We find that most families maintain some kind of contact with us for about a two-year period, varying widely in terms of the actual therapy time depending on the family's own unique growth pattern.

Setting the stage for the next meeting. We do not experience each therapy session as having a beginning, middle and end, either. In our earlier training in individual therapy, we had this view of therapy—the beginning was a kind of warming-up period consisting of small talk, catching up on what had happened since the last meeting, or dealing with various forms of resistance. The middle part was the deep discussion, interpretation, and abreaction. The end was a kind of wrap-up, summarizing what had occurred during the session and what that meant in terms of the patient's growth. In process therapy, we are often into areas invested with deep feeling in the first few seconds or certainly the first five minutes of the interview. The interview may even begin in the waiting room where the therapist picks up a salient meta-message about the family or one member of the family, and he may plunge right into that perception the minute the family sits down in the session. Also, sessions often end simply when the time is up and the family may be left with unresolved anxiety and confusion. We do not operate on the premise that we have to water everything down and spoon feed it to families in small sips. It is often important to leave families with anxiety—not enough to overwhelm them—but enough to push them into using their own resources and working with the therapist, not expecting to be spoon fed.

However, when possible, we do try to build a bridge to span sessions and to teach the family to do this for themselves as part of their learning about the natural growth process. For example, a family may have an experience of deep tenderness and intimacy in a session. The therapist then lets the family members know that they may have further such experiences during the week, they may find themselves getting into moods of depression or irritation, or they may feel very distant from each other. It is important for them to understand that, whatever the reaction, it will be valuable material to look at and understand, at the next session, in terms of what it means in their ongoing growth process. It is important for them to understand, however, that nothing that happens can take anything away from the experience they have just had or prevent that from occurring again. Each new experience usually triggers thoughts and reactions or other feelings people don't even know they have. So, it is important to see subsequent events as tools to open up new understanding rather than conclusions that the experience that preceded these events was not real or was bad in some way. The therapist is thus teaching the family that growth means always moving into new, uncharted territory—not always successfully. He helps them shift their focus from outcome to flow.

Shifting the survival framework. We think that the concept of emotional survival as it relates to the family system is so important that we have devoted a whole chapter to it later on in this book. Suffice it to say here that most of the families who come for treatment are operating with a tacit understanding among them that they have to function in certain prescribed ways in order to preserve the family unit on which they are depending for emotional survival.

For example, they may believe that it is necessary for everyone to always be agreeable, nice, and reasonable, and if anyone is disagreeable, unreasonable, a bitch, or a bastard, the family and marriage will disintegrate and the children be left homeless. Another family may operate as though their survival depends on not criticizing mother and on protecting her. If they don't protect her, she will die, have a nervous breakdown, or leave. If she leaves, the family will fall apart because she is the real backbone of the family, holding everything together. That may be so even though the family outwardly labels father as being in charge. A third family may operate as though it is dangerous to directly assert any real feeling. They may close off such assertion with denial, withdrawal, game-playing, or the hot potato routine.

Now, the therapist, with his interventions consisting of outspoken observations of the obvious, will quickly begin to puncture the family's survival myth. He may comment to the first family that he is getting bored with their reasonableness and is about to go to sleep. On one level, he is simply stating the obvious. Probably all of the family members have felt the same way, but of course never mentioned it in order to preserve their facade. Now, on the deeper level, the simple act of mentioning that reaction validates that feeling for all the family members so that they can no longer pretend to themselves that they don't feel that way or that there is something wrong with them if they do. They may think: The therapist (an outsider who is also a respected authority) has the same reaction I do!

However, if they accept that reality, then some change must be considered and that is where survival is threatened. The therapist may therefore get tremendous resistance to the simplest observation. When this happens, he knows he is in survival territory. Then it becomes important for him to explore with the family the importance of their maintaining a reasonable framework, how that framework gained such importance with them, and what each of them would feel he might lose if that framework were to change to allow room for some feelings that weren't so reasonable. The therapist must respect and appreciate that the family is not being obstinate but that on some level they are genuinely panicked and need to be handled firmly but gently. The therapist can offer support and validation to their value system, but ask them to simply consider, without making any decisions, whether it might be possible to begin to make some room for the parts of them that were not always reasonable, nice, or agreeable. At this point it is important that the therapist not get into the trap of convincing the family. It is a temptation to try to superimpose his own value system, perhaps. However, the therapist does need to make it clear to the family what he sees as the price they are paying to keep their system closed to the areas of growth that require more freedom. He needs to let them know that change would not be easy for them—might even be very frightening, because they have learned their ways of behaving through their life experiences and those ways have served them very well in many instances. They are now, however, at a new stage of growth where those ways don't work as well or where different ways are needed. The point is that continued growth and change are certainly possible, but will not be easy, and the genuine respect of the therapist for the difficulty of such a shift is a vital support to the family.

With the second family we mentioned, the therapist may comment that it looks as though the family has a rule that no one can criticize mother. In this instance, the survival myth is also punctured with that remark, but the family is not so threatened because mother does not fall apart when the therapist confronts her. In fact, she may even look a little relieved. When the therapist proceeds to question her about whether she knew family members thought her so fragile and how she feels about such protection, she may begin to express herself in a way that is relieving to other family members and the survival shift may proceed with minimal trauma through subsequent sessions.

The third family may require very direct confrontation from the therapist early in the therapy and the therapist may take the risk to break their survival framework because it is impossible to work in or around it. So, he may take the plunge and hope to pick up the pieces as he goes along. He does this by pinning the family members down, not allowing them to change subjects, shift contexts, or drag him down with their hopelessness and guilt trips, or manipulate him in any other way. He keeps confronting them with their manipulations until they have no way to go but to leave or begin to come out straight. Since their survival is being threatened so directly, they may react violently. If the therapist holds his ground and does not allow himself to be manipulated, intimidated, or seduced, they will often respond with relief and then work very hard in therapy. They trust him because he does not panic, attack, or withdraw in the face of a storm, so they know he will not desert them physically or emotionally during their process.

Pinpointing the change and keeping the system open. When a family system begins to change, each move to open the system produces a counter-move to reclose it. An important technique to prevent closure is to pinpoint the opening move and lay a base under it. For example, a family may come into therapy with the mythology that if men are strong, they don't come out with their feelings; they appear self-sufficient and stoical. Then, in one of their therapy sessions, the father begins to express some of his scared or sad feelings, perhaps even begins to cry. At this point, the therapist first blocks the rest of the family from rescuing him. They may do this by changing the subject, with disruptive behavior, or by trying to give to him physically with the end result of cutting him off from his feelings. As the therapist blocks any of these moves, he tells the family members that they do not need to rescue the father, that he is not falling apart in a destructive sense. Everyone experiences feelings of helplessness, inadequacy and fear at times, and the ability to express these feelings is an important strength since it makes it possible to work these feelings out rather than carry them like a heavy weight inside. This is what we call a structural comment designed to give all family members, including the father, a new way of looking. Such structural comments regarding alternative ways of looking, behaving, and being, enable the family to build a new framework of values, thoughts and actions for maintaining an open system.

The therapist may then check out with each family member what he or she is feeling while the father (or husband) is experiencing his pain. The therapist is careful to differentiate with them what they are feeling rather than what they are thinking. Family members tend to give judgements or opinions about what is happening to the other person and usually need to be taught how to stay in touch with themselves during someone else's emotional expression. Teaching them how to stay in touch with and respond to their own feelings is another step in building a structure that allows the unblocked flow of feeling in the family and therefore keeps the system open. Family members may often express pain, concern for, or empathy with the father. At that point, the therapist can ask the father how he would like family members to take care of him. This is another structural comment which builds in three new factors: it gives the message clearly that it is not only all right, but it is important to allow yourself to be taken care of at times; it implies that each person in the family may be different in how he or she wants care; and, it indicates that each person must be able to ask for what he wants clearly so that he will not be intruded upon. Giving, even when impelled by the best of intentions, can be intrusive if it does not fit what the receiver wants or needs at the time.

The next structural step in this particular process is that the therapist asks other family members to be clear about whether they can or cannot give as the father asks. The therapist clarifies that each person is different in terms of what he can give and it is important that each be clear about what his abilities and limitations are in this respect so that he will not overextend himself and establish a barrier of harbored resentment which closes the system. The final step in the structure is that the therapist teaches the father to hear these expressions of other family members as clear statements about who they are and how they are different from each other and from him, and not as a lack of concern about him or a lack of desire to give.

This structuring process must be followed with each new opening flow of feeling in the family to help the family integrate the new feelings with new knowledge to build a solid foundation for continuing growth in an open system on their own.

Positive system error. The therapist may at times allow himself to become a part of the family system in the hope that by starting exactly where the family members are, he may be able to connect with them more easily and lead them slowly out of their system. The principle is similar to that used by the psychiatrist who temporarily becomes part of his patient's delusional system. It is often effective with families who are so frightened to move out of their system that they do not respond at all to a therapist who is discrepant with the system. An example would be an extremely repressive, judgmental system in which survival is based on following rigid rules about what is right or wrong, good or bad. The therapist may get right into the system, become very reasonable, stay on a content level as though he were a teacher, judge or other authority. He would give the family a great deal of support for their hard work and their virtues with recognition that those values have accomplished much for them. He would then slowly begin to introduce slight changes which would increase their openness to a small degree, and he would use methods to do this that were congruent with their system—like reasonableness, scientific exploration, and logical choice. Hopefully, all of this would lay the base for the beginning expression of some feeling in the family. Then the therapist would go through the structuring process described under the previous heading. Obviously, this would be slow, painstaking work and the therapist would have to understand, at least in the beginning, that minute expressions of feeling in a family like this constitute a big gain.

This technique is also helpful in another kind of family in which one or more members is highly manipulative. The therapist out-manipulates the manipulator as a way of blocking the manipulation (you can't con a conner!) and at the same time he puts the manipulator off balance and therefore open to change. The therapist may do this in a variety of ways that fit his own personality and his feelings at the moment. He may mimic the other person's behavior; needle him to open and direct anger, be sarcastic, laugh, or fall asleep at the tragedy performances; or simply ignore him until he comes out with a feeling to which the therapist feels he wants to respond. Now, to use this technique the therapist must feel comfortable with it, otherwise it will fall flat. So, a therapist who originally grew up in a reasonable family system and who has grown past that point, will probably be better able to handle the judgmental family described above without falling asleep in the process. On the other hand, the therapist who has had to acknowledge and work through his own manipulative process will usually feel much more comfortable and easy with an extremely manipulative family. We think the positive system error is a technique used only in extremes where nothing else seems to work and must be a technique with which the therapist is comfortable to the extent that he can easily move in and out of the system and be in charge of the process.

Another aspect of the positive system error occurs when the therapist gets caught in the system, catches himself in the error, and uses his mistake to promote understanding and to model the ability to admit error without depreciating self.

The therapist may suddenly become aware that his posture (slumped), tone (lifeless), and voice (droning), are congruent with the family's depressed, hopeless image. In another instance, he finds himself arguing with family members about who is right or wrong. In still another family, he finds himself in a convincing, defensive stance. In each instance, he can become aware of what is happening because he senses internally that he is no longer in a flowing process with the family, but is hooked on content. At that point, he can own his error with humor ("I got sucked in again!"), or with a simple statement of fact. However, he recognizes the nature and power of the system with understanding and a willingness to explore, not with judgement or blame, i.e., "Let's take a look at what is going on with you and with me that we allow ourselves to get into this unrewarding negative process."

Chapter 8

INTERVENTION TECHNIQUES (INTRAPSYCHIC LEVEL, DYADIC LEVEL AND PROCESS LEVEL)

The second treatment aspect of the family system which we'll discuss here has to do with techniques connected to the intrapsychic level of intervention. These techniques are ways to treat the individual within the interaction framework of the family system, and ways of doing individual therapy which take into account that part of the individual's natural growth process which took place interactionally as well as the development of his self-esteem and self-expression. These techniques are as follows:

Ghost analysis. The ghosts are the parents of the husband and wife in the family, who are not present in the interview and perhaps, not alive at all. However, they may be incorporated as judges into the internal structures of husband and wife so that they (the grandparents) are still very much in control. The therapist, in his role as enabler to the family system in developing and maintaining the interactional flow, always moves to the close-off—the person who consistently breaks or interrupts the interaction. For example, a family with two daughters, 13 and 15, comes into therapy because the mother is concerned with what she feels is rebellious behavior on the part of the 15-year-old and because her own reaction to such behavior is punitive to a degree far out of proportion to the stimulus. The father agrees that the daughter is negligent in what he considers very necessary and reasonable rules for taking her share of responsibility in the family. He also feels that his wife overreacts and that while he can support her with the rules, he cannot support her yelling and screaming and over-severe punishment for the girl's infractions.

The youngest daughter has much the same picture as her parents describe; she does feel, however, that while the rules are reasonable, her parents are overly rigid in enforcing them. The oldest daughter admits she frequently flaunts the rules deliberately and doesn't know why she does it. With encouragement from the therapist in terms of exploring her feelings about being in this family, she indicates that she often feels unappreciated and that her mother uses her as a scapegoat when she is upset about other things. In the process of enabling the family to share their feelings with one another, the therapist becomes aware that the interaction breaks down in two places: between the mother and the oldest daughter and between the father and everyone in the family. When the mother and oldest daughter begin to talk to each other, the mother's body posture, tone, and words are always distancing even when the girl is coming out clearly with her feelings in a non-defensive, open way. The therapist makes this observation as the same block occurs several times and suggests that perhaps something in the mother's own experience with mothering is getting in the way. As this mother recalls her experience with her ghost (her own mother), she recalls that her mother was demanding, perfectionistic, and distant with her. The therapist then asks her to use the gestalt therapy technique of placing her mother in a chair in front of her and talking to her about her anger and hurt about this as well as her yearnings in terms of what she really wanted from her mother. The purpose of this technique is to get her in touch with her buried feelings that are getting in her way to connect with her current family, and to bring her internal interaction into the interactional framework of her present family. As she begins to talk to her mother, she lets herself feel her own pain and anguish about her lack of mothering. She also gets in touch with the reality that she has resented giving to her daughters the freedom and understanding and nourishment she never got. She is particularly resentful with the oldest girl because she reminds her of herself as a girl since she expresses the rebellion that she herself felt, but never could express as a child. As she shares this, the daughter really gives to her mother for the first time in the sessions, and offers that she really understands her mother's pain and resentment. At that point that two make a connection on a feeling level. Then the youngest daughter begins to offer that she has some feelings, too, but has kept them to herself because she had previously felt it was best in this family to stay out of everyone's way. She and her sister and mother then really begin to share and the flow of energy shifts to the three of them, leaving the father outside.

When the therapist moves to include him, the father consistently responds to the rest of the family with wooden expressions of concern, understanding, thoughts, and ideas but does not share any of his own feelings. He consistently maintains the facade of a nice guy who is always in control. As the therapist pinpoints this, the other family members begin to share with the father how frustrating his behavior is to them and how hungry they are to know his real feelings rather than experience him as a robot. When confronted by them and the therapist, he indicates that he has learned his way of being in control; it is the only way he knows, and he does not want to give it up. The therapist then moves in two directions with him—to let him hear from his family what this is costing him with them and to explore how and why he learned this way of behaving in his origin family. It becomes clear from his and his wife's descriptions of his parents that he survived by being a good boy who never talked back and was always reasonable. To have done otherwise would have made him an outcast with his parents. However, even though they are both dead, he is still behaving as though they are right and are hovering over him making sure he continues to behave according to what they expected. Therefore, his structure of who he is and how he behaves is built around them and not around who he really is and what fits him. In this instance, the therapist recognizes that to change would mean giving up his image of himself—for something or someone he doesn't even know about yet. To do this, he would have to begin to expose feelings that don't fit the expectations of his parents. Out of that exposure and exploration of those feelings, he would slowly have to build a new structure based on his own uniqueness—who he is, how he feels and what fits him in terms of values, behavior, and goals. The therapist recognizes that would be a frightening and difficult thing to do, but that it is possible. If he doesn't go that direction, he faces further potential breakdown in his current family.

Non-verbal behavior. The therapist attempts, in a variety of ways, to teach the individual to pay attention and learn to listen to the way his body talks to him. In the beginning of therapy, sometimes people feel the therapist is criticising them when he comments on the discrepancy between their words and their body messages. The therapist must make clear to them that he is trying to help them be aware of and use this additional valuable resource as a way of deepening their understanding of themselves as well as a way of expanding their communication avenues with others. Again, the purpose of the intervention is to shift the individual from a judgmental view of himself to one of exploration and discovery. We frequently say to a client, "Everything that comes out of you is valuable and therefore useful in facilitating your growth."

Discrepancy analysis. We've discussed this technique in detail in terms of the interactional framework. The technique is the same here except it has to do with the individual's discrepancies in his manifestation of himself—his verbal contradictions, the discrepancy between his verbal and non-verbal behavior, discrepancy with the family system, and discrepancy with his manifestation of himself and the therapist's internal experience of him. The father in the last example was discrepant with the family system in that his denial and repression of his feelings was incongruent with the family's increasingly free flow of expression so that all of the energy in the family gravitated to him as the controlling factor. In addition, his statement that he liked his pattern of operating and that it was rewarding and comfortable to him did not fit with the therapist's experience of him as depressed, weighted down, and sad. In this particular instance, the family members also experienced him in this way.

Primary process. Techniques in this area of exploration usually have to do with individual therapy. However, there are times when primary process is dealt with in the interactional framework. When we talk about primary process we are referring to preverbal blocks in emotional development. For example, an infant who is deprived consistently over a period of time will cut off his ability to feel, and will withdraw as his way of protecting himself from pain which he does not have the structure to handle. As he gets older, that infantile pain remains deeply buried and he builds a whole structure of relating that protects him from ever having to open up that pain. If, however, his growth takes him to the place where these defense structures break down, he may seek out therapy because he no longer has enough energy to hold down that pain and at the same time to do all the other things that are creative and rewarding to him. Also, he may find he can only go so far in his relationships and then he has to cut himself off because intimacy triggers a resurgence of that early pain. For him, then, the therapy process would involve individual work to enable him to feel the agony of that deprived child as the child experienced it at six months or a year or whatever. As the feelings wash over and through him, he has then faced and survived his worst fears and can lay them to rest. Then the therapist can help him to understand and integrate that experience into his structure of who he is so he can let go of his internal picture of himself as a deprived second-class citizen and begin to explore what he wants now and how to get it in ways that fit him.

Now, in a family session, an individual may be so blocked by his primary process that he is simply unable to respond in any way to others in the family. Family members may be doing everything including hitting him and wrestling with him, but nothing penetrates. If he is aware that he is cutting off to this extent and wants to change that, then the therapist may offer to work with him individually within the context of the family session, at least for that particular session. If all in the family are willing for this to happen, then the therapist may use bioenergetic techniques, group therapy techniques, or an internal imagery trip to help the individual open up. With the bioenergetic approach, the therapist might ask the client to lie down on the floor on his back with arms and legs relaxed so that his physical system is as open as possible. Then he might suggest deep breathing exercises or physical exercises such as kicking and pounding to build up the energy and help the person get in touch with what he is feeling.

Group therapy techniques might involve having other family members physically hold him, surround him, or sit on him depending on what feelings the therapist felt might be getting in the client's way. The physical pressure on him might help rage to surface. The bodies around him or holding him might encourage yearning or helpless feelings to surface.

The imagery trip has to do with having the individual close his eyes and take a trip inside of himself without forcing himself in any direction or holding on to anything that emerges. Whatever images, sensations, feelings, blank spaces or fantasies emerge, the therapist asks the client to let himself sink into the experience without pushing or holding on, just to see what that particular place is like for him. This technique is very helpful for people who are blocked by rage at being programmed all their lives. The technique is polarized from any hint of programming because it is based on the assumption that anything that emerges is valuable even if it is blankness or space, and that all he has to do to learn is to just experience what that state is like for him. There are no expectations and no prescribed outcomes. As the individual slowly becomes aware of this on a deep level, his defenses begin to move slightly and feelings begin to emerge.

The therapist then integrates this experience back into the interactional framework by checking out each family member's experience while this was going on and by explaining why the individual must go through this process and how it affects the family system. He may then offer to see this client individually to continue this process until he is able to be enough in touch with his feelings that he can take part in the interaction of the family, at which time they would resume treatment as a family unit.

In the third aspect of the family system—the dyadic level—we have already discussed many techniques in detail in the previous chapter on the dyad, including those dealing with discrepancy analysis and non-verbal behavior in couple or two-person therapy. However, there are two additional techniques which we want to discuss here. The most important has to do with shifting the survival connection in a marital pair. In a dysfunctional family, the parental or marital relationship often operates as though the husband and wife are feeding off of the same bloodstream. He sees her as his judge who is in charge of whether or not he is okay as a person. Therefore, he does not hear her feelings as statements about her; he hears them as judgements about, or demand on him. She operates as though she cannot survive without his love, that she is nothing without it. Therefore, she hears his feelings as criticisms of her or indications that she has failed in some way. Thus clear communication is impossible between them because each is defining himself around what he thinks will please or hold the other one rather than around his own identity. The therapist's first step then is to make it clear to each, via his observations about their interaction, how much power each is giving the other.

As the therapist comments on the discrepancies and the blocks in the couple's interactional flow, he will begin to get statements like "I can't say what I really feel because he will leave me," or "I can't tell her what I feel because then she won't love me." Then it becomes important for each to understand that by not coming out with their real feelings, they are building up hidden resentments that are destroying the relationship in insidious ways. If they begin to express themselves clearly, they may lose the relationship. However, they also stand a chance to build a relationship based on the solid foundation of who they really are. If they continue to give each other power over their worth and play games about their feelings, they can be sure the relationship will founder. It may dissolve more slowly, but their experience up to now indicates it doesn't have a chance if they continue in their current pattern.

At this point, the therapist needs to recognize with them that they are not just talking about changing the base of their relationship. They are talking about each of them giving up defining self around someone else in favor of defining self around their individual uniqueness. That means letting go of any parent, judge, or any measuring stick outside of themselves. Each would have to trust that he is basically all right, would not really destroy or hurt others or drive them away from him, and each would have to begin to build a structure of who he is around what fits him rather than what is right or wrong, good or bad, or produces certain outcomes. That is a major internal shift, and the individual feels as though he is risking his emotional survival by going into totally unknown territory when he makes that shift.

As a couple, each needs to know that when he lets go of his old way of connecting, he will move into a desert phase in his relationship in which it looks as though there is nothing between them. That may not be so at all. What is happening is that there is an in-between period in which the old way of relating doesn't work anymore and they have not yet developed a new way to take its place. They need considerable support from the therapist at this point to understand this phase of process and to enable them to begin to experiment with new ways of expressing themselves to see what fits each of them and what works with the other. As each begins to get clearer sense of who he is, he begins to see the other as a separate person, not an extension of himself. Then they can begin to explore whether or not they really fit and how they really feel about each other. It is impossible to accurately assess the depth of feeling one person has for another when he has given the other power to determine his worth.

During this process, the children may or may not be involved. We leave them in the sessions until it is clear where the marital relationship is and that the parents are ready to make a shift. However, whether they stay after that point depends on how involved they are in the marital relationship and on whether the parents are better able to focus without the children there. In either case, we would bring the children in later, when a new marital base has been established, to integrate the family into the new structure.

The other technique we will discuss here has to do with incongruent interactional flow. In this process, the couple may look as though they are coming out with feelings, and the body, tone and verbal messages may be congruent. However, the effect of one's expression is to push the other away rather than make contact. For example, they may be expressing anger, but it is coming out in the form of conclusions and closure rather than an open-ended sharing, that is:

He: "I can't stand you, you don't care anything at all about me—"

She: "I'm furious at you for never listening to me and always being more interested in your job—"

He: "You're a bitch!"

She: "Bastard!"

The anger never gets beyond this stage of name calling, assaultive, actually distancing interaction. It is as though there is an invisible wall between them and their feelings get only as far as that wall, but do not connect with each other. True contact interaction requires that each individual be able to stay in touch with his own feelings but also be able to empathize with where the other one is on a feeling level even though he doesn't understand why the other feels as he does nor does he agree with his feelings. This is the kind of interaction the therapist is working for; otherwise, people might just as well stand in separate rooms and scream at the walls. Interaction must have contact as well as ventilation to produce growth.

In the fourth aspect of the family system—the process level—these are the major techniques that will shift a session from the content level to process:

Non-verbal. We've discussed in detail elsewhere the techniques for bringing the non-verbal behavior into awareness in the interactional framework. Suffice it to say here that the non-verbal behavior is the most reliable resource of information that we have as therapists. When in doubt, follow the behavior rather than the words. This is particularly true in working with children. Many times, in working with families whose verbal facility masks the process, the therapist can do whole sessions asking the family to communicate without words, in order to get through to the feeling level. Non-verbal sessions with couples are extremely valuable in discovering the blocks in their relationship. We have used gestalt and psycho-drama techniques like: having the couple Indian wrestle to see how each handles his or her power; having one person hold an object, usually a large pillow, and the other try to take it away from him—then reversing the roles; having each play the other and mimic how the other appears to him or her; or having them face each other and look at each other, responding only to their own internal stimulus for action and not to any expectations they perceive from the other.

Modeling of the therapist. Whether or not the therapist is congruent with the system will depend on his clinical judgement about how fast the family is able to move into process. If the system is so destructive that any delay would only reinforce its destructiveness and lose the family anyway, he will immediately be incongruent with the system—break the family rules—and move as fast as possible into process. He will also move into process rapidly if the family appears strong and ready to move. He will be congruent with the system, as we discussed earlier with the judgmental and manipulative families, when the family requires support and a slower build-up before moving into process, or when congruency with the systems appears the most effective way to get the family off balance and thus into process.

Discrepancy between hopes and expectations. We have noticed that families with delinquent children often are families who try very hard to do right by their children and have high expectations of themselves and the children. Frequently, an effective technique with them is to encourage them to explore their feelings about their high hopes for their children and the fact that they haven't been able to communicate these aspirations effectively. Such an intervention spans the space between logic (with which they are comfortable) and the beginning exploration of their feelings of helplessness and pain. Therefore, for families who are outcome or goal-oriented, talking about the difference between their hopes and expectations makes sense to them and can become a beginning wedge into process.

Therapist exposure. One of the main advantages in seeing the whole family in treatment is that it seldom happens that everyone in the family will support the denial defense pattern all the time. Usually some member will give you an opening. However, when that doesn't happen, the therapist's use of himself becomes the crucial factor in opening up process. His willingness to keep coming out with his inner experience of being with the family is incongruent with the family system but at the same time does not directly attack their defenses. For example, he may offer to them that he is in a bind with them. If he doesn't do anything he isn't doing his job. If he does intervene or comment, he gets no response. Then the therapist may just sit and let the anxiety build up. All his comments and interventions make clear to the family what he feels his role is, what his boundaries and expectations are, and what he considers the family's responsibility is in the therapeutic, discovery process. He doesn't take over and make the family problem his problem; he doesn't make the family an extension of himself so that whether or not they work is a matter of choice for them and not a statement about his worth, and he isn't outcome-oriented. He doesn't give the message that the family should or shouldn't do anything—he simply makes clear to them their choices as he sees them. He also attempts to take the stigma of right and wrong off those choices so that whether or not the family continues in therapy depends on what fits its growth process at the moment rather than what the family should do.

Message analysis. Sometimes in families some very powerful messages are sent on a content level and not understood, clarified, or responded to by other family members. If the sender does not then pursue his message or back it up with some kind of action, the transaction is incomplete, adding to the general sense of frustration and isolation in the family. Teaching families to complete verbal transactions to the satisfaction and understanding of everyone in the family will automatically move the family into process as feelings are then pushed to the surface which were previously covered over by vagueness and lack of clarity.

Socializing. With some families who are unsophisticated regarding psychological awareness, home visits can be a way of bridging the gap and meeting them halfway. The therapist has a chance to see the family in its natural setting which gives impetus to his ability to evaluate process. The family has the opportunity to be with the therapist in a social context in which they are in charge of the setting and this often helps to break down barriers. The therapist can make definite differentiations between social time and therapy time while in their home, and perhaps later transfer the family to his office setting when the ice is broken. We realize that many therapists do not have the time or flexibility to do home visits on any kind of regular basis, but we feel that it would be very helpful to make a few home visits in the process of getting training in family therapy just for the experience.

Use of congruent imagery. A therapist may find himself sitting down in a session with a family and experiencing all kinds of images about the family. He may look at the father and have a mental picture of a small boy crying; he may see the whole family having a picnic and playing games in a park, and the images may appear frequently at different points in the session. If the family is fairly sophisticated psychologically; if they have a fairly solid structure out of which they are operating; or if they trust the therapist to a high degree, then the therapist can confront them with his imagery. It is a very effective tool for moving rapidly and deeply into process. If the family is not ready to move that fast, the therapist can file the data he receives in this way for use to himself in clarifying the direction of treatment.

Shifting the survival framework. The shift into process is for some families a survival shift. These are families who have their whole way of operating built around protecting each other from their feelings. Therefore, they have to change their whole structure in order to express how they feel directly to each other. In other families, they do not need to change their basic structure totally, only to expand and/or modify it. For them, survival is not threatened by the shift into process. It is obviously vital for the therapist to assess accurately whether the shift into process involves a survival threat to the family so that he can respect their resistance, give them an understanding and appreciation of the reasons for it, and give them a clear picture of the choices involved in considering a change. Usually the therapist can tell whether survival is involved by the pervasiveness and rigidity of the protective structure, or by the combined, universal strength of the family's resistance to all attempts on his part to get into process.

Structuring to maintain an open system. In the process area, such structuring is done by allowing some sense of completion in the expression of feeling so that the homeostasis is maintained. For example, if the client's words are expressing fear, but the behavior is saying he is ready to move, go with the behavior, even if it means putting pressure on the individual or family to get the feeling out. Once they get into process, people expect the therapist to respond to what they feel, not what they say. If he does not, they will assume that he is afraid and will close off the process. Once the feeling is out, then it is important to make room for the reactions and responses of everyone in the family, again for the sense of some resolution. Now, in this context we are not talking about resolution in the sense of problem-solving or finding answers, but more in the orgastic, rhythmic sense of the flow of feeling.

Chapter 9

CONCEPT OF INTEGRATION IN THERAPY AS COMPARED WITH THE NATURAL GROWTH INTEGRATIVE PROCESS

In the natural growth and integration processes, the infant, when stimulated by a feeling, experiences and expresses it throughout his entire organism. When a baby is unhappy, he cries, his whole body gets red, every muscle feels and expresses the pain in some obvious way. When he is happy, he laughs, gurgles, waves his arms and legs—his whole organism is suffused with the feeling—it flows unblocked through every part of him. That process alone will produce growth. The ability of the organism to experience the unchecked flow of feeling pushes him into deeper levels of his own consciousness resulting in an opening, ever-expanding, evolving awareness of himself. If the child is adequately nurtured and not intruded upon, that process is his major growth process through the first year of life. Family interaction is not yet a major factor, except indirectly if it interferes with his nurturing or results in intrusion upon his process. If the family is experiencing any sustained trauma such as illness, deprivation or unhappiness between the parents, the resultant disturbance in the family equilibrium may interfere with their ability to give the child their time and affection. The primary form of intrusion that impedes an infant's growth is unresolved tension on the part of either of the parents. If either parent is experiencing pain, deprivation, or unhappiness inside of himself but represses it to present a seemingly calm exterior, that split produces a peculiar kind of tension in the parent to which an infant is extremely sensitive. If that split is prolonged over a period of time, the end result is that a large part of the child's energy—which he would normally use for his own deepening exploration of himself—must go to handling the tension he perceives from his parents. Depending on the amount of energy he has available to him, his growth may then slow down, stop momentarily, or become totally blocked, at which point he regresses behaviorally.

After the age of one, the child's direct interaction with his parents and his observation of their interaction with each other assume equal importance to his continued self-exploration process. At this point, the optimum conditions for the child's continued growth are the expression of nurturing from both parents without strings attached, and a solid family structure. This form of nurturing has to do with parents' ability to separate their feeling for their child from their expectations of him. They see him as a separate entity who has his own unique way of developing and growing; not as an extension of themselves whose obedience or lack of it determines whether or not they have succeeded or failed as parents and as people. Thus, they teach their child the family rules by giving him choices. "If you keep throwing the ball in the house, I'll put it away." "If you don't go to bed on time, you can't watch Sesame Street tomorrow," and so on. They don't give him the message, directly or indirectly, that he is bad, sick, stupid, or crazy if he doesn't see things their way. If he chooses not to obey, it is because he wants to try his own way, he doesn't understand, or he is upset about something that he is having difficulty expressing. The parents may not like or tolerate his disobedience, but they don't see it as a deliberate attack on themselves. They recognize that while they may be able to govern their child's behavior, they cannot control his feelings.

So, they offer him ways to express his differences or disagreements that are acceptable to them. One father might put on the boxing gloves with his son; another might allow his son to say, "I hate you." It doesn't make any difference what expressions are available or if each parent has different expressions he can tolerate. What is important is that the child gets the message that while he can't act any way he wants in the family, he can feel any way he wants without being depreciated or ostracized. On the contrary, he is encouraged to feel and to learn ways of expressing those feelings that others in the family can hear and to which they can respond.

Very small children can easily learn to differentiate that what works with one person may not work with another, and they need teaching from each parent as well as older siblings about how they can best communicate their feelings to each of them.

In terms of structure, the child needs to know that when he expresses his own feelings, he will get congruent messages back from his parents in response to him. If a parent is angry on the inside, but adopts a calm, controlled exterior, the child picks up the discrepancy and gets anxious. If this is a consistent occurrence, then a child must begin to use part of his energy for mind reading that would normally be utilized for his own continued growth both inside of himself and in exploration with others. He can no longer just be concerned with how he feels and how that affects others. Now, he has to be concerned about what they may be feeling that they aren't saying and how to discern clues that might give him some inkling of what they may be experiencing inside. In addition, he has to be concerned that obviously there are feelings you are not supposed to express and he is not sure what those are and why they are taboo.

If, on the other hand, he trusts that parents will be honest with him about their feelings, then he is free to utilize all of his energy for experimenting with his feelings and finding out through trial and error what are the best ways of expressing himself that fit him and work with other people. He trusts that other people will take care of themselves and are not helpless, so he does not grow up a rescuer. He trusts that others will respond to him on the basis of what they like or don't like and not with judgements about how terrible, selfish, or stupid he is, so he doesn't grow up a manipulator. He trusts that others will really hear his feelings and respond appropriately, so he doesn't grow up feeling ineffectual and inadequate. If a child has the nurturing and structure we have described, he will, by the age of three, develop a sense of self-esteem which nothing from that point on can shatter. We think that most of the problems we see in adolescents really have little to do with adolescence but have their roots in this period from one to three.

With the optimum growth conditions we have described, a child of six will already have a fairly strong sense of who he is; a structure which he will expand and modify as he matures, but which will serve him all his life. From six to adolescence, his primary growth process will be the interactional one—learning how to adapt to the outside world. He is concerned with social skills, intellectual and physical development as they relate to performance in the group, and the integration of these skills into his internal structure of who he is.

The integration process occurs in this way: The child expresses a feeling in the moment, spontaneously and impulsively—tries it on for size, so to speak. As he externalizes his feeling in words and/or action, he determines whether that particular way of expressing fits him—makes him comfortable or dissatisfied. He will toss out that way of expressing and try out another, either from his own imagination or in imitation of someone else. If he is satisfied, he then checks to see how that expression affects the person to whom he is relating. If it works in terms of his feeling good about himself in the interaction; if it then fits with his image of himself and the value system he has in his head; and if it supports his self-esteem and doesn't depreciate him, then he will incorporate and integrate that way of being into his internal structure of who he is. It becomes a part of his identity. If he does not feel good about himself and the interaction, he may try other ways until he finds one that fits. He may pull back to let himself come together inside before he tries again. He may seek help or advice. Or, he may go through a period of confusion and anxiety before he does any of the above.

At this stage of growth, it is very helpful if the parents can perceive their child's natural rhythm, which is his unique way of meeting the world, and teach him to understand it, appreciate it and not to fight it. This is often difficult for parents to do because their own growth rhythms may be totally different. For example, a father's natural growth rhythm may be that he handles a new situation by jumping in, splashing around, and picking up the pieces later. His son, however, may meet new situations by standing back, looking everything over carefully, and then jumping in. It may be difficult for this father not to push his son, and it may be hard for the son to appreciate his own rhythm as simply different from his father's and not less than.

In adolescence, the individual is concerned with the understanding, development, and integration of power and intimacy, strength, and tenderness. Here, again, the self-exploration and the interactional processes become equally important. It is in this period that the person stretches. He tests his strength sexually—how many can he or she attract, how many can he make, how much control can she exert over males with her budding sexual desirability? Such manipulations are part of the normal growth in this period. Adolescents also push themselves physically—again testing power, strength, limits. The more solid the preceding family and emotional base, the more the individual will stretch and the more areas in which he will stretch. Adolescents also have great drive spiritually. Unfortunately, in our culture, spiritual development gets tied up with organized religion which often destroys the whole creative, spiritual process with an avalanche of shoulds and guilt-producing judgements. Without such distortions, adolescent spiritual development might proceed into the psychic, metaphysical arena—a worthy doorway into adulthood in that such study encourages the individual to look inside of himself for answers and to develop his awareness of his unity and flow with the world around him, both tangible and intangible.

The adolescent needs very adaptable parents who can allow him to take increasing responsibility for his own decisions as his judgement matures. He also needs approval of his cockiness and bravado. Parents don't have to approve of the ways in which adolescent power tests itself, but they do need to encourage and appreciate the power. Adolescents do not need Calvinistic restrictions to prevent them from becoming cocksure or swell-headed or, worst of all, selfish. They need just the opposite. They need help in learning how to revel in their energy, power, and ability to feel deeply and explosively, and they need the protection of their parents so that they have room to learn how to express these feelings constructively. If parents can learn to respond to the adolescent's power with understanding and sensitivity, they automatically preserve his vulnerable, open quality. If they brutalize him by depreciating, repressing, or responding negatively to his power, they force him to close off his deeply tender, sensitive, poetic side. If they support his power, he will be able to protect his sensitivity in terms of the rest of the world without having to close it off. It they do not support his power, they leave him defenseless and he is forced to close off to survive.

In order to achieve the deepest intimacy and sustained creativity, the adult must have an integrated balance between strength and tenderness. He must be able to experience himself as a feeling person without guilt, shame, reservation, or fear. He must be able to make his boundaries, limitations, and demands explicit, and trust that he is best able to get what he wants and needs by being himself.

INTEGRATIVE PROCESSES IN THERAPY

Very few families come into therapy ready to learn how to grow or to further enhance and add to their growth processes. Most families come because they are in pain and want relief or resolution. Many times they are operating out of a survival framework that is the antithesis to growth because it is a closed system. So, the therapist may have to do major surgery with a family before they are even able to learn about growth. He has to help them get through their defense system and develop a beginning sense of who they really are individually, and then assist each in building a new structure to fit his real identity as well as a new structure for relating as a family. Many therapists work with people through the defense system and into a new sense of themselves and stop there. We feel that is just the beginning—that most people need just as much help to develop growth processes that will enable them to maintain an open family system as well as develop intimacy and creativity. We feel that a therapist operates something like an elevator with a family. On the way down through the defense system, he will model and teach the same growth processes that he will model and teach on the way back up as he is building from their new base; but the family will hear and use them differently in each place.

For example, in the beginning of therapy, the therapist may make it very clear by his words and behavior that he does not see any feelings as destructive. The way in which the feelings are expressed may be destructive or unworkable, but the feelings themselves are always valuable and only need a more appropriate form of expression to prove their value. That concept, in the beginning, is both frightening and reassuring to a family—frightening because it implies they have to change; reassuring because they get the message that there is nothing wrong with them—only with their modes of expression. When they have let go of their old ways of behaving and are ready to experiment from a new beginning, that concept is very exciting and they are quick to grasp it and experiment with it. However, the fact that the therapist has taught and modeled the same concept earlier increases the speed of acceptance and integration of this concept into their new structure in the building phase of treatment.

In addition, during the tearing down phase of treatment, by his modeling and teaching, the therapist is presenting himself as a bridge. Thus, the family, when it lets go of its manipulative, judgmental, or repressive structures, will look to the therapist as a survival person until they can develop new ways of being and relating to each other with which they feel some sense of competence and security. During the building phase, they see the therapist as someone who presents a solid structure against which they can bounce their new ways of feeling and expressing. They have developed a trust in him that he will give them congruent messages in response to anything they throw at him because they have tested this out thoroughly in the earlier phase of treatment. They would never have given up their old structure unless they trusted him in this respect because families, couples, and individuals must have someone solid to bounce against in order to make a major structural change.

In addition to providing this kind of solidity during the building phase, the therapist also gives the family constant feedback about where they are in their growth process. He may experience that an individual is in the one- to three-year-old stage emotionally in which he is using most of his energy for exploring himself as a feeling person and therefore doesn't have much left over for the rest of the family. People need to understand that when they let go of the external structures around which they have defined their identity, they will return to the place in their emotional development where they originally cut off and adopted that external facade. This may be a totally different place for each person in the family and each needs to understand and make room for the other in this respect. Once the defenses are down and people are ready to grow, growth can be very rapid in this process. Someone can be in the three-year-old phase one week and up to adolescence the next. The important thing is that they understand this process and are encouraged to savor each stage of growth. We always ask them to milk every drop of experience in the "second time around," since this new structure they are building will last a lifetime.

The family now becomes an experimental arena for each person to begin to explore his feelings with trust that others will understand and encourage his process. In other words, the current family unit, with the help of the therapist, begins to do for its members what the parents' origin families did not do and what these parents could not do earlier. Thus, the children are integrating knowledge about parenting at the same time they are experiencing themselves differently as children in this family. The parents are integrating knowledge about themselves as parents to their children in different ways as well as about themselves as children in relation to their parents and to the therapist, in terms of his meaning to them as a survival person.

In this integration process, the therapist teaches family members how to give and receive feedback so that each can benefit from the other's insight, knowledge, and experience. When the whole process of experimentation, feedback, determination of fit, and development of structure—both internal and family—is made explicit so that all family members have conscious knowledge of what they are doing and what stage they are in, there is tremendous pleasure and excitement in the building process. We always tell people that one advantage of going through your emotional development when you're already an adult is that it moves much faster, and it is often less painful and much more pleasurable because you're aware and in charge of it every step of the way.

Chapter 10

BUILDING THE INTEGRATIVE STRUCTURE (INDIVIDUAL)

The integrative structure has to do with the internal framework around which the individual has built his identity. It includes his value system, intellectual and body images, ways of manifesting himself, framework for giving and receiving, ways for handling change, loss, frustration and intrusion, and processes for promoting growth and enhancing self-esteem. All of these aspects of the individual's identity are integrated into what we call his sense of himself as a whole person. Since the individual is an organism operating in balance within himself and the world around him, any distortions in his internal framework will automatically produce distortions in his marital and family framework. As therapists, we are constantly concerned with this balance. Therefore, we may enter his world wherever he experiences pain—in his individual adjustment, in his marriage or in the family system. However, no matter where we enter, we will then work with him toward balance in all three of these areas, if he is willing.

We do not consider that therapy is at an end just because the client once again feels in charge of his problems and able to handle them. We feel that is just the beginning; the real goal is for him to feel in balance within himself and the world around him. In order for an individual to achieve such balance and thus to be able to follow his own process, he must have a strong internal structure which he trusts. Otherwise, he will cling to his external supports and be afraid to risk going into new areas of growth and change. Therefore, we feel the most important job of the therapist is to teach people how to build integrated internal structures that will make it possible for them to achieve their maximum potential for growth and development of their creativity. Our methods for enabling individuals, couples and families to build such structures are as follows.

INDIVIDUAL

The first step in working with an individual to help him develop a structure that fits him is to develop a trust relationship between the therapist and client. The trust is based on the therapist's clear presentation of his role with the individual. He is not in charge of him, responsible for him, or obligated to do anything except be himself. The therapist must believe and operate as though the best gift he can give his client is to be as clear as possible about who he (the therapist) is and what he can offer, as well as what he expects from the client. In this way, he gives the client someone solid to bounce against (in terms of self-expression), which was something the client did not receive from his parents, without becoming a parent or parental with the client. Instead, he teaches the client how to parent that part of himself which is young, undeveloped and afraid, and how to raise that part of himself and integrate it into his total structure of who he is.

For example, a man grows up in a family in which any assertion on his part is greeted by his parents with withdrawal or attack if that assertion challenges them in any way. So, perhaps he learns by age three that he cannot come out directly with his feelings and get what he wants. His parents will give to him only if he doesn't ask at all, asks in a devious way so that it doesn't look as though he is asking (gets affection by getting sick), or gives them something he knows they want as a way of seducing them into giving to him what he wants. He learns how to manipulate. By the age of five or six, he has stopped developing an internal structure based on a sense of who he is openly and directly, and has a good start on developing a structure based on getting goodies and avoiding pain without taking any responsibility for his actions. This structure may work very well for him in allowing him to grow up with a minimum of trauma in his particular family. The problem is that once he becomes an adult and is interested in a different kind of life for himself, he is still stuck with a structure that protects him in a family situation that won't allow openness, and that same structure also ties him to those kind of relationships.

At the point where he realizes he is unable to make a different kind of life for himself, he may come into therapy. What he doesn't realize is why he cannot get what he wants and what it will cost him to shift his internal structure so that he can. Without knowing it, he operates on the basis of his early life experience which is that no one can love and accept his real self and that if he is honest about his feelings he will be alone or hurt. He must pretend to be someone else in order to survive and get what he wants. Therefore, he alternates between trying to please, and having temper tantrums along the line of "keep your damn old jack!" The first may win him friends, but he feels cheated and uneasy because they love him for what he does, not for who he is. The second pushes people away who are really capable of loving and the only ones who stay around are those who, like himself, are afraid and so low in self-esteem that they will hang on even though they are being dumped on. Either way, he never wins, he always loses, and he confirms what he was led to believe earlier—that no one can ever love and give to him for himself.

After years of such experience, his self-esteem becomes very damaged so that by the time he gets into therapy, his pain may be intense. However, his self-destructive process is so ingrained that he will do his best to prove the therapist is like everyone else even though he wants desperately for the therapy to work. He will run through his repertoire of manipulations—seduction, intimidation, withdrawal, helplessness, hopelessness, and limit testing. He will begin to trust the therapist if the therapist does not get caught in any of these, but is able to stay with himself and be clear to the client about what he (the therapist) sees, hears, and feels. Confronted with seduction, the therapist may make a comment like, "I appreciate your compliment, but I feel a little uneasy, like I'm being had in some way—is that just me, or is something else going on?" With intimidation: "I'm not here to convince you about what you should do or that I'm right and you're wrong. All I can do is let you know what I see and hear and feel in relationship to you and to what I feel may be going on inside of you. I don't have any investment in whether or not you change or continue in therapy with me. I'm concerned about you, but I'm not in charge of you and think you are perfectly capable of deciding what's best for you."

If the client withdraws and the therapist feels something is going on even though the individual isn't talking, he may just sit with him through that stage without any prodding. If the therapist feels he is being manipulated, he may offer that he is getting annoyed and doesn't want to just sit as he doesn't feel anything is going on and doesn't want to waste his or the client's time. If the manipulation is one of helplessness, the therapist may say, "I get very strong vibrations of helplessness from you—not from anything you say or do. It's more of a feeling that I should do something, that I'm somehow responsible for whether or not anything happens here." With hopelessness, "I can't give you a reason for living—that has to come from you. I can help you understand what's getting in the way for you to get what you want in life. However, you have to come up with the wants."

As the client tests the therapist's limits, it is very important for the therapist to be clear without punitive or withholding. He may say to the client, "I think you handle the world by manipulating and that you're very good at it. I also think you need to understand that you learned that way of relating in order to survive and that you are lucky you were smart enough as a child to figure out such a way. It got you through some difficult times. However, now that way of relating no longer fits and is, in fact, hurting you by preventing you from getting what you want. It's an old friend that you can appreciate for getting you out of a tough spot; now you've outgrown that process and have to move on. The first step in doing that is for you to recognize that you are manipulating. The process is so much a part of you that you often do it automatically without even realizing it. So, I'm going to call you every time I experience a manipulation—not for you to then use to criticize yourself or attack me. Instead I want you to consider my feedback, decide if my perception is accurate and then determine whether or not you want to keep that kind of manipulation or give it up."

Thus, the therapist divorces the process from the person's identity—he is not a manipulator except by choice. He has *learned* how to manipulate for very good reasons and must respect that reality rather than use his awareness to judge and depreciate himself. To judge and depreciate himself only keeps him in the manipulative framework. Therefore, if he wants to stay a manipulator he can continue to judge and depreciate himself every time he finds himself manipulating (positive double-bind). The therapist in this way models a new way for the client to look at himself.

In our experience, the main deterrent to a manipulator changing his mode of expression is that if he admits to himself he is manipulating, he automatically is overwhelmed with guilt and self-recriminations. This is because he gets in touch with the real feelings underneath the manipulations which his origin family condemned. In addition, he begins to get in touch with his overwhelming outrage and pain connected with their lack of support to the point that he feels overwhelmed, out of control, and panicked. So, he adopts a denial and distortion system which enables him to rationalize anything he does. By the intervention described above, the therapist gives him a way of looking at his manipulation without experiencing guilt and all the concomitant processes that triggers. He also models what real parenting can be like and teaches the client to respect and nurture the child inside himself. The client may be 35 years old and very accomplished in many areas. However, he is still six years old emotionally because that is the point at which he stopped developing himself in relation to his own impulses, needs, and limitations, and started developing himself in relation to protecting himself from others and getting what he wanted without being vulnerable to attack or intrusion.

As the client begins to accept feedback from the therapist about his manipulation, he begins to experience a differentiation between the manipulative behavior and what he is really experiencing internally in the moment. When he becomes aware of this discrepancy, he then begins to assess on an emotional level what the manipulation does for him and what it costs him. As he allows himself to experience the results of his choice, he is then forced to make his choice more explicit—either to stay where he is knowing what is involved, or to change because he cannot knowingly stay where he is. Either way he goes, he is already breaking his internal structure because he is taking responsibility for his choices. If he chooses to change his manipulative pattern, he will begin to experiment in expressing the feelings to the therapist that he has previously been holding back. The therapist must respond on two levels—first, recognition and support that the client is coming out directly; and second, how he (the therapist) feels in response. The message is "I appreciate and respect your coming out clearly—I see that as a gift to me. I also will be just as honest in my feelings toward you even if I think you won't like them." In this way, he does not infantalize the client as a helpless infant who needs to be protected and coddled; he treats him as another adult who needs support, but is in charge of his own learning. He again models parenting as support of assertion—both directly, by complimenting the assertion—and indirectly, by responding in kind. The client then learns he can take help without being depreciated in the process. The client then integrates what he hears from the therapist ("You are in charge of yourself"); what he experiences with the therapist (the therapist does not take over, intrude or back off); and what he experiences within himself (intimacy can involve sharing deep feelings without a loss to either participant in the process). Thus, the beginning base for a new internal structure is established. This process is repeated with the therapist over and over as the manipulative defenses crumble and the client gets in touch with his real feelings.

As the manipulative defenses crumble, the early pain that the young child experienced (prior to his cut-off and shift to a manipulative structure) begins to break through the denial system and move to a higher level of consciousness. At this point, the client will begin to panic because he feels himself losing control. He may experience this loss of control as a feeling of internal chaos, emptiness, intense pain that doesn't seem to be related to anything concrete, or a feeling that he is going crazy. As this point, he needs solid support from the therapist in four major ways. First, he needs for the therapist to let him know where he is in his growth process—that early pain which he had previously repressed in order to survive and grow is now beginning to emerge. He needs to just let himself experience the feeling without trying to analyze or understand it. Secondly, he has to experience those feelings so that he will no longer have to carry them around as dead weight, use energy to keep them repressed, or allow them to prevent him from utilizing and understanding those parts of himself that are buried under that pain (usually the vulnerable, sensitive, creative child inside himself). Third, the therapist encourages him to set his own pace for dealing with his pain—experience it as much as he can when it emerges without pushing himself or holding on—allow his internal self to set its own rhythm—feel to the extent he is able in the moment and let himself cut off when it fits without making judgements or programming himself in any way. Thus, the therapist teaches him to begin to get in touch with and appreciate his own natural growth rhythm. And last, the therapist indicates that he will ride closely with the client through this feeling area, not taking care of him, not intruding, but simply experiencing his feeling with him. He will occasionally intervene to encourage the client to stay with the feeling or to share his own imagery or gut sensation, but always with the understanding that the client ignore the intervention if it is at all intrusive.

At times, in this process, the client may appear as though he is totally oblivious of the therapist. He may be writhing on the floor with the experience of early pain he cannot even elucidate. However, the presence of the therapist is vital in this experience. Clients have expressed to us later, in evaluating their experience, that they constantly felt the therapist's presence even though they may have had their eyes closed or backs turned during the process, and that experience of the therapist being there on a gut level made it possible for them to stay with the pain and ride it through. It is as though the therapist is experienced as a solid wall, not pushing them, but supporting their experience of their pain by not backing away from it or being afraid of it. Again, this is the support they did not receive from their parents. Rejecting, depriving, or intrusive parents are usually running away from or repressing their own pain which the child's growth experience triggers, and the child interprets this behavior as an indication that he is overwhelmingly bad or unlovable.

When the therapist respects his pain and sees it as unpleasant and difficult to experience but necessary to his growth and development, then the client feels free to let go into the pain until it runs its course. When he gets on the other side of that pain, he knows on a deep level that he can survive emotionally alone; that there is no longer anything inside himself which he has to fear. At that point, his survival shifts from clinging to external supports and defending himself against pain to committing himself to his own growth and the development of his uniqueness and creativity. Once that shift is made, he starts to build his identity all over from the point at which he originally cut off. Since he will be building on two levels—the self-esteem and the relationship—as in the natural growth development, the therapist may work with him and with his spouse, children, lover, friends, as the need emerges. The therapist will need to shift back and forth between individual and relationship therapy according to the way the client's progress emerges. The self-esteem level is developed as the client experiments with expressing his feelings spontaneously, openly, and directly. That process alone is self-appreciating. The therapist teaches the client that the expression of feeling will automatically produce growth because it opens up new areas of feeling and understanding inside oneself.

Therefore, if the individual's meaning for living is attached to growth, there is no way he can lose. Any time he comes out with his feeling in a way that is fitting to him, he will learn and grow by that expression. That process is the cake. If others respond and give him what he wants—that is the icing. Thus, the client learns to shift from outcome to flow because his goal is growth rather than specific concrete result. The client then proceeds to develop according to the integrative process we described in the chapter on natural growth, with these additions. He has the help of the therapist who gives him feedback on the way he experiences the client's assertions in terms of congruency, clarity, and authenticity. If he has a spouse or family, he will also have to develop a new structure for relating as a separate whole person in an open system at the same time he is building a new identity for himself.

Our experience has been that people usually take about two years to build a solid internal structure with which they feel comfortable and secure. As they learn the processes for facilitating their own growth, they use the therapist less and less—usually only for giving them feedback when they seem to run against a block, or to help them clarify an experience they have just been through so that they can integrate it into their structure. The therapist teaches the growth processes during the building-integration phase and we'll go into those in detail in Chapter Eleven.

Chapter 11

BUILDING THE INTEGRATIVE STRUCTURE (MARITAL AND FAMILY)

In an intimate relationship, legal or otherwise, two people may be operating as whole, separate people, but have a low level of integration in the relationship. Each may have his survival attached to who he is and to his own growth, but at the expense of the relationship. These people may need help in learning how to deepen their intimacy without infringing on their individuality. It is as though their sense of themselves as individuals is clear and well-formed, but their sense of themselves in relation to others is less well-developed. They can walk away or let go easily if things don't go well; indeed, it is far too easy for them to walk away and take care of themselves. Thus, the marriage may offer connections in a few areas or go to a certain depth and not farther. They find excitement and express creativity in other areas of their lives. The areas that need to be opened up in these relationships are those involved with hurt and disappointment. Usually, because these people are strong, they often get strong messages from others who want to be taken care of. Thus, they have learned to shy away from hurt feelings—their own and others—as a form of self-protection. They do not know how to express hurt or to hear someone else's pain without feeling responsible, as though they have to do something because they are strong. Their ability to turn away from suffering has conserved their energy and made it possible for them to achieve, but it has also limited their depth. The therapist can respect their unwillingness to wallow in pain, but he also disclaims their difficulty in understanding and using it. He teaches them that pain is simply a teacher. We do not experience it unless there is no other way to find out what we need to know. The hope is that as we get more in touch with the processes necessary for growth, we won't need pain as a teacher.

With this interpretation, the therapist makes it possible for the couple to look at what is disappointing and hurtful to them without feeling as though they are burdening each other or losing control of themselves. As each begins to share his hurt without looking for a solution or explanation, he may get in touch with the dependent, child-like parts of himself he has never allowed himself to see and explore.

In other words, the ideal base for a marital relationship is that each partner have a strong sense of himself as a separate, whole person whose survival is attached to himself and to his own growth. However, with that as the base, the relationship must have room for each of the partners to parent each other at times, to be children together, to be siblings, and to be friends. All those areas need to be developed to realize maximum growth potential in the relationship and enhancement to the individuals involved. Therefore, with couples who already have a sense of separateness, the therapist works for a balance within each and with each other by the exploration, development, and integration of all these levels into their relationship structure.

So, when couples come for therapy not because they have a problem but because they want to grow or deepen their intimacy, we explore their ability to be mother and father to each other, to play as children, to share as siblings, to respect as friends, and to demand what they want as lovers. Many times people are aware of these many aspects of their relationships, but it is very helpful in solidifying and enhancing their structure to have these aspects labeled clearly.

When the marital relationship is such that the emotional survival of the individuals involved is attached to the relationship itself, we bring that observation out into the open and let them decide whether or not that arrangement is fitting to them. Thus, they get the message from the therapist that there is no one way or right way for a marriage to be. Whatever works and fits the people involved is a good marriage. Whatever way they go involves choices and therefore costs something. If each individual's survival is connected to his own growth, they both risk the possibility that the marriage won't accommodate their individual changes. If they opt for preserving the marriage no matter what, they may have to curtail their individual growth considerably. Sometimes people make a conscious choice to pursue their individual growth, but are unable to follow through on it. When that happens, we ask them to consider that perhaps the family they have created with their marriage is a much better family than the ones in which they grew up. If so, then maybe they are using this family to finish growing up and when they do, they can then decide what kind of marriage they want either with one another or with other people.

Thus, they learn to shift their way of looking from why they don't do what they want to what it is they are learning by their current experience. That makes it possible for them to take responsibility for their situation without using the reality to depreciate or judge themselves. If they choose to preserve the marriage, but seem to keep rocking the boat, we ask them to consider that maybe their heads are making a choice that other parts of themselves are sabotaging. We suggest that they may be ambivalent about what they really want and to recognize and let themselves experience their ambivalence without feeling as though they have to make a choice. Thus, we teach them to stay with their process and we make this possible by the message that ambivalence is not a bad place to be—it is simply part of the growth experience. If they allow themselves just to feel both sides of their ambivalence—to flow back and forth between what it feels like to go one way and what it feels like to go another—a decision will gradually emerge. Thus, they integrate into their repertoire a new way of making decisions by letting them evolve.

Sometimes people come into therapy thinking that their marriage is falling apart and they have to get a divorce which they don't want. A divorce may not be the answer at all. They may be at a place in their relationship in which the old way of connecting doesn't work anymore. Let's say, the husband was the father and judge, and the wife was the dutiful, awe-struck little girl at the time of their marriage. Since that time, each of them may have grown to the point of greater self-assurance so that he doesn't have to play god anymore and she doesn't have to pretend she is passive and helpless. However, when he tries to express some of his needs—which he has previously hidden—and she tries to make demands and set limits for herself, they seem to clash. The therapist first of all helps them to see that the old way of connecting is dying, and to make room for each of them to let go and to mourn that old way of being. He recognizes with them that they do not as yet have a new way, so that they are in a very frightening, unsteady framework with each other. Thus, they have a chance to integrate their loss and at the same time make room for a new beginning.

When a couple makes a decision to give up using the marriage as a survival framework and to come together as two separate, whole people, they need a great deal of help from the therapist in defining and clarifying what structure of relating fits for them. They need support through their desert period so that they don't make rash decisions based on the emptiness they feel in their relationship at this point. Also, it is important that they don't push for a connection out of their fear of losing each other, simply because such pushing will not work and will only build resentment. They have to stay with the vacuum and let feelings emerge gradually which will lead them to new ways of being with each other. As the therapist holds them to this process, he teaches them respect for their own and the other's natural rhythm—an understanding and respect for such rhythm is vital to the formation of a new structure for relating. It requires a trust that they will get what they want just by being who they are and not by grasping, holding on, or maneuvering desperately.

The next important step is for each to learn how to say no and how to ask clearly for what he wants. Deep intimacy is not possible unless people can clearly honor their boundaries about what is intrusive to them, and can express their desires without equivocation, defense, or explanation. The other part of that process is that each learns to hear the other's expression of his limitations and demands as a gift—a way of keeping the connection open and clear—even though he may not like or be able to respond positively to such expressions. The therapist enables both to keep open in this respect until they are able to experience the results of that kind of freedom and honesty. Once they realize that they feel relieved and much more responsive to each other, even though they don't agree on everything, they will adopt and integrate the process as their own. The other awareness that evolves out of their process is that they cannot really hide how they feel in these areas of boundaries and wants; their feelings will come out more slowly and in devious ways if they are not honored directly. Therefore, they really have nothing to lose, and they stand a chance of a rich, free relationship if they take the risk to be who they are in direct and fitting ways. The extra added bonus in this process, no matter what the outcome, is increased self-esteem and self-awareness. Once a couple has learned to connect survival to self and growth, recognize and appreciate their own and the other's growth rhythm, and to be clear with each other about wants and limitations, then they will know very quickly whether or not they fit with each other. If they decide they do not, then the therapist needs to help them recognize that they have used the relationship to promote their own and the other's growth. Any relationship that does that is not a failure.

Thus, he teaches them to connect success to growth and not to outcome. With that understanding they can appreciate each other and grieve over their loss without guilt, self-doubt, or self-depreciation. They can understand that they chose to leave the marriage because they did not fit together and not because there was something wrong with either of them, or because they didn't care or try hard enough. They can respect and appreciate themselves and the other for following the process through to the end. Thus, the experience can be integrated positively as a building block to help them determine the kind of marital relationship they do want and to find it.

If they decide they do fit with one another, they may want to take time to just be with each other and experiment with the new growth processes they have learned. They may at a later time return to therapy for additional help in learning how to use their imagery, phantasy, and intuitive levels of communication to deepen and enhance their relationship. Mrs. Luthman discusses the possibilities in the intimate relationship in detail in another book.*

Some couples may come into therapy because they want to separate and are somehow unable to do so or want help in doing it as constructively as possible. The goal of the therapist in this instance is to assist them in staying with their process so that they can experience the separation in all of its aspects in a growth-producing way. Then there is no left-over internal baggage and they can integrate the experience as a building block toward the next state of their growth. We have observed the following steps in the separation process.

Usually one partner, let's say the husband, realizes he no longer feels strongly enough toward the other to stay together. However, he has difficulty being clear because he does care about his spouse and doesn't want to hurt her. The therapist usually has to pin him down until he can differentiate the fact that while he feels a commitment and a familial connection with his wife, he does not feel a male-female connection anymore and can no longer deny that in himself. The wife may try in many ways not to hear him, but the therapist keeps confronting her with what he is saying and asking for her

---

* S. G. Luthman, *Intimacy–The Essence of Male and Female,* Nash., (November 1972)

response. The wife may then admit she really doesn't want someone who doesn't love her in the way she wants to be loved, or she may maintain that she wants him no matter how he feels about her. Either way, the therapist encourages her to come out with her feelings and asks the husband to hear her without taking care of her or defending himself.

The next stage is panic on the part of the wife. She may get hysterical, threaten suicide, or just go into a deeply grieving, frightened state. It is very important that the therapist be able to hear her pain and give her plenty of room to express it, but not be seduced into reassuring her that her husband will change or that she will immediately find someone else. The husband, at this point, is often withdrawn as though he has to close off his feelings in order to follow through on his decision. The therapist can recognize this with both of them without pushing him to get into his feelings.

The next step in the process is often a euphoric state on the part of both of them. He has moved out and found an apartment. They have told their friends. She has learned that while she is in pain, she is not going to die, and is rather proud of herself that she is surviving. He is also proud of himself that he was able to follow through. The therapist reinforces and supports that pride because it accurately denotes their growth. However, he also gently chides them that in many ways they are not really separate. They still call each other regularly, go out on dates, occasionally sleep together. He doesn't criticize that behavior, but questions what it implies to both of them. The husband may then say that it keeps him from having to face and deal with his dependency. His wife is still doing his wash, maybe even cleaning his apartment. The wife says it makes her feel they aren't really separated and that there is hope. When that is clarified, it becomes clear to both of them that they are playing a game that is torturing to both of them.

At this point, they make the decision to separate a congruent one, and then the death hits both of them. Their reaction may be surprising to them. Each of them gets in touch with whatever early infantile feelings the marriage masked. The husband may begin to experience a deep depression which has nothing to do with the marriage but is connected to his loneliness as a small boy which he has never let himself experience before. The wife may get in touch with the rage she felt toward her father who could only accept her as a sweet little girl, and not as a strong woman. She has some of the same rage toward her husband, but now she realizes the rage really belongs to her because she has pretended to be passive and clinging to please men. As she has begun to cope with being alone, she has begun to experience her real strength and with it her rage at having denied her real strength for so long. Each of them may then need individual therapy to deal with those parts of themselves that the relationship hid.

The next stage is that both of them have begun to date other people and with the therapist's help to separate their anger and grief toward one another from the feelings that belong elsewhere which they have projected onto one another. They may even be able to express some appreciation toward one another for their ability to follow through on their process to this extent. The therapist supports the fact that they do have great respect and concern for one another in order to do this and that it is a gift.

At this point, the immediate crisis is over. They may go their separate ways for some time and come back later to deal with their anger, love, and grief as a way of totally finishing. They may find, after taking responsibility for themselves and working out some of their own problems, that they care more for one another than they realized and want to try again. Or, they may decide on divorce and proceed to end the relationship legally. The therapist gives them much support for their growth during this experience, clarifying what he has seen as the destructive parts of their connection and the growth-enhancing parts. He encourages them to keep open to their process, recognizing that nothing is ever totally ended, but that each experience flows into the next.

To build an integrated family structure, it is necessary to move back and forth among the individual systems, the marital framework and the family system, to incorporate each change into each of the individual structures, the marital structure and the family structure. Thus, therapy begins to follow the ebb and flow of the natural growth process. Each individual has a unique rhythm; each dyadic interaction has a unique rhythm, and the family system as a whole has its own unique rhythm. As each individual in the family learns to understand and appreciate this phenomenon, the family beings to emerge as a dynamic organism with a life of its own, functioning as an open system. In other words, the family's structure of relating built around an understanding of process and a respect for rhythm becomes an entity separate from the individuals involved. Thus, it is possible for imperfect individuals to develop a perfect process which permits them to grow individually, relate together or in dyadic units, disagree, or separate—and the experience is always growth-producing without any loss of self-esteem, creativity, or individuality.

The first step the therapist follows in enabling the family to build this process is to help its members to shift their goal from outcome, in terms of concrete results, to growth. For example, the family shifts from worrying about why Johnny is a failure in school to exploring what his lack of performance means in terms of his growth rhythm. Maybe it means that he has a kind of preparation stage—a period during which he is withdrawn, disinterested, and passive—which is his way of preparing himself internally for a new growth phase. Once this is understood, then they can begin to explore what the preparation place is like for each person in the family. For one it may be a type of depression that is not related to any real event. For another, it may be a period of internal chaos or confusion. Usually, family members have previously depreciated or criticized themselves and one another for these moods because they were "unproductive." With help from the therapist, they begin to appreciate these states as not only important, but the life-blood of the growth process. For it is in these states that the head and body activities are turned off and the gut has an opportunity to digest, assimilate, and integrate prior experience as well as anticipate, explore, question, and prepare the organism for the next leap.

Johnny's lack of performance may also be an expression of some process that is going on in the family that is not overt. The therapist teaches the family how to look at behavior in terms of what message is being expressed rather than whether or not it fits some external image of how the family and individuals within it should be. They may discover that Johnny's behavior is expressing the sadness or pain of someone else in the family who is not in touch with those feelings and has been unable to express them openly. Therefore, Johnny's behavior is then seen as a prod to get that family member to take more charge of his feelings. The therapist then explores with Johnny and with the family how he could get the same message across without having to hurt himself to do it. Thus, the family's level of awareness is automatically lifted.

Johnny's behavior may be a statement that some area of his own growth is being inhibited. The therapist encourages him to consider and look at this possibility without the accompanying judgement that something is wrong. He also teaches Johnny to let the family members know whether he wants help from them and what kind, or whether he simply wants his own space to work things out for himself. Thus, the message is that it is all right to ask for help if that fits your process, or it is all right to demand space if that is what your particular growth phase requires. Either way, the individual remains intact. He can ask for help without feeling less, or he can refuse help without feeling he is being ungrateful or disrespectful. He has learned that both processes are important for growth and development.

Another important concept in the family's structure is that connection is not based on physical presence, sameness, or words and actions. It is based on an internal commitment that is the result of interactional experience and not an act of will. Once the family members understand this, they can allow each other great freedom to move out, drift away, or experiment individually. This kind of commitment operates oblivious of time, space, or distance. If family members begin to accept this concept, they can learn to be aware of each other's process without words, even at a distance or over time. When they come together, they can pick up on their internal connection easily if they are not masking it with anxiety, recriminations, or projections. In other words, there is no longer any fear of loss. The commitment is there; it is real and it is not based on externals so there is no way to lose it or control it.

Once individuals in the family have understood and accepted the above concepts, then the therapist encourages each member to explore with other family members what he wants from the family in terms of nurturance and structure and what he wants to get elsewhere. In what ways does he want to depend on the family, what does he want the family unit to do for him, what does he want to do for the family unit? Other family members then define whether or not they can meet these desires and/or to what extent. Then each person is clear about what he can receive from the family and what he has to get elsewhere, and other family members are freed from guilt and doubt about whether or not they are fulfilling their responsibilities. In the process of exploring these areas with family members, the therapist teaches them how to do this kind of exploration for themselves so that they can continue this process as needs, demands, ability and willingness to give, change and develop.

Another important concept in the family structure is for family members to understand the value of allowing themselves to teach and be taught by one another. Many families do not realize that everyone in the family has something to teach and something to learn. For example, the three-year-old in the family can often teach others how to fantasize, how to play, how to get in touch with their feelings. Three-year-olds are very close to the feeling area, because they haven't yet learned how to use words to cover up. Therefore, their behavior is often a reliable barometer as to where the family is in process. Eleven-year-olds can teach family members what it is like to face a major growth change because they are usually letting it all hang out for the world to see—they are overwhelmed and everyone knows it. If other family members allow themselves to be open to the eleven- or twelve-year-old's process instead of trying to rescue or ignore the child, they can get in touch with their own feelings about change and development and learn something about themselves. The adolescent can often teach family members new skills and philosophies that go with his or her generation. Parents can teach children how to stay with their feelings and be true to themselves through every crisis, and they can teach each other and their children about maleness and femaleness.

With a structure built out of these concepts, family members are then able to leave the family when it fits their process without a loss to themselves; they can learn about giving and receiving based on a comfortable sense of who they are in terms of their limitations and wants; they can pay attention to and develop great respect for their own natural rhythms; they can relate to others out of a sense of separateness and wholeness; they can shift from child to adult, from parent to friend without trauma or loss, and they can learn the true meaning of commitment. What else could anyone possibly want?

Chapter 12

LETHAL VERSUS GROWTH PROCESSES

We think that family therapy is really a teaching process. We teach families to become aware that some of the ways they have learned how to function actually sabotage their hopes and produce destructive results. When they become aware that the root of their failures or destructive outcomes lies in their manner of operating and not in their basic make-up, then they may be willing to risk change and move into new ways of manifesting themselves.

We have broken down some of the common processes which we have observed as producing destructiveness and closed systems in families. They are as follows:

1. Any comment family members make about another is viewed as an attack, whether the comment is a question, a compliment, or an actual criticism. For example, a child tells a parent he doesn't like something. The parent could explore why the child feels that way and use that knowledge to learn more about himself, the child, or both of them. Instead, he immediately starts to defend himself or criticises the child for lack of appreciation.

The husband may indicate to his wife that he feels very depressed. She doesn't offer him an opportunity to ventilate about his depression, or to explore why he feels that way. She manages to convey the message that if he expresses any unhappiness, it is a deliberate attempt to criticize or depreciate her. Or, the husband may tell the wife that he loves and appreciates her, and she looks at him suspiciously without responding. Now, it may be entirely accurate that there have been instances in which he flattered her to get something.

However, if she views every positive comment from him as an attempt to manipulate, there is no possibility for change.

A sister offers to help her brother with his newspaper route so he can get through earlier. He makes a sarcastic response indicating that he sees her offer as an intrusion and an indication that he isn't capable of doing his job.

All of these examples are connected to the same end result—no one gets too close to another. That way, no one gets hurt or disappointed too much, but on the other hand, neither is there any nurturing or deep sharing.

2. The fact that family members may be very different from one another in the way they think, behave, and function is experienced as a threat rather than an opportunity for learning, for growth, and for excitement. Thus, if a member expresses his differentness, he is accused of a lack of respect or love for other family members. For example, one child may have a very different learning rhythm from that of other children in the family. He may be uninterested in school through elementary and even high school. He may have to work for awhile or explore himself more before he can focus on a definite educational or work goal. Another child may be a loner in comparison to the rest of the family in that he is not group-oriented. His family can hamper his development by giving him the message that this is wrong or bad, and by pushing him in another direction. Such differences are particularly hard for parents to accept when they feel they are giving the child an opportunity for an education they never had, or when they are concerned about their own adequacy as parents.

Children in the same family may be quite different in the ways in which they communicate. One child might be quite verbal and be very willing to come home from school and give everyone a full account of his day. Another child might view the pressure from the family to report as an intrusion. He may need room to let his day's experience come together for him inside of himself and then he will communicate what and when he wants to. He may never be as verbal as other family members, so they will have to learn to live with his flow between verbal and non-verbal states. If they could observe his difference as an opportunity to learn, they might become more observant and responsive to his non-verbal communications. That might put them in touch with parts of themselves they might not otherwise perceive. Because they talk so easily, the talk sometimes covers up their more quiet internal states.

3. The expression of anger is viewed as an attack rather than an attempt at contact. This is one of the most destructive of the lethal processes because anger is very much attached to aliveness, sexuality, and creativity. To repress it is to deaden oneself in all these areas. The family unit is the most effective training ground for learning productive, non-destructive ways of expressing anger. When that training ground is unavailable, the growth of all family members is set back many years, if not permanently. If family members can see the expression of anger as an attempt to make contact and therefore as positive, then only the ways of expression are criticized and there is plenty of room for trial and error. Expressing anger becomes a way of saying, "I don't want any barriers between us," rather than, "I want to hurt you."

4. To express tenderness means to make oneself vulnerable to attack, ridicule, or disappointment. We have seen families whose warm, tender feelings were so restricted that family members were actually in physical pain. Family members do not see the expression of their tender feelings as an opportunity to enhance their own growth and for each to learn about his ability to feel and be a loving person. They see such expression as valuable only if it produces a guaranteed outcome. Since previous experience has led to disappointment or hurt, they refuse to risk again, often not realizing they are closing off their own growth as well as any possibility for change in the family system.

5. The expression of sadness indicates weakness, lack of strength and dependability. Tears are tantamount to disaster—anyone who cries is falling apart. In some families, this is permissible for the females as they are not expected to be stable, dependable, or in charge of themselves—an additional destructive side effect of this process. Thus, men have no room in the family to be taken care of and women have no room to be strong and to take charge when it fits. This further permeates the system to the extent that children are seen as incapable of giving. Thus, parents must always be strong and protect the children from their feelings and can never let the children have the opportunity to take care of them. So, children may learn how to take the care they are given, but they never learn how to give care. Also, they don't have the self-enhancing opportunity to know that they have something worthwhile to give to their parents; that they are really people, not just leeches or incompetents.

6. Everything must be reasonable. With this process, spontaneous expression of any feeling is usually viewed as a lack of control and therefore undesirable. Feelings must be justifiable and rational in

order to be expressed. If someone is angry, his first move is to decide whether or not it is righteous indignation. Then he talks about what made him upset, and what the other person or persons ought to do about it. The discussion then ends up a lecture or if there is interaction, it sounds like a United Nations meeting. In families like this, homeostasis is dependent on the external controls of logic and reason. Family members do not understand or believe that they have any internal controls that will guide them if they react spontaneously and impulsively.

7. Everything must be nice and polite. With this process, there is no anger or open disagreement in the family at all. In our training courses we often ask trainees to simulate a family, and use these processes to experience the results internally. For example, we ask them to try to plan a trip—each one wants to go to a different place, but cannot say so directly. Each must try to get what he wants without disagreeing or being impolite. The internal end result of this process for everyone participating is always an intense desire to run away or to murder somebody.

8. Love is equated with being dutiful and obedient, "If you love me, you will do what I want, think what I think and feel as I feel." Since love is equated with behavior, other expressions of love are unappreciated or ignored. Thus, the individual gets the message that he is loved only for what he can do and not who he is, resulting in great damage to self-esteem. Family members seldom hear praise or encouragement for what they do—after all, it is expected that everyone does his duty. Why should anyone be praised for something he is supposed to do as part of the privilege of being in the family? This process produces escalating resentment and depression resulting in acting-out behavior periodically on the part of one or more family members to provide a safety valve for all. Without the acting-out, there is internalization of the resentment and depression and subsequent severe physical symptomatology.

9. Intimacy is viewed as frightening. Intimacy is not perceived as an opportunity for sharing, enrichment, and nurturance; instead, it is viewed as a potential threat. Very often, the underlying fear is that of inadequacy. Individuals doubt their abilities to please one another. The message is, "If you get too close and know me too well, you won't like me or I won't be good enough for you." Or, they feel they will be intruded upon or swallowed up if they get too close because they have difficulty setting limits and holding their boundaries. Thus, when they have a very close experience, it is often followed by a fight

or a withdrawal. The homeostatic rule—don't get too close—is maintained.

All of these lethal processes are based on each individual's underlying sense of himself as destructive and worthless. He assumes that if he does not have external controls, he will hurt others, or be isolated, or abandoned. Therefore, he develops ways of functioning that protect him from revealing himself and from being confronted with the feelings of others in the family. Such ways are always destructive and sometimes lethal to the point of actually producing physical death. At the Institute we hope that in the future we can do research on the possible relationship between these lethal processes and illnesses like cancer, heart attack, arthritis, and other crippling or terminal illnesses. We believe that we can perceive incipient physical death in a family via the meta-messages and the extensiveness of lethal processes, but this facet of our work has not been scientifically validated.

Once a family has become aware of the lethality of its processes and is willing to go through a period of disruption and chaos necessary to develop a new system, the therapist can then begin to teach them processes for maintaining an open system and for maximizing the growth of individuals within the system.

The most important growth processes we have observed are:

1. Feedback is perceived as necessary to growth. Family members encourage each other to comment on how they see each other, to express how they feel openly and spontaneously to each other, and to be as honest as possible about their feelings. For example, a son comments to his father that his father's judgmental attitude irritates him. If father agrees with his son's perception that he is being judgmental, he simply responds to his son's annoyance with his own feelings—"That's too bad about you!" "You can be irritated all you want—just do what I tell you." Or, "I'm sorry you don't like it, but that's the way I feel." Whatever his response, the issue is not resolved in terms of agreement or compromise, but all the feelings are out in the open in a non-destructive way, so there is no excess baggage of buried hurt or resentment. Thus, no one loses. Loss is not equated with disagreement; it is equated with intrusion, attack on one's self-esteem, or vindictive withdrawal.

If the father did not intend to be judgmental, he can explore why his son perceives him in that way. His son may be able to offer him some information that indicates he was coming across in a way that didn't fit him. If so, he has learned something useful to him and his son has been able to give to him. Both win. If he finds his son has distorted his communication, the father can clarify his message. Again, both win because the son has learned something about his father and the father was able to make himself understood.

2. The fact that family members may be very different is viewed as exciting rather than a source of threat or attack. Family members view their differences as opportunities for exploration, change, learning and enjoyable stimulation. For example, a husband may like to plan a trip in methodical, step-by-step fashion and his wife may prefer to just start out and see what happens. If he doesn't condemn her way as stupid and she doesn't depreciate his as boorish, then the difference does not lead to a power struggle. Instead, they can begin to experiment with various ways of handling a trip and may be surprised at the results. They may find that each really likes the other's way better in some instances; they may develop a combination of the two, or they may end up exactly where they started. However, even in that instance, they have grown individually and have enhanced their relationship because they have given and received the message of respect for their differences. They have been willing to experiment and perhaps learn from each other which is a much more valuable gift to their self-esteem and their relationship than whether they agree on a specific trip.

3. Disagreement is viewed as an opportunity for learning rather than a loss. The family does not live with the mythology that agreement is connected to love and closeness. Nor do they believe that all issues have to be resolved or brought to a compromise. They do believe that there must be room for feelings to be out in the open and then the issues will take care of themselves. Therefore, disagreement is viewed as normal and acceptable, not in any way connected to separation, attack, or disaster of any kind.

4. Family members separate internal intent from external manifestation. Thus, if daughter does or says something that hurts mother's feelings, mother does not immediately jump to the conclusion that daughter intended to hurt her feelings. She checks first to see if the way her daughter expressed herself was congruent with the message she intended to get across. Thus, there is room for error in the family without being labeled a bad person. The space to make mistakes, knowing others will assume innocence until proven guilty, is vital in developing spontaneity and aliveness in family communication. Even if the mother's perception of the daughter's message was accurate, the mother will respond with her hurt feelings rather than

by attacking or withdrawing. Again, the assumption is positive—that the daughter may not have intended to hurt and didn't realize her message would have that effect. If it turns out that the daughter did intend to hurt, the mother may respond with her own hurt and anger. However, she also checks out at some point what may have happened in the daughter's experience that made her want to hurt her mother. Again, the underlying message is that the daughter is not basically a hurtful person. So, if she behaves in a hurtful fashion, there must be some other reason.

Thus, family members know they will have support even when they make mistakes connected to not being in charge of their feelings and therefore coming out in destructive ways. With such support, they have the opportunity to get in touch with feelings they were not previously aware of with no damage to self-esteem. For example, a child in the family may shop-lift some article from a store. When confronted by his family, he may be rebellious and depreciative in his response. The parents may then enforce restrictions or some other form of discipline for his behavior, but they will also question what upset or hurt him so much that he would behave in this way. Thus, he pays for his behavior without feeling ostracized or depreciated, and he has the support of his family to search for a better understanding of himself.

5. Family members know how to report self and keep the way open for connection, intimacy, and growth. This means an individual can stay with his feelings, keep coming out with his feelings, and not become judgmental, attack, jump to conclusions, or cut off communication totally. So, a parent may say to a child, "Dammit, cut out that noise—it's driving me crazy and I can't get anything done!" If the noise doesn't stop, he may say, "If you don't stop, no television tonight!" The message is connected to the parent's feelings and to choices—the parent never implies that the child is bad, sick, stupid, or crazy. Neither does he imply that the child would behave if he loved and respected the parent. The child may then stop the behavior, but respond to the parent with his own anger and hurt, "You never let me make any noise—I hate you!" The parent tolerates the expression of feeling because he is only concerned about the behavior. In this way, the connection is kept open between the father and the child. The child keeps the connection open by expressing how he feels at the restriction. That makes it possible for either of them to come to the other at a later time and talk about the problem. Family members recognize that an open, flowing connection does not require

certain kinds of behavior, agreements, or compromises. It requires that each person be willing to stay with an interaction until all the feelings are expressed and nothing held back. If they are commited to staying with the feeling flow, then the system will remain open and unblocked even though everyone doesn't always like the end result in terms of decisions or feelings.

6. One of the most important growth processes is the ability to receive a stimulus, savor the experience, and allow the action to flow from the savoring process. For example, a sister may do her brother a favor which makes him feel very warm toward her. If he can let himself just experience his warmth without feeling embarrassed or obligated to respond immediately in some way, then he can use the experience to get in touch with his ability to feel loving and warm. That experience alone will produce growth. The infant grows in this way. When he is happy, his whole body is suffused with the feeling and his whole body expresses his joy. Being able to savor a feeling enables an individual to constantly probe deeper into his inner capacity for feeling. Depth is learned—it is not automatically there. As the brother allows himself to let his warmth flow over him, his response to his warmth will flow from that process in a way that is fitting and natural to him. If his sister can do the same, they will be able to get the most nurturance out of that interaction and deepen their experience and knowledge of intimacy.

7. Another important growth process is the ability to experience feeling without blocks. Each individual in the family is able to stay with and follow through on his experience of anger, sadness, joy, warmth, loss, or whatever he is feeling without cutting it off because of embarrassment, awkwardness, or fear. In addition, other members of the family can stay with that individual without intruding on his feeling or taking him away from it. Thus, the message is that there is great respect and appreciation for feelings in the family system. Because of this each individual is enhanced and his growth is encouraged.

8. Emotional survival is attached to self and personal growth. Children, of course, are attached to their parents for emotional and physical survival in their early years. However, if the parents give their children a solid structure to bounce against as we discussed earlier, and model that their own emotional survival is not attached to the family, then children will make their survival shift to themselves very early, often around twelve or thirteen.

9. When emotional survival is not the focus of the family homeo-

stasis, then the attention of the open system is on contact, sharing, enrichment, and fulfillment. Such an open system with those goals makes for a lively, sometimes exhausting interaction. However, the rewards are great in terms of aliveness and creativity for every member of the family. With such a system, parents can reap tremendous benefits in learning more about human nature from their children who are each unique and totally different from each other and from the parents. We believe that the human potential has only just barely been tapped. To open up pathways for that potential to develop requires the development of family systems geared toward the appreciation and encouragement of uniqueness rather than clinging together defensively.

Chapter 13

TREATMENT OF FAMILY SYSTEM IN RELATION TO TREATMENT OF INDIVIDUAL MEMBERS

In the treatment of a family unit, the therapist moves back and forth between working with the family system as an entity and working with the individual members of the family. He lays the base for this in the beginning of therapy by letting family members know that in the treatment sessions, individual members will periodically receive the major focus of treatment. This does not mean that that person is the sick one because each person in the family will come into focus at various times in the process. It means only that the therapist will move in the direction of whoever is blocking the interactional flow at any point in time.

In the natural growth process, such blocking always takes place either because of past distortions in learning or because new stages of growth are opening up and the individual is confused about where to go. For example, a family may come into treatment with vague symptomatology—one of the children is underachieving in school, another is having nightmares periodically, and a third child is overly rebellious. No one is in serious trouble, but the combination of difficulties is beginning to cause the parents some concern. The therapist asks the parents to begin to share their concern with the children. As the parents do this, the therapist observes that the children look down at the floor or fidget as their parents are talking to them, and he comments on this. The children admit they have difficulty looking at their parents directly. The therapist gently probes regarding the reason for that difficulty and one of the children comments that when he looks at his parents, his mother looks sad and his father looks angry. The therapist asks him to say that directly to his parents, which he does, and he asks the parents to respond to the child. The mother is surprised that her children are so aware of her inner feeling. She responds that she is not sad so much as she is feeling lonely. Her husband seems to be more and more distant, spending a lot of time at work and coming home exhausted and withdrawn. The therapist asks her to begin to share her lonely feelings with her husband, which she does. He sits, unmoving, and looking very closed-off from her.

Up to this point, the flow of interaction has been moving very slowly, but congruently, from children to parents, from mother to child, and from mother to husband. At this point, the interaction is blocked by father's closed-off appearance and lack of response. Therefore, the therapist moves to the father, commenting on his closure and his lack of response. He asks the father to close his eyes and get in touch with what he is feeling inside. The father says he is feeling as though he is facing a brick wall and unable to get over or around it. The therapist asks him to just experience his frustration and helplessness without forcing himself to move in any way. As the father does this, he starts to cry. As he cries, the therapist encourages him to let himself go as far as he wants to and just experience his tears without being afraid or analyzing himself. He tells the rest of the family that the father is getting in touch with new parts of himself, and that they do not have to worry about him—he is exactly where he needs to be.

When the father recovers, the therapist asks him to share what he is experiencing with the rest of the family. Thus, the flow is back into the interaction. The father begins to tell family members that he is feeling helpless and overwhelmed both by the problems at home and at his work. The therapist has to hold him to the feeling level because he easily gets into explanations, history, or rationalizations. As he expresses his frustration and helplessness, he appears much relieved. The therapist gives him support indicating that everyone has feelings of this kind—it is part of being alive. If a family has ways for such feelings to come out without seeing them as an indication that someone is falling apart, then individuals can experience relief and refreshment which makes it possible for them to cope more effectively. Thus, the therapist is supporting the father's feelings as normal, and at the same time providing a base for the whole system to begin to develop processes for expressing and responding to these kinds of feelings.

When the therapist asks the family to respond to the father, the children indicate they are relieved but somewhat scared because it is so different for their father to express himself in this way. The youngest child begins to share how he sometimes feels scared and helpless and he and his father make a feeling connection at this point. The therapist asks the wife to respond to her husband's feelings and she closes off, saying she doesn't know how to respond. The therapist then moves to her and asks her what she is experiencing inside. She has difficulty getting in touch with her feelings, so the therapist asks her to take her time, forget about the rest of the family, and just experience herself. She reports that she is feeling frightened. When the therapist explores this with her, she reveals that she is afraid she cannot take care of her husband's feeling and she is afraid she can't depend on him. The therapist comments that she seems to react as though she has to be strong and follow through in some way when her husband is down and that if she does this, then she may not be able to depend on him to take care of her anymore. He wonders where those messages originated with her—where and how did she learn those assumptions?

At this point, the wife gets into her relationship with her original family and her father in particular in terms of her life experience that led her to those distorted assumptions. It may be clear that her perception of herself as inadequate on a feeling level and of men as being unreliable is not going to be resolved in one session. She needs more individual work to understand and integrate her past experience so that she can proceed with the family interaction. Therefore, the therapist may recommend that she have some individual sessions for that purpose at this point, and at the same time proceed with the family sessions to continue to integrate her learning into the family interaction. Thus, both she and the rest of the family are clear about what the therapist is offering and why.

Again, the therapist makes it clear that he may recommend individual therapy or some other adjunct to family therapy at various points in the treatment process when it evolves that a family member is blocking the interaction in some way. He indicates that this is a common process because people learn and grow on many different levels and we try to fit the treatment process to the natural growth rhythm. Our purpose is to help people get to where they want to go in the fastest and most effective ways possible. Again, offering additional help is not an indication that the therapist sees a family member as being in a worse condition than others in the family; it simply means that he sees an area of concern or confusion emerging that would best respond to another approach in addition to the family work.

In some instances, the therapist may discontinue the family treatment for awhile to give an individual time to work out his blocks to interaction because the block is so great that the family cannot move until something changes. In this instance, he may see the family once a month or once every two months to check the homeostasis. Sometimes, when one member of the family is in individual therapy, it may skew the family balance and they need occasional sessions to support them until the individual is ready to relate back into the family. In other instances, the changes in the individual who is in therapy alone may trigger the exacerbation of symptoms on the part of some other member of the family who may then also need some form of individual or group therapy to deal with his problems. Or, he may need a family session to understand what his symptomatology means in relation to what is going on in the family system.

Family members need to understand and make allowances for the differences in individual rhythm in relation to growth. Often, a family member will criticize or depreciate another because he does not respond in a certain way or wish to continue treatment at a particular time. They see his refusal as a lack of caring for the family, stubbornness, or revenge. The therapist enables them to see that that particular member may have a different rate of growth and may have to take time to assimilate what has already happened in therapy and experiment with what he has learned before he is ready or able to go on. The therapist may then begin to explore with the family the different growth rhythms of each family member and how those differences cause difficulty and misunderstanding in the family. He indicates to them that rhythms are not susceptible to change by an act of will. They are innate, and asking someone to alter his rhythm is like asking him to change his eyes from brown to blue. He teaches the family that rhythm has to do with the unique way in which each individual meets the world—how he adapts to change, how he responds to new situations, how he makes decisions, how he relates to others, how he learns new ideas and behavior, and how he handles trauma and problems. The rhythm differences can best be seen in very young infants. Some will meet the world moving and making noises, while others are equally alert but much more quiet, and there is a multitude of differences in between. This does not change in the adult, so the more active one may see the quiet one as disinterested or incompetent and the quiet one will see the other as domineering and intrusive if they do not understand and appreciate rhythm differences.

The therapist teaches the family members to understand and appreciate their own and the other's rhythms so that they can differentiate what behavior is related to processes they can change, and what is related to rhythms for which they must learn understanding and adaptability. For example, parents may complain that they relate very well to two of their children, but cannot understand or relate successfully at all to the third child. When the therapist explores their interaction with them, he may see that the third child is very different in rhythm from the rest of the family. He appears hyperactive to them, but he is really only extremely curious and energetic. Other family members operate at different levels of evenness, but they all have a steady flow with no real extremes in highs or lows. The third child, on the other hand, is quite volatile, and very aggressive—he learns by pushing the limits to the maximum and by leaping in where angels fear to tread without worrying about the consequences. No amount of reasoning reaches him. He only responds to cause and effect. If the parents lay out his choices clearly and enforce the discipline part of the choices consistently, he will channel his energy constructively. However, if they are inconsistent or judgmental or depreciative of him, he will become rebellious and totally uncooperative. This is understandable when you realize that his parents are really asking him to be and learn in exactly the same way that others in the family do and the basic uniqueness of who he is is not being recognized or appreciated.

Once parents understand that his way of growing is related to his own natural rhythm and is not indicative of a lack of respect for them or a deliberate desire to antagonize them, then they may be able to treat his behavior as a normal phenomenon and provide the structure he needs for his testing and experimentation without damaging his self-esteem. Also, the child needs to understand and appreciate that his parents' rhythms are different from his and it is difficult for them to understand and appreciate the way he learns. Thus, perhaps he can learn very early to respect the rhythm of others and not see their responses as a depreciation of him as much as a statement about their own frustration and confusion about how to relate to someone who is so different.

With this understanding, perhaps each can learn from the other. The child can begin to appreciate his parents' stability which is very helpful to him as he is learning how to channel his intense energy and gusto. The parents can begin to see the creativity and aliveness which is often more apparent at an early age in a child of this nature. Once differences can be understood in terms of rhythm rather than perceived as statements about the relationship, then everyone seems more able to relax and learns to flow with one another. The therapist makes it clear that rhythm differences always make for more friction in relationships, so family members need to make allowances for the fact that they will periodically get on each other's nerves because they are different in a basic area, and not because there is anything wrong with any of them.

The therapist can support the parents in that this child will be more difficult for them to raise because he is least like them. We always have more difficulty with people who are very different from us. However, this child will also provide them with a challenge for learning and developing new understanding and skills within them selves. The therapist makes clear to the child that he may sometimes feel left out or misunderstood in the family, but that it is important that he appreciate and honor his own uniqueness even though he may at times feel lonely because of it. He is not lonely because people don't love or care about him; he is lonely when he is most in touch with how different he may be from someone else he loves. However, those moments pass and he will find that uniqueness to be his most prized possession.

Chapter 14

CONCEPT OF ENDING THERAPY IN PROCESS THERAPY

As we indicated previously, there is not definable beginning, middle, or end in the family therapy process in the same sense that we originally learned about in therapy. When a family is ready to stop therapy either indefinitely or for a limited period of time, we get some concrete clues, but mostly they are intangible. We see the concrete clues as follows.

One of the things we look for is the family's ability to understand, experiment with, and incorporate the growth processes we have discussed into their own system and family structure. Once family members feel clear and secure with those processes, they have the basic tools for continuing their growth on their own.

Another clue is the ability of family members to communicate with clear, congruent messages and sustain interaction on their own without assistance from the therapist.

The children are clearly unhooked from the parents in terms of having to rescue them, express feelings for them, or interfere with their own growth processes in order to draw attention away from parental pain. Sometimes children can be very subtle in this respect. For example, a child may sense that a parent is upset or annoyed about something and deliberately pick a fight to give the parent an opportunity to vent his rage and frustration. Neither parent or child may be aware of what is really going on until both examine their real feelings. The child may realize he did just pick a fight out of the blue and really didn't feel angry until he had contact with the parent. The parent may become aware that he was carrying around excess baggage in the form of unexpressed feeling. The child then needs to get the message from the parent that he (the child) no longer needs to do this; that the parent is capable of handling his own feelings and he doesn't want the child to cut into his own growth processes by making himself such a scapegoat. The parent then needs to be aware of clues in his behavior that will let him know when he is holding something back and not dealing with his feelings. Perhaps he has headaches, gets a little low, becomes very irritable—everyone has mood states or body indications that tell him that something is going on which he needs to notice. It may take time for the individual to educate himself to be observant of these indications, but the effort to do so is well worth it in terms of the savings in energy, time, and family equanimity.

The parents operate as separate, whole people no longer dependent on each other for emotional survival. They are beginning to explore ways of relating that pertain to getting more out of the relationship and finding creative outlets for themselves individually. Each takes responsibility for his own state of happiness or despair—he or she does not any longer expect that the other spouse is on this earth to make his mate happy. Therefore, if one is happy, he can respond to the sad feelings the other one may be experiencing; but he does not let his mate's sad feelings take him away from experiencing and enjoying his happy feelings to the fullest. In addition, the partner does not look at his staying with his happy feelings as a loss or threat to the relationship. If one is unhappy, he takes responsibility for correcting that condition without looking to the other for a solution or panacea.

Individuals in the family have achieved a balance—at least a beginning one—between their interaction and sharing within the family system and their efforts to experience and express each one's individuality outside the family unit. Family members see the flow of individuals in and out of the system as desirable and beneficial to the family unit.

Family members have shifted from manipulating, grasping, and clinging, to a relaxed trust of each one's growth process and of the growth flow of the family system. Thus, they can adapt more easily to change within or to trauma from the outside, without blocking in panic.

Now, the intangible clues to ending therapy have to do with the subjective experience of both the therapist and the family about where they are in their growth process. For example, a therapist may be on his way to his office for a session with a family and he has a fantasy that they may be going on a trip. When he arrives at the session and begins to explore where the family is, they may say that they thought about missing next week's session so that they could go to the mountains. When the therapist shares his fantasy with them, they may realize that they are talking about something more than just a trip. They are getting ready to use what they have learned to try their wings and explore on their own. They may want two or three more sessions to get used to the idea of being without the therapist and to further solidify their learning, but they realize that it fits for them to leave therapy.

In another instance, the family may come in with a tale of gloom about how terribly things are going in the way they used to be ten or twelve sessions ago. Although they are talking about how terrible everything is, the therapist is feeling very light and finds it difficult not to smile. He shares this with the family. They look at him as though he is crazy, but then one family member comments that she has had occasional flashes of feeling over the last week that they were ready to stop therapy and that thought scared her a little. The therapist asks family members to explore that idea and as they talk with each other, they reveal that all had some sense that they were coming to some kind of a close. However, none wanted to face that because he was not yet sure he could sustain what he had learned on his own. The therapist explains that he also feels they are ready to experiment more on their own, but that they need occasional feedback from him until they feel more solid about their new processes and systems. He indicates that they can arrange the therapy structure to fit their natural growth process and suggests that they meet once every two weeks or once a month for a few sessions and then evaluate where they are.

In another example, the therapist gets a premonition before a session with a family, who is usually very prompt and reliable, that they aren't going to come, even though they haven't notified him. They do not come, but they show up next week on time and ready to go as usual. They seem exuberant and lively. When the therapist explores the absence with them, they indicate they decided to play hooky and the whole family went to the beach, had a picnic, and played all day. There is an impish quality about their report as though they feel a sense of accomplishment in being able to be totally irresponsible. The therapist comments on this, and with much surprise, family members agree that they do feel that way. The therapist then suggests that for them this was a major growth experience because they are normally reliable and responsible to the point of rigidity and sometimes harm to themselves. He indicates that perhaps this experience means that they are beginning to appreciate themselves more and to take better care of themselves so that they can balance their responsible structure with nurturance.

The therapist also explores whether their missing a session was in any way a statement about where they are in therapy. The father indicates that he has had vague thoughts about this in the sense that they have been coming to therapy for some time and have worked very hard and are very pleased with what they have accomplished. He doesn't feel they have gotten everything they need from therapy, but he does feel like enjoying himself for awhile and not working so hard. Other family members support this, with some trepidation. The therapist feels good about that perception and says so. He doesn't feel they are avoiding or covering or resisting in any way. He feels they are just getting in touch with gradually loosening their controls and enjoying their first burst of freedom. He supports the family in this and encourages them to enjoy themselves as much as they possibly can. Not only is it a good idea, but it is essential for their growth that they learn how to let go and enjoy. He agrees that they will need additional help later in integrating that experience into their new structure and in learning additional growth processes. Therefore, why don't they plan to meet again in three or six months when the family is ready to work again?

This family is so committed to growth and has such a strong base with the therapist that he is not concerned about their following through with this plan. If he had some doubts, he would say so to the family. "I agree you need this space, that it is important for you to have time to explore this new process of letting go and soaking up good feelings. However, I also feel it is easy for you all to get so active and involved in your many interests that you may not continue your process. If you are concerned in the same way, we can do one of two things. We can plan a definite appointment three months from now to evaluate where you are and whether you need more time or want therapy at that point. Or, we can explore what the clues may be in your own interaction and individual processes that will let you know when you are ready to come back into therapy." If the family decides on the latter, then the therapist and the family together can explore what these signs might be. There may be a mild sense of tension on the part of all the family members; one child may get overly active or rebellious again, some somatic complaints may develop, parents may find they are spending less time with each other and their relationship has stopped progressing, or the family may become aware of a general anxiety not related to anything concrete and not a real problem, but noticeable. The therapist indicates to them that it is important for them to understand that none of these signs will mean that they are regressing or are back where they started, even though they are similar to symptoms they originally experienced before they started treatment. At this point, they mean that the family is ready for a new growth spurt and need to come into therapy to understand what that new growth direction is and what may be getting in the way of proceeding with it. In this way, the therapist teaches the family to look at symptomatology as a guideline to new growth rather than an indication of regression or a breakdown.

In normal growth this is what symptomatology is. We don't like the term symptomatology because it implies pathology, but we use it for want of a better term. In normal growth everyone experiences symptomatology of practically every known variety at one time or another. Most children have periods when they lie, steal, have temper tantrums, rebel, act out, and become obnoxious. There is a serious problem only when these symptoms persevere. Otherwise, they disappear when the normal growth problem has been worked through or when new growth occurs. The symptoms simply provide periods of delay and temporary release while the organism is coping with change or trauma. Now, once a family has shifted into a growth framework, the symptoms have the same meaning as in normal growth even though the same symptoms may previously have denoted serious pathology in the family. The difference has to do with where the family is in process both in the concrete and intangible data we have just discussed.

Now, the concept involved here is that there is a process flow which develops over time between the therapist and any family with whom he has considerable experience, and that flow is not tangible or concrete in any way. It is as though the family has developed a trust in the therapist based on his understanding and support of their natural growth rhythm, and the therapist has developed a trust in the family's final commitment—no holds barred—to their own growth. Once that trust is developed, there is no more resistance on the part of the family and no more concern on the part of the therapist as to whether the family will stay with its shift. Therefore, the family is able to leave its defensive position with the therapist and be totally open to him. The therapist is able to leave his doctor-patient framework and operate with them as people who are coming from the same place he is. He may have more experience with the growth structure and have developed his own internal structure much more than they, but they see the world the same way in terms of their commitment to growth and aliveness. Because of this, their deeper non-verbal, non-body aspects of communication open up to each other, and there is much more communication on the fantasy, imagery, dream, and sensation level.

With this kind of communication, a family can come back to a therapist after a six-month, year, or even longer absence, and in one interview, he can experience where they are in their growth process. Because of the depth of their connection, the therapist has a basic feel for where the family is in process. He is able to pick them up on that level which is much more readily available and valid than any other level, especially over time. For example, a family may have come into treatment originally because of a twelve-year-old son who is not in serious trouble, but is obnoxious and rebellious at school and at home. The family has a repressive structure and the therapist works with them in the family unit for a year, with the marital pair, and occasionally with the boy individually. The family breaks its old repressive structure, and begins to develop a new base for its system which allows family members more room for expression of feeling within the system and development of individuality both inside and outside their system. At this point, the father is transferred out of the area. A year and a half later the family returns to the area and shortly thereafter arranges an appointment with the therapist. When the therapist sees the family, it is obvious to him that they have continued with their growth. There is a noticeably increased meta-message of lightness, fluidity, and freedom. The therapist does not experience anyone in the family as blocked, holding back, or depressed in any way. The communication is clear and direct.

The family has come in because the father and son seem to be getting into frequently lively battles and the father is saying he doesn't understand what this is all about and more important, he doesn't want to use his energy in this way. He would like his son to go off and solve his own problems, so that he (the father) could concentrate more on his own growth. The son feels he wants more room to do things his own way. He is now fourteen and interested in experimenting. The therapist comments that it is interesting that both he and his father want the same thing—what's the problem? The mother is very much involved in her own growth. She has gone back to school, developed many new creative interests, and is perfectly happy to let the males in the family slug it out. The therapist experiences her message as congruent with her internal state. He also experiences the father as ready to erupt totally out of his old individual structure, which was rather passive, quiet, and methodical. He comments to the father that he senses that the father's growth has brought him to the place where he realizes that continued growth for him does not mean modifying and adding to his old structure; it means giving it up completely, with the awareness that he may not really be anything like the image with which he had chosen to live. The father is very responsive to this and indicates that he has known something was happening but was not sure what because at times he feels ready to explode. The therapist indicates that the father is ready to let go of his old structure totally and suggests some bioenergetic therapy because he senses there are some intense pre-verbal feelings which the father needs to experience in a safe area, otherwise they will overwhelm him as he moves into a new space. He experiences the boy as wanting more room as he says; but also experiencing some qualms at his own withdrawal and absorption with himself. The therapist offers this and the boy confirms that that is what he is feeling. The therapist then offers that the father's current state is only temporary until he gets through this stage of growth, and suggests that the family make room for both the father's and the son's annoyance at this current stage. In other words, they don't have to like it even though they understand and want to go through it.

The therapist also suggests the boy isn't getting much support from his father at this point because it takes all the father's energy to cope with where he is. Therefore, he suggests a group for the boy to give him a sounding board to explore the effects of his new experiences until his father is again able to connect with him. Thus, the therapist labels the process of where the family is in their growth based on his past knowledge and experience with them, his subjective awareness of where they are based on his deep connection with them, and the verbal affirmation they give to this diagnosis. We don't think it would be possible to accomplish this much in this short a period of time with a therapist who did not have that process connection to the family.

Chapter 15

CHOICE OF THERAPY METHOD

Family conjoint therapy is not a panacea; it is simply an additional method or tool to add to our framework for stimulating and enabling growth. We are beginning to believe that there are few, if any, people who cannot be helped. Failures in treatment are due more to a lack of knowledge than anything else and, as such, can give us impetus to explore and experiment with new ideas and techniques.

In some instances, family or individual therapy might be equally appropriate methods of choice. However, even if individual therapy is the appropriate choice for on-going treatment, the assessment of the individual's adjustment in the family may be a vital diagnostic tool. The establishment of personal identity and choice of distortions and defenses are largely determined by the person's experience in his family. Thus, diagnosis may be faster and more accurate if the therapist is viewing the individual interacting with the source of his transference than if the therapist is attempting to diagnose the individual through transference to himself. Also, a family diagnostic session may indicate that others in the family need treatment also, or that family treatment should be concurrent with individual treatment to maintain homeostasis and prevent sabotage of the treatment process.

In some instances, family therapy may be the only effective therapy method or the most appropriate; in other cases it is contraindicated. We'll discuss both in this chapter.

INDICATIONS FOR FAMILY THERAPY
AS THE TREATMENT OF CHOICE

If the symptom-bearer in the family is a child, we think it is impossible to accurately diagnose the meaning of the symptom or to treat the problem without seeing the whole family in the treatment process. In our experience, the child's symptomatology is always a reflection of some destructive processes which are operating in the family as well as indications of the inhibition of growth in his individual development. The only time we have been able to successfully treat a child apart from his family has been when the child is emotionally emancipated to the point that he is no longer dependent on them, can differentiate between their negative processes and his own, and is able to seek nurturance from other people and situations even though he may still be living at home.

Family therapy can be very effective when individuals have such a rigid denial system that the therapist cannot break through. It is very difficult for all family members to cooperate in maintaining a solid front of denial; it is impossible if there are children in the family under five. Their behavior will consistently give away the family secrets. For example, a family with five children, the youngest of whom was three, came to the Institute because the oldest boy was truanting from school and the school insisted the family come for treatment. They persisted for three sessions with the stand that there were no problems in the family except that the boy simply needed to grow up and be more responsible. In the third session, the three-year-old, who had previously spent most of his time under the table (to the extent that the therapist had to get down on her hands and knees whenever she talked to him), came out from under the table and announced loudly to the therapist that "Daddy never kisses Mommy when he comes home at night." Family members tried to laugh this off, but when the therapist asked the parents to talk further with their three-year-old about this, it was evident that he was very concerned about it. That opened up the fact that the parents were feeling a lack of connection with each other, but had been very afraid to discuss it. They felt that admitting that problem was tantamount to destroying the marriage, but they were forced to see that they had no choice but to deal with it since the problem was evident anyway, even to their youngest child.

Sometimes the one-to-one treatment relationship is frightening to a person. He may be afraid he is seriously ill; that he will reveal too much and that the therapist will think he is crazy. Or, he may fear being overwhelmed by the therapist, because it is a temptation to him to let someone else take over and control him.

In some instances, the individual feels so diffuse and unstructured about his own identity as male or female that he may be overwhelmed with either homosexual or heterosexual (or both) impulses toward the therapist. If the individual's life experience of intimacy has been consistently hurtful, he will do better in a treatment situation such as a family or group where intimacy is not immediately forced upon him. He has time and space to move in at his own pace, under his own controls.

Impulse-operating people (manipulators, psychopaths, whatever terminology you prefer) will usually not stay with a one-to-one relationship or a group situation long enough to develop a transference or relationship. However, such a person often will respond to family therapy because the treatment-focus is on his family system with which he is already involved and on which he is usually very dependent. The importance of that connection will often hold him in treatment until he has enough experience with the therapist to find out that everyone is not out to control him. Then he may begin to relax enough to take a look at whether or not he wants to change.

When the therapist and client in individual treatment are stuck and therapy is not moving, a family session may be very useful in revealing how the therapy is being sabotaged by the client, the family, or both.

Family therapy can often be amazingly effective in unhooking children from their rescue operations with their parents in a short period of time. Sometimes, even when a family does not continue in treatment, one or two family sessions will enable a child to see that while he affects and is affected by the problems in his family, he is not responsible for them. This may enable him to begin distancing moves—he may make major investments in school, hobbies, peer groups, church, or other relatives and friends. This may clear the way for his emancipation when the family does not change or when the process of change is very slow.

When the family is out of control with no one in charge, then family sessions are helpful because the therapist can take charge, thus reducing anxiety so that whatever treatment is appropriate can be determined. The therapist does not take over—he takes charge by establishing the limits within which he can work and holding the family to make choices about treatment based on those limits. For example, a family may be prone to uproar interactions and the therapist may outshout them or even pound the table to bring order. He then tells them that he's stopping that interaction because he can't work with it, because it isn't working for them and it's destructive to them as well. If the family continues its uproar no matter what he does, he may kick the members out of the session with the understanding that he'll try again with them next week. Usually, if he makes it clear he will not be intimidated, they will relax and begin to work. If not, he may offer to them that this is obviously not the kind of help they want or need since they cannot work within the limitations. Thus, he makes it clear they are making a choice, by their behavior, not to continue treatment. However, he does this without implying they are wrong or bad because they do not go along with this method of working—it simply does not fit them. Even though they stop treatment at this point, it can be a growth experience because the therapist has structured the experience into a matter of choice without guilt—a process discrepant with their diffuse, unstructured system.

In some families, the system and interaction are built around a scapegoat. One person in the family is the source of all difficulty and the message is that if he dropped dead, the family would work beautifully and everyone would be happy. He may be a delinquent child, an alcoholic father, a schizophrenic parent or child, a drug addict, or just a consistently obstreperous type with a chip on his shoulder who sets himself up for attack—of course, everyone else always takes the bait.

It is almost impossible to deal with this phenomenon without the whole family together, since each person plays into and reinforces the pattern in almost equal intensity. The pattern is always a cover for unexpressed pain in the family as well as unresolved conflict in the individual who has assumed the scapegoat role. For example, if the scapegoat allows himself to continue in the victim role, he does not have to take responsibility for himself or risk asserting himself. By keeping the focus on himself, he may be covering a psychotic process in another family member or a potential crisis in the marriage. Therefore, other family members attack him overtly, but support his delinquent behavior covertly by giving him double messages, not following through on discipline, or giving him non-verbal cues which hint they enjoy his behavior.

The therapist may need other observers: sometimes an individual is giving a picture of his experience as honestly and accurately as he can, but something is missing. His report seems discrepant with the end result and with the way he feels. Therefore, the therapist may suggest a family session to get the whole picture. Each person in the family may see the same event in entirely different ways and it isn't until all these parts are put together that a clear picture evolves of the family and the individual's process.

CONTRA-INDICATIONS FOR FAMILY THERAPY

Some families are threatened by the interactional framework and it is discrepant with their life style. An extreme example of this was a family we saw at the Institute who were referred by school officials. The fifteen-year-old daughter, youngest of five children in the family, suddenly began to fail in school. In one session with the family, the therapist learned that there was almost no family interaction. The only time family members were all in the house at the same time was at breakfast and even then they did not eat together. Each even had his own dishes and took care of his own cooking and cleaning. The father went camping alone every weekend and other family members all went their individual ways. The therapist found it impossible to get any sustained communication going in the family. With much probing, she learned that the daughter's troubles started when the mother began baby-sitting a working neighbor's six-year-old girl in order to make extra, badly needed money. Apparently, the only nurturing the daughter had been getting came from the limited amount the mother had to give which was now going to this younger boarder. The therapist then evolved a plan for the daughter to get extra attention from the teachers, the school psychologist, and a group at the agency to provide nurturing which the family was totally unable to offer.

Some families are so infantile that if the therapist focuses on one person, everyone else feels left out to the point of sabotaging the interaction, and no amount of support and structuring on the part of the therapist cuts any ice. In this instance, the therapist may have to have family members in individual therapy until the self-esteem levels are high enough to permit them to accept feedback from the therapist and one another.

We think family therapy is contra-indicated when one member of the family is operating out of an extremely rigidified, paranoid character structure. Because the family therapy method produces increasing intimacy, it alienates such a structure which is built to keep a hostile world at a distance. Therefore, the structure itself has to be dealt with in the individual before family therapy can even be considered. Now, in this instance we are not talking about a psychotic person. We are talking about a character distortion in which the individual has built his entire identity around a logical, systematic, often materially successful way of operating. The problem is that the whole castle is built on the erroneous assumption that everyone is hurtful including himself and the best protection is insulation. So, family therapy is a life and death threat to such an individual.

In some families, individuals will deliberately lie about what is happening outside the interview experience. The therapist saw one family treated at the Institute for several months and felt he was doing everything appropriate in terms of the treatment approach, but nothing was changing. He then discovered inadvertently from someone else who knew the family that the father had been conducting an affair with a neighbor woman for eleven years. Everyone in the family knew it but it had never been mentioned. When the therapist found this out, he called the father to say that obviously such an important aspect of the family situation could not be ignored and had to be brought up in the next session or treatment wouldn't go anywhere. In this instance, the family terminated treatment. A more experienced therapist would have terminated the family much earlier on the basis that if he could find no major error in the treatment approach, the family must have been holding something back.

When the parents in the family see their problem as a marital one and are able to separate themselves from the children so that the children are not extensions of themselves, then we will focus on the marital pair. We may have an occasional family session to see if the parents are being clear with the children about the changes they are experiencing and if the children can handle these changes. However, the family is not the treatment unit.

MOVEMENT FROM ONE FORM OF THERAPY TO ANOTHER

When a family or couple or individual comes to the Institute for treatment, we are prepared to move in a variety of directions depending on our assessment of what would be the fastest and mose effective way to get at the problems. It has also been our experience that a family may begin with one form of treatment and move to another modality several times during the process of their therapy, depending on where their growth takes them and how they can be reached most effectively at different stages of growth. For example, a mother may call us and ask for help regarding a fourteen-year-old child in the family who is beginning to exhibit some delinquent behavior—lying, truanting school, some suspected sexual acting-out. We indicate to the mother that since a child is involved, we would like a session with the whole family first to understand what each person's perception of the difficulty is so that we can get a complete picture of the girl in relation to her family. We indicate that our function is not to solve a problem for a family but to enable the family to understand the reasons for the problem and develop ways of solving it for themselves.

In the session, the family interaction reveals distance—family members sit with restrained postures, limited body movement, and father does most of the talking; a judgmental framework—father's talk is liberally sprinkled with shoulds, mother complains her daughter doesn't seem to appreciate what they do for her, and other family members' comments have to do with good and bad, right and wrong, and the family has a rule that no one talks about feelings. Each time it looks as though someone is going to cry or get angry or express sadness, there is an interruption or change of subject.

The therapist comments on these observations and adds that he feels sadness as he sits with the family. At this point, the focus shifts from the delinquent girl to the whole family in terms of all of their unexpressed feelings. This focus holds for several sessions as the family members begin slowly to open up their concerns and needs. At this point, the focus shifts to the parents. The mother begins to tell the father that he doesn't make room for her or appreciate her, and her husband lets her know that she doesn't take care of his feelings when he needs her and that he would like to be able to depend on her more. The girl's symptoms have abated by this time; she is relieved that her parents, especially her mother, are taking responsibility for their feelings for the first time. Other children in the family have ventilated their feelings and seem detached from the parental difficulty and more interested in their own lives. The therapist feels that both parents are people who have worked very hard all their lives and received little nourishment either from their origin families or each other. Therefore, he feels that a few sessions in which all his energy and attention could be focused on them would be nourishing to them and more helpful to the whole family in the long run.

He explains this to the family and then begins to see the marital pair alone for several sessions. In the process of confronting each other with feelings they have been repressing for years, the father begins to question whether he wants to continue the marriage. As the therapist explores this possibility with both of them, the father realizes that he really doesn't know what he wants. All of his life, he has been so used to doing and being what other people expected of him that he has never had an opportunity to explore what fits for him and what he really wants. He doesn't know how to relate to his wife from the standpoint of his limitations and needs because he doesn't know what they are. He was raised in a family in which his physical needs were well provided for, but there was little contact and he remembers feeling very lonely as a child. Since he does not seem to be closed off from his feelings, but simply unsure about them, the therapist recommends group therapy for experimentation with his feelings in a safe arena. In addition, he would have a variety of models to use for developing his own internal framework.

The wife realizes that she has played a passive, unassertive role for years and has been afraid to express her strength. However, she feels that that role has gotten her nowhere at this point, and that she has to change to make room for the more powerful parts of herself. She grew up with a passive, withdrawn mother who may have been potentially psychotic. The therapist then has her see a female therapist individually to give her help in learning how to develop both her strength and tenderness and balance those parts of herself. He feels she could accomplish this better with a female who could give her a model of feminity that was not passive, because she associates femininity with passivity.

As the husband begins to become more aware of his identity and the wife more expressive, the therapist brings them back together to explore how they fit from these new places. Depending on what emerges from those sessions, there may be more family sessions to integrate the changes into the system or to explore a separation.

The decisions to move from one therapy modality to another or from one therapist to another are made jointly by the therapist and client based on the stage of growth that has evolved as both see it; the therapist's evaluation of the best approach; and the client's reaction and validation of the move. As in everything else in family therapy, such decisions are process moves determined by tangible aspects such as the client's historical development, the current interaction framework and the client's current growth stage, and subjective aspects such as the feeling experienced by both therapist and client, based on their deepening level of communication.

Therefore, clues to possible shifts in the therapy process can emerge out of fantasies, imagery, dreams, and meta-messages.

Some of the clues that suggest movement from one form of therapy to another are as follows:

An aspect of growth emerges that does not fit with the current treatment modality. For example:

1. A person who has been in individual therapy now feels his self-esteem has developed to the point where he is willing to experiment with his assertions. He is doing this at home, work, and with friends but is having difficulty. Both he and the therapist decide they need to take a look in a therapy situation to see how his assertions break down interactionally.

2. A family in treatment finds its interaction consistently blocked because one member closes off. Individual therapy may be appropriate for him if he needs help in getting in touch with what he feels or building his self-esteem; or group therapy may be the treatment of choice if he can take feedback and respond more easily to people other than those in his family. That experience may give him the necessary support, clarity, and assurance so that he can then later hold his own with the family.

3. A person in individual therapy keeps focusing on the interaction in his marriage even though he says he wants to deal with himself. He may need support in facing the difficulties in his marriage and preparation to do so by dealing with his fears about it.

4. A couple who has difficulty making space for themselves within the family unit may need support from the therapist in taking time for themselves with marital instead of family therapy.

A couple who cannot take feedback from each other or their children without getting defensive may respond to a married couples group in which they can see themselves in others and each can more easily take feedback about himself from someone else's husband or wife.

In marital or family therapy, one individual drops the external structure with which he has survived and finds that underneath he is diffuse, chaotic, and unable to relate to others. He needs the room and support of individual therapy until he can build a beginning base for a new structure of who he is.

An individual has a solid defense structure which his wife or family cannot break through. The therapist suggests a group with a co-therapy team as leaders and a group focus on Gestalt techniques. Thus, the individual has increased pressure from the group and two therapists to break through, and he has the security of two therapists to help him pick up the pieces when he does.

An individual in marital, family, or group therapy breaks through his defenses and gets in touch with infantile, pre-verbal, unfocused feelings. He is referred to an individual therapist who will work with him with bioenergetic and other physical techniques geared to making room for such primitive experiences.

Some individual in the family wants privacy to deal with aspects of himself separate from his family, and this does not interfere with the family or marital process.

A couple with no models as a basis for developing their own marital framework may be referred to a married couples group to get an intimate view of how other marriages operate which they can use as a sounding board for developing their own marital framework.

A young person who is ready to leave his family unit, but is having difficulty taking the first step, may benefit by a group which he can use as a bridge to being totally on his own.

Thus, movement from one form of therapy to another is determined by the client's flow between the development of his self-esteem plus his internal structure of identity, and the development of his ability to make connections with others in a meaningful way; whether or not he needs feedback from others to facilitate his awareness, or space to allow himself to emerge from inside, and occasionally shifts in therapy are made on a trial and error basis to break through—if one thing doesn't work, try the next.

We also sometimes move clients from one therapist to another. Sometimes, this is simply because one therapist may be better at dealing with a specific stage of growth than another. However, most of the time the shift is made because we think the client needs a therapist of the opposite sex to the one with whom he has been working. Such moves are based on this concept: We believe that in the natural growth process the child may get the same message from both parents, but incorporate it in different ways. If the mother says it is okay to cry, the male child incorporates this as permission and validation from the opposite sex that he can cry without a loss to himself. If his father says he can cry, the male incorporates this as affirmation from a male of his maleness and assimilates processes for expressing sadness into his male identity. The same message from both also adds another dimension which is a solid acceptance of this part of himself which no one or nothing can later shake.

Now, in the therapy process, if the individual had an early base of male-female interaction between his parents and himself so that he has awareness and some clarity about both the male and female parts of himself, then the sex of the therapist may be unimportant. However, in many people either the male or female part is unclear because of an absent or withdrawn parent and the individual feels off balance. Therefore, we duplicate the natural growth process to solidify and give impetus to his growth. For example, a male client has been seeing a male therapist for some time. He has developed a sense of himself and a solid structure inside, which is defined around himself. However, he is a little afraid to assert himself with women because his experience of women as whole, real people is nil. His therapist refers him to a woman therapist with whom he can test out what he has learned against a female reaction he can trust. As he experiences her response, he can incorporate those parts that fit with what he has already learned about himself from his own insides and from his male therapist. The other reactions he gets from her that he isn't sure about, he can use as a base for experimenting with other women. At least, he knows from his experience with her that he isn't way off base as far as women are concerned and, knowing that, he has more courage to explore. Having a solid male and female reaction enables him to feel more clear and more comfortable with all parts of himself whether he is relating to male or female.

We also frequently use a co-therapy team with some families, couples, or individuals such as the following:

An individual has no male or female model either because his parents were psychotic, he was an orphan, or his parents were not available enough to him. A co-therapy team gives him a parental base which makes it possible for him to simultaneously test out his expressions with immediate male and female affirmation and validation. We find this speeds up his growth process considerably and is more effective.

A family who is draining or exhausting to work with, or whose process is extremely manipulative or destructive, benefits greatly by a co-therapy team. Two therapists make the task easier and more comfortable for the therapists themselves, which obviously benefits the clients. In addition, it is more difficult for the therapist to get caught in or stay in the system if he has a partner to bail him out. Also, the interaction in many of these families is very fast, and with two therapists, nothing is missed.

A couple who is ready to work on their intimacy in depth can really benefit from the interaction between their male and female co-therapists. Of course, that requires that the co-therapy team have a strong intimacy base and we'll go into that in detail in a later chapter.

The co-therapy team provides a parental base, a male-female interactional model and two therapists—therefore two trained observers. It is the fastest form of therapy we know and therefore not recommended if clients are not prepared to move that rapidly.

PART III

BASIS OF CHANGE

Chapter 16

SURVIVAL MYTH

This analysis of the survival myth began as an inquiry into Family Conjoint Therapy; who needs it, when it is most effective, and how it works out in combination with other therapeutic methods. The investigation covered twenty families who were studied for a period of a year at the Family Service Agency of Marin County.* In each of these families, a child was the identified patient who precipitated therapy.

DEVELOPMENT OF THE STUDY

A first impression was that symptoms severe enough to bring a family to the attention of a clinic or agency occurred in families in which children are given the message that the family's emotional survival is in some way dependent on them. The original definition of emotional survival was then rather naively stated to be the parents' ability to remain together and perform their parental functions. Three types of family psychological survival patterns were distinguished—family survival dependent on one parent, the other parent consenting; survival dependent on one parent, but with the second

---

* These were families seen in therapy by Mrs. Luthman when she was Casework Director at FSA of Marin and Dr. Kirschenbaum was the agency's consultant in family conjoint therapy (1965-1967).

parent undermining the first; and survival totally threatened and the family disintegrating since neither parent is dependable.

Viewing families in treatment as exemplars of these three patterns, we soon observed that there was a correlation between symptomatology and survival patterns. Families in the first group, parents and children alike, shared repressive symptoms such as headaches, enuresis, stomach disorders, and phobias. Those in the second shared delinquent symptoms such as car thefts, school problems, running away, and sexual acting out. The third group showed suicidal symptoms, either verbalized threats or actual suicide attempts, and extremely self-destructive behavior such as narcotic addiction. At this stage of the study we began to correlate survival patterns with other family patterns in communications, interactions, and roles development. From this data, the following observations were made.

SURVIVAL OPERATION SIGNIFICANCE (SOS) WITHIN THE FAMILY SYSTEM

It became apparent that a disturbed family's interaction and communication pattern, covert rules, and symptomatology may define the pattern of survival on which the family operates. The family system is geared toward defense of the illusions shared by each family member about the role each must play in order to support the parental relationship and thus maintain the family balance. This is referred to subsequently as the Family Survival Myth. The twenty families studied were differentiated by three types of survival myths associated with the symptom classifications described above.

THE REPRESSIVE FAMILY

This type of family is moved by the myth that psychological survival depends on the repression of oral aggressive feelings. The substance of the myth is that impulsive expressions of feeling are precipitant actions, will bring about loss of love, even abandonment, especially when these feelings or actions are released in the face of opposing feelings or actions of other members of the family. In the marital relationship, conflict is eliminated by the sharp separation of the roles of the husband and wife. Each adult has specific areas of decision-making where there will be no interference from the other.

Joint decisions are reached only in areas relatively free of conflict. Needless to say, this parental relationship may appear on the surface to be productive, serene, and free of symptoms. For example, in beginning interviews with these families, interaction does not reveal open conflict between the parents. The wife is the family spokesman but assumes this role with the obvious consent and even encouragement of her husband. The husband can be articulate, however, and is so especially when asked for cooperation or elaboration of his wife's opinion. The parents' communications are reasonable and intelligent; they do not interrupt, refute, or argue with each other. Indeed, there is little or no interaction between them and each tends to direct his remarks to the therapist. When questioned by the therapist or the other spouse, each will comment on prior statements without distortion in the interpretation or response.

The conflict in this type of family is indicated in two ways—by the parents' disqualification of their own feeling, and the anxiety evidenced by the children's behavior.

The parents, first of all, will suppress or disqualify for discussion any comment on their deeper feelings. The serious symptoms of the children will be detailed but no mention is made of the deep pain the parents must feel about this behavior. Their descriptions of problems are lucid, but restrained to the point of sterility. They will wonder if possibly the children's behavior is normal and that parental concern is unfounded. This indecisiveness concerning a need for therapy is demonstrated by the fact that while nothing is held back in describing the family's symptoms, the problem is, in effect, denied by the repression of affect and the verbal disqualification of the seriousness of the problem.

The extreme pain in the family is evidenced in the interviews by the anxious behavior of the children. They are, to varying degrees, out of control. They giggle, interrupt, cry, throw temper tantrums, or change the subject. Constantly moving, they squirm, cover their heads, or hide under tables. The parents either ignore this behavior or make ineffectual attempts to limit it. They may lecture, reason, plead or cajole, all of which conceals the irritation or anger they feel at the children's behavior. There are usually clear-cut overt rules in the family which get verbalized but somehow never really enforced. For example, the children's bedtime may clearly be understood to be at 8:30. The children's persistent attempts to stay up later are countered by the parents with attempts to persuade them that the hour is reasonable, for their own good, etc. The parents feel frustrated and hurt when these arguments prove ineffective, and underlying their surface feelings are deep perceptions that they are failures as parents, which brings their own worth into question. Out of this perception and its accompanying guilt, the parents redouble their efforts to give to their children so that the children will not feel unhappy or unloved. The covert rule in the family is that everyone must feel the same way about everything. Any expression of individuation will make other family members feel hurt and inadequate. It is by appearing to be hurt or treated unfairly that children in this family manipulate their parents most effectively. The parents always respond to these particular stimuli no matter how unreasonable, and are quick to attempt to convince the child otherwise. Conflict between the children evokes parental efforts to arbitrate the dispute. In this way these conflicts become a question of which parent will concede the most to which child. Children in the family become frightened and angry because of their ability to control the parents and their anxiety is expressed in body language. The purpose of the covert rule in the family is to defend the Survival Myth—the necessity for repression of oral aggressive feelings.

Since the covert rule of the family—that every member of the family must respond with the same feelings to every situation—is established to defend the myth that survival depends on repressed aggressions, the child affected by the rule becomes certain that normal growth is impossible for him. He fears that if he continues to grow normally, that is, to test his relations with his parents in terms of boundaries for himself, he will force his parents to protect themselves by abandoning him, thus threatening his very survival. Father will withdraw and mother will become very hostile. The child then torn between losing his protectors or stunting his normal growth, becomes immobilized by unexpressed rage and fear. Out of this internalized aggression, his symptoms are projected: difficulty in eating and sleeping, headaches and stomach pains, enuresis, phobias.

In the origin histories of parents in these families, the common message was that the parent of the opposite sex was "overcome" by the aggression of the other parent. The end result was a feeling of being left out as a child. This is not usually verbalized and is frequently not conscious.

In relation to the origin histories, the Survival Myth in these families further implies that husband and wife must protect each other from their feelings or they will lose each other and be alone. This means not surviving because the feeling of aloneness is comparable to the feeling of abandonment as a child. It implies that in order for their children to feel loved and to "belong" they must protect the children from their feelings. Aware of this apparent need for constraint, the children reciprocate by understanding that their feelings in turn must never be expressed to their parents. By protecting their parents in this fashion they feel they will insure against their own abandonment. That the Survival Myth is imposed upon the children quite early in their lives is evidenced by the high level of tension when the family is together. The myth is constantly reinforced moreover when on rare occasions the repression mechanism falters or fails. The violence of exploding feelings too long held in proves again to all members of the family that feelings *per se* are dangerous and to be avoided at all costs.

THE DELINQUENT FAMILY

The Survival Myth of these families is that one parent cannot survive the sexual-aggressive impulses of the other. The function of the identified patient is to act out the impulses of one parent and displace the impulses of the other parent onto himself. He enables the family to stay together by protecting the child-like parent. In effect, he becomes the scapegoat in order to protect the weaker parent; in his perception, the weaker parent will collapse without this sacrifice. Usually the identified patient will be of the same sex as the parent he protects, or if not of the same sex, will possess a personality akin to that parent.

In interview sessions it is early noted that one parent, sometimes subtly, will attempt to disqualify the other in the family interaction. This is accomplished by various devices: interruption when the other is speaking, or finishing the other's sentences, speaking for the other spouse or commenting inappropriately on what the other has said. The identified patient is generally stoical, even sullen, in appearance. He *looks* like a scapegoat. The other children in the family are also taciturn with little spontaneity of speech. The parents monopolize the conversation which is invariably permeated with accusation and blame. This ranges from a subtle implied blame to overt attack. The wife, for example, will say that she cannot be a competent mother because she has to work for a living. By tone and manner she implies that if her husband supported the family more effectively she would not have to work. The husband may complain that he cannot control the children because his job forces him to travel. The implied criticism is that his wife could control the children during his absence if she were a more adequate woman or if she did not undermine his authority. The parents' accusation of each other may be much more overt, but even then there will be a projection onto the identified patients as the real cause of the family difficulty. Frequently everybody in the family, parents and children alike, will assent that the family would have no difficulties were it not for the scapegoat child who, along with the others, tenaciously agrees to the validity of the role he plays.

This type of family will openly discuss rules for family conduct, but they can never agree what these rules should be or how they should be carried out. If a momentary agreement is reached, one or other of the parents will undermine it. In carrying out the Family Survival Myth, the dominant though concealed family rule is that the family may have no rules at all. Only in this type of disorder can the scapegoat child perform his role in acting out for the parents.

The symptoms are predominantly sexual if the identified patient is an adolescent—car and liquor stealing, sexual acting out, expressed fear by the parents about sexual acting out on the part of their children even though this is not the case, playing the truant from school, usually with children of the opposite sex, etc.

In the origin histories of these parents, there was a seductive relationship with the parent of the opposite sex, unrelieved by the other parent because of a detachment or ineffectuality, and unresolved. These people then marry others who will parent them or whom they can parent. The Survival Myth implies that grown up sexuality is destructive. The child in this marriage then acts out the fear and rage of the child-like parent's unresolved Oedipal feelings. The other parent has handled his or her unresolved Oedipal feelings by repression and rigid control and is extremely threatened by the child's acting out. However, there is secondary gain in terms of his own sexual feelings which can more safely be expressed toward this child than toward the marital partner who might abandon or devour him. By triggering these parental responses the scapegoat in effect brings onto himself the sexual-aggressive feelings of one parent and acts out the sexual-aggressive feelings of the other.

The symptoms of the identified patient begin at the Oedipal stage with resistant behavior. This is succeeded in latency by passive resistance and in adolescence by open rebellion. The Survival Myth is continually reinforced by the family's irrational fear of the child's developing sexual impulses, which in turn produces behavior that validates the myth that sexual impulses are dangerous. The Survival Myth is very difficult to break through because everyone in the family gains from it. The scapegoat has mixed feelings about the sexual stimulation he is receiving. The other children use him as a buffer which permits them to escape conflict. The parents use him as a release for their sexual-aggressive feelings which they cannot release with each other. Should the scapegoat burden become too heavy, the child may leave or get himself removed from the family. At this juncture another child always takes over for him. If the burden eases and the crisis temporarily abates, the original scapegoat may return. There is a continuing pattern of seduction in these families. The parents seduce the identified patient into being the scapegoat; he seduces them into giving him control in the family. The parents seduce the other children into validating their judgement of the scapegoat by giving greater approval to them. The other children seduce their parents by agreeing with them so as to remain free of conflict. The members of such families will try to seduce the therapist, try to get him either to act as a parental stand-in or take sides in any conflict which may arise between the parents and children. These families generally withhold vital information. The parents especially will conceal their own earlier acting out or that of their parents in origin history material.

THE SUICIDAL FAMILY

The Survival Myth in these families is that no one can function alone; that no member is whole without the others and that, therefore, the family cannot survive if any member leaves it. They are all caught and extremely frightened. In interview sessions, it is impossible to distinguish which are the parents and which are the children. The interplay of family activity consistently screens off any effort at discussion of real issues or areas of conflict. Interaction consists of constant, universal disqualification. Coalitions constantly shift depending on who is being threatened. Disqualification may take many forms. Uproars occur during which everyone talks at once and no one can be heard. It may be evident in the inability to verbalize at all with communication unexpressed in the form of depressive body language—grimacing, sighing, looks, belches, hanging heads, hiding beneath hands, glasses, or clothing. It might appear in schizophrenic-like movement from one unrelated subject to another. A family member comments, then responds to the therapist's reflection of the comment with a denial. Family members never respond to one another's comments with appropriate follow-through.

The communication pattern, in short, is a defense against ever revealing anything of significance. This is revealed when one member will deny that another member really feels the way he says he feels. A member may misinterpret a family member's comment and respond according to that interpretation. Or, again, they may lead the communication into another channel entirely and be quite able to continue this *ad infinitum.* The end result is that the whole conversation is nonsensical. Their nonverbal expressions are all too clear, however, as by tone of voice and facial expression they show their feelings of being hurt, attacked, and misunderstood by one another.

There are no overt rules in these families. The covert rule is that no one can make a mistake without appearing bad, sick, or stupid in the eyes of the others in the family, since any action by one member is always seen as a reflection on all the others. Because the family members believe that any clear expression of feeling may damage all members of the family, the family system works against pinning anybody down. The function of the identified patient in the family is to act out the aggressions of both parents, while at the same time providing them with support and reassurance. The Survival Myth implies that neither parent can survive without the other and without the children the parents cannot survive. The children indeed provide warmth and understanding for the parents, and an opportunity for the release of their feelings. Through the children the parents can cling to one another without really dealing with each other because the children are the communication media.

Origin histories of the parents in these families reveal detachment and lack of involvement with any parent. The childhood experience is one of distance. Therefore, these people cling to each other like lost children, unable to function as adults with each other or as parents. The marital Survival Myth is that neither of them can survive without the continual approval of the other. Each needs validation of his own worth by the approval of the other. Therefore, every source of conflict is skirted, masked, or denied, but not dealt with and, of course, not resolved. In this family system no one is in charge. Therefore, the symptom is severely self-destructive—threats of or attempts at suicide, narcotic addiction, etc.

At this stage of the study we realized that we had discovered something more meaningful and basic to the practice of family conjoint therapy than we had known before. The focus of further investigation was therefore shifted to exploration in depth of the meaning of psychological survival in the family. A definition of survival thus evolves into a much more complex and elaborate concept basic to the overall functioning of the family system.

THE MEANING AND IMPORTANCE OF FAMILY SURVIVAL

The significance of family survival patterns has been alluded to by Virginia Satir, but up to this time no systematic analysis of Survival Significance in families has been attempted. Satir writes: "Parents are automatically survival figures because the child literally depends on them for physical life; later need for love and approval from them becomes invested with like meaning. In addition, the way the parents structure their message to the child will determine his techniques for mastering his environment. It is not only his present, but his future survival which is in their hands. As a result he cannot afford to ignore messages from them, no matter how confused. . . If he is threatened by some event of survival significance, some happening which says to him 'you do not count; you are not lovable; you are nothing' the defense may prove unequal to the task of shielding him, and a symptom will take its place."*

Through our experience with family conjoint therapy at the Family Service Agency of Marin County, we have come to believe that all families to varying degrees are struggling with a sense of survival significance, deeply rooted and central to the functioning of the family. In this chapter we therefore hope to make clear both the meaning of *Psychological Survival Significance* within the family system and its implications for the assessment of families in terms of diagnosis and treatment requirements.

Survival significance exhibits itself on two levels: the physical, and the psychological or perceptional. A sharp distinction must be made between the two. Physical survival concerns itself with external threats to the existence of one or more members of the family, even to the entire family. Here a gun is pointed at someone's head, or

---

* V. Satir, *Conjoint Family Therapy*, Palo Alto, Science and Behavior Books, 1964.

some other threat just as real: abandonment, starvation, grave illness or physical violence. These threats of death may be so terrifying that one or all in the family may deny the very existence of the threat by distorting their view of the world about them. *Psychological survival implies a fear of loss to self quite as strong as the fear of actual death.* An example will illustrate: A husband stares at his wife who interprets the look to mean that her husband no longer loves her and is going to abandon her. In a panic she begins to behave as if a part of herself is being destroyed. The stimulation of the look may be neutral, but the perceiver invests even a neutral stimulus with feelings of being abandoned and unprotected. The interpretation and terror are based on a combination of two things: the wife's perceptions of what such looks appear to mean in her past interactional experience, and her current self-esteem which has to do with the feeling that she is not a whole person without her husband. Therefore, loss of him makes her incomplete as though a part of her dies with such a loss. It then becomes possible for the slightest communication involving any difference of feeling to carry with it the threat of loss of a part of self. Thus, death, a force external to the individual, removes that individual's choice. Divorce implies choice and therefore the threat of divorce by a husband is perceived by his wife as a rejection, an underlining of an impression that she is "no good," that no one can love her. This rejection of one spouse by the other repeats an earlier familial pattern in which failures of the parents were perceived by the child to be the result of his own unworthiness.

Psychological survival as a central system concept must answer two major questions: how does each family member perceive his own need in relation to the family unit, and how does each family member perceive the negative implications in the threat of loss of one or more family members or of his own individuality within the family system? The question basic to psychological survival then involves, "What will happen to me if. . . ?" To the husband and wife in the family, disturbance of the family balance may mean many losses in their relationship with each other—loss of the opportunity to take care of and be taken care of, loss of recognition and respect, of the stimulus of sharing and intimacy, of the assistance each brings to the rearing of the family, loss of companionship and of feeling protected, loss of financial security, and help in the support and rearing of the children. To the child, severe family imbalance may mean the loss of one or both parents. This in turn may be seen as the loss of a buffer against the world, the loss of a place to turn to when hurt, the dissolution of home as a haven of safety. It may mean that one parent may walk out or be hurt physically, leaving the remaining parent to "fall apart." When this happens the child feels, "I will have no one. I shall be alone. I shall lose everything."

Thus is the behavioral sequence in the dysfunctional family repeated over and over again. A neutral action stimulates a threat of loss. This perception feeds upon and stimulates the low self-estimate of each member. As a result it seems necessary to maintain the family balance at all costs to prevent any change which might further diminish each individual's sense of worth.

FAMILY SURVIVAL MYTH VERSUS REALITY SURVIVAL CONCEPTS

The survival myth has to do with the illusion shared by family members that they have to maintain their existing familiar ways of relating in order to survive psychologically. They regard their ways of relating as the only possible means for them to survive in the family unit. When pain results which precipitates them into therapy, there is a contradiction inherent in their request for help in that they wish the pain to be assuaged without changing the existing manner of relating necessary to their concept of survival. This is the basis for family resistance to treatment and is thus the therapist's dilemma. If the therapist accepts the myth as a reality, he cannot be effective as a treatment force since he operates in such a way as to reinforce the family's basic distortions.

In viewing the dysfunctional family, we see that the perceptions of each family member about his own survival and that of his family are neither clearly formulated nor openly labeled. Yet family members respond with a high degree of sensitivity to the implied threat that disturbance of the family balance may result in the individual's psychological death. That their fears are never clearly verbalized implies that perception about survival appears to result from acquired, conditioned, interactively reinforced experiences absorbed by the individual from infancy to adult years beginning at the preverbal level of experience. From this it may be derived that the individual's emotional maturation occurs on two interrelated levels: his perception of who gives what to him in response to what he does or doesn't do (self-esteem), and his perceptions of how others in the family respond to each other, what kind of interaction results, and how this interaction affects his own development (interactional-perceptual).

An example illustrates these two levels. In a therapy session the father is having difficulty getting his children to sit still and be quiet. He wants his wife's help, but doesn't ask for it because he is afraid she'll laugh at him. She possibly even thinks he is inadequate for not being able to manage alone. He sighs, appears to glare at his wife who in response interprets this look to mean that she had better not interfere. Offended, she withdraws into herself. The father in turn interprets her withdrawal as a lack of concern for him and reacts with anger toward her and the children. This reinforces the wife's distorted perception that nothing she does or can do pleases her husband and underlines the husband's belief that his wife is completely uninterested in how he feels. The children's perception is that the expression of their desire to behave as they wish results in friction between their parents, a friction that carries with it a threat of loss of parental understanding and approval, even the possible loss of the family home.

All of these interactions are primarily nonverbal and are based on assumptions equally nonverbal but accepted as facts. Through these interactions, assumptions about survival harden into fixed generalizations reinforced by repeated reactions whose meaning is never explained. By this process the understanding of each family member as to what will happen as a result of direct contact with other family members becomes rigid and certain without ever being discussed.

Because the Reality Survival Concept is so closely related to treatment and the transition from the Family Survival Myth to the Reality Survival Concept is so complex in operation and implementation, we will discuss it in detail in the next chapter.

Suffice it to say here, the *Reality Survival Concept* is premised on the hypothesis that all people who are committed to a dynamic family system are also oriented toward growth and creativity. The therapist's task is to stimulate the troubled family so that it can provide the nurturing which will allow its members to develop as individuals and at the same time enjoy family endeavors which result in positive joint outcome.

For each individual, the reality survival concept provides two aspects, one relating to physical care and well-being, the other to opportunities for creative growth. For adults creative growth must involve areas of shared intimacies and mutual goals. For children, growth involves help in learning how to make intelligent vocational, marital, and other primary choices. Growth in a child implies a preservation of parental balances, rather precarious at times, between providing him with chances to make selections appropriate to his age and assuming responsibility for making decisions too weighty for his immature judgement. *A family becomes sick when members perceive efforts toward growth as a threat towards survival of their family unit.* To illustrate, we can utilize the example of family interaction described earlier and point out that the therapist must puncture the Family Survival Myth by labeling the behavior observed in the family to elicit an explanation of real intent and feelings of husband and wife. Of course, the timing for such a puncture must be based on clinical judgement and is preceded by considerable cushioning by the therapist. The nature of this cushioning and of the puncture process have been discussed in earlier chapters of this book. When the puncture takes place, the open labeling of feelings perceived as threatening to survival can precipitate a crisis in the family. It is at this crucial point in the treatment when family secrets and deep feelings about one another are made public that the therapist must deal directly with the deep pain all family members are experiencing.

We think the Reality Survival Concept is based on the premise that each person in the marital relationship must operate as a whole person. By this we mean each may be dependent on the other in many ways but not for survival. Each is responsible for his own growth through open and direct expression of his desires and limitations. The marital partners must be able to accept such expression from each other as an indication of their differentness. This involves perceiving differentness at its best as potentially enhancing to the relationship, and at its worst as somewhat limiting; if perceived as an attack or intent to undermine, the relationship cannot grow. A "working" marital relationship in reality, then, is not a blending or meshing of two individuals into a whole person. It is the accomplishment of two individuals who remain intact in their individuality so that their individual growth evolves concurrently. Ideally, the growth of each is then enhanced by the growth of the other although it may be in a different direction or at different rates of progress. This is accomplished because of the process utilized by each to express himself and perceive the other's individuality without threat.

The task of the therapist is to enhance the individual's self-esteem. Then he is enabled to operate as though he counts by expressing himself clearly. In addition, family members must learn new ways of looking at and dealing with such open expression from each other.

The method most useful in accomplishing these two goals is then dependent on the degree of self-esteem in the individual and the degree of threat in the family interaction.

In summary then, Reality Survival Concept theory must concern itself with: diagnosis of the Survival Myth as it applied to a particular family; conditioning of the family with regard to its survival fears; puncture of the myth and persuasive relabeling of the positive intent in family members' responses previously perceived as threatening to the family solidarity; and finally, guidance of family members toward an understanding of how their Survival Myth began, developed, and eventually became an ineffectual defense mechanism for protection against pain.

Chapter 17

SHIFT TO SURVIVAL
CONNECTED TO GROWTH

The nature of the survival shift has to do with the movement of the individual away from an external support to an internal framework and process as the basis of his meaning for living. Whether or not he lives or dies emotionally is no longer dependent on whether he has a certain relationship, family structure, home, job, business, erection, looks, or performance ability. It depends on his ability to express his uniqueness in ways that are fitting to him and on his ability to grow emotionally. Therefore, as long as he feels himself moving and developing, he will function relatively symptom-free. All of the external supports mentioned above do not become unimportant—they simply assume a different place in his life. He will no longer try to be a square peg in a round hole. His relationships and work will have to fit him in such a way that they will not impede his growth because with the survival shift he has made, death is now associated with impeded growth rather than with aloneness or the failure of any experiment or experience.

The individual more and more experiences himself as a dynamic organism, always in flow. He is able to stay with sadness when he experiences it because he knows that if he simply relaxes and goes with whatever he is feeling, his natural flow will carry him back up again to moments of serenity and joy. He does not have to hang onto his joyous moods for fear of losing them; he can relax and savor the joy without worrying about when it will go because he knows his process will eventually bring him to this place again.

None of this implies that the individual becomes a loner—quite the contrary. For the first time in his life, he is able to really see other people as entities separate from himself rather than extensions of himself or objects to be controlled for his own protection or sustenance. This means he is now able to form relationships at a depth which was not possible before. Love and respect are based on a perception of the other person's essence and uniqueness rather than his ability to serve or please.

When the individual shifts his survival from his marital and family structure to himself, he takes the risk that the marriage will no longer fit him. The original marital connection was based on defending himself against being alone and having to face unresolved pain and conflict, and that defense is no longer necessary. Therefore, the marriage must have a different reason for being in order to survive. Much of the time individuals do not even know what they want in a marriage once they are devoid of the survival need, let alone whether or not they have what they want in this marriage. Thus, when the individual begins to give up his marriage as a survival framework, there are certain danger signals and pitfalls the therapist needs to be aware of both in the individual's adjustment and the marital relationship.

First of all, an individual may be potentially suicidal. He will frequently have suicidal thoughts and fantasies, even though there may be no real danger of suicide. These are related not so much to any desire on his part to die, but to the fact that a real death is going on. The old structure around which he has built his identity is dying. Since he has no sense of himself separate from that structure, he experiences himself as dying. For example, a man has built his identity around a judgmental structure of right and wrong, good and bad. He may be in a miserable state most of the time because of this structure, but it is familiar and at least he always knows where he stands. If he gives up that structure and his wife as his judge who keeps him in line, he has nothing to take its place immediately. He is in a no-man's-land of confusion until he begins to develop a structure based on what is fitting to him. That no-man's-land can be experienced by him as death. We have found that when we label the process for individuals and let them know that while it is a terrifying experience, the feelings are appropriate to the magnitude of their changes, they can usually ride it through. If people know where they are in process, they can tolerate almost anything. We let them know there is a real death going on, that they need to grieve for their loss even though it is a desired loss. The old structure is like an old friend who served them while they needed it, but is no longer useful and has become destructive.

In another instance, the individual may become so inundated by early pain and internal chaos when he lets go of his protective structure that he is temporarily in danger of making a suicide gesture. We have found the most reliable resource for perceiving this possibility is the therapist's subjective experience. If the therapist begins to experience death fantasies or intense anxieties or fears related to the client, it is important that he share this with the client and work out a protection plan to carry the individual through the initial stages of his shift. Usually this is only a matter of a few weeks until the individual is able to begin to mobilize and begin to rebuild a new structure. During that interim period, additional sessions may be necessary to give the client an opportunity to vent explosive rage or infantile terror. The therapist also provides much structuring to enable the client to understand where the overwhelming feeling is coming from, why he needs to experience it, that it will pass, and what it means in terms of his growth process.

For example, a woman who married at eighteen to escape a sadistic father, has maintained a passive role in a marriage with a man who is kind to her, but very withdrawn. She has related to this husband as father, judge, and god until she grew to a point where this framework no longer fit her. However, as she let go, she got in touch with her rage both at this man who she feels does not give her his feelings and at her father, whom she experienced as cruel and intrusive. She experiences the rage as suicidal urges until the therapist gets her into gestalt sessions in which she talks to both her husband and her father (via the empty chair), and the anger surges to the surface. The therapist may enable her to further ventilate with physical activity such as hitting, tearing up cloth, biting or whatever form her rage takes. He then prepares her for the possibility that, as she gets on the other side of the rage, she may get in touch with great emptiness or terror and talks to her about possible safety valves for handling this.

In other words, the client is totally aware of the therapist's fears and perceptions in relation to him through this process because the therapist is clear with the client that a major shift is taking place and extreme reactions are normal. Therefore, they must plan together accordingly. Very often, if the client knows the possibilities he can expect and what they mean, he is less panicked and more able to be in charge of himself when they happen.

Another danger in this process is that of a temporary psychotic episode, usually in the form of dissociation, diffusion, chaotic behavior, flights into paranoia, or withdrawal. Again, such an episode is not abnormal behavior in relation to this process. It is simply a validation of the massive strain on the organism that this kind of shift entails. For this reason, we would not attempt to facilitate such a shift with anyone with severe physical illness that was already putting a maximum strain on the body. People often have somatic symptoms during this process—temporary rise in blood pressure, pain, dizziness, nausea, cold, and extreme fatigue. Again, we see these all as indications that the energy required to make a survival shift is enormous. The client needs to understand this because he is usually only aware of his symptoms and not of the energy he is expending.

In terms of the psychotic episodes, if the individual understands that they are psychotic only by symptom description, and appropriate in relation to his process, he can allow himself to experience them without becoming fixated at that level. If he can allow himself to experience them, he can begin to understand their meaning in terms of his origin family, his historical experiences, and his current growth process. The feelings he experiences during these episodes may be related to his origin family in that he is now allowing himself to experience feelings that he never owned as a child, but has buried all this time. Or, the feelings may not be his, but may be reflections of internal processes he perceived in his parents and accepted as his own. Therefore, part of the reason for his need to go through this experience now is to differentiate what belongs to him and what belongs to them. We have worked with individuals who were not psychotic themselves, but had psychotic parents. If they had difficulty differentiating their parents' craziness from their own feelings as children, they may be still carrying their parents' psychotic processes as their own. If such is the case, they often can't know this until they act them out and find out they really don't fit and they can then discard them.

Because of the magnitude of the survival shift and the pitfalls we have discussed above, we think there are certain vital conditions that must be recognized by both the therapist and the client in order to successfully accomplish such a shift:

Support. During this time, the individual's survival shifts to the therapist, but not in the sense of the therapist's taking care of him as though he were a child. Rather, it has to do with his being able to rely on the therapist to present a consistently solid front to which he (the client) can relate. The therapist gives him continuous feedback about what his feelings and experiences mean in terms of his on-going growth process so that he has a kind of touchstone. The therapist is not afraid of the intensity of his feelings but keeps relating them back into the client's growth flow. Thus, the client looks to the therapist for the structure he needs until he can rebuild his own. The therapist is careful not to intrude or to take over from the client even in his most vulnerable moments, but he is very solidly there, giving the client both his own feelings and his assessment of the client's process.

The therapist is readily available during this time, or makes sure someone else is who knows the process, so that the client is never very far out of reach of his touchstone.

Nurturance. The therapist makes sure with the client that he has resources available to him during this time whom he experiences as nourishing. These need to be people who will just be with him without giving him advice or taking him away from his process. If he doesn't have anyone or enough resources of this kind, the therapist may offer additional therapy during this period in the form of a group or increased numbers of therapy sessions. We had one client see three different therapists, each once a week for a three week period, until he got through this crisis. He had never had a male connection as a child and was breaking through a female-connected survival framework. So, we gave him three male therapists in addition to a male-female co-therapy team who were the basic therapy unit.

In addition, we explore with the client what kind of experiences are nurturing to him—reading, bubble baths, hiking, whatever—and encourage him to do whatever feeds him without taking from him. We indicate that such experiences are as vital as actual food during this process. Also, we suggest that he put no extra strain on himself, like going on a diet, changing jobs or any other external stress he can avoid.

Commitment to change. In order to attempt a shift of this kind, the individual must really be committed to growth for himself as the only way he can go. Most of the time, people will not even attempt a survival shift until they have arrived at a place where they know they cannot continue to survive as they have been operating. It is as though the individual knows he can't continue to live the way he has been; he doesn't believe he can survive any other way, but he has no choice but to try on faith that maybe he can make it by learning how to be himself, to do what fits him, and trust himself totally.

The individual must also be willing to live with a lack of structure. We think this is even more difficult than the original crisis precipitated by the shift. It isn't so dramatic, but the lack of structure is painful to experience, especially since the individual may experience this lack for several months until he begins to get a beginning sense of an internal structure based on his real needs and limitations. The individual really feels he has nothing solid to hold onto. He is trusting his insides to guide him when he has absolutely no previous experience that they will guide him in a positive way. He must be prepared to let himself be awkward, adolescent, unsure, and confused because he is in brand new territory and much of his past experience will not be of help since it was based on something other than what fits him. He can use the therapist to keep himself on course and for feedback to help him integrate his experience, but no one can alter the fact that the trip is a painstaking, cautious one which cannot be rushed or made easier.

Chapter 18

POSITIVE DOUBLE-BIND
MAJOR INTERVENTION FOR CHANGE

We think the positive double-bind is the major tool for producing change. It involves a subtle process which we will make a beginning attempt to delineate here, but we think that much additional research and exploration needs to be done to fully understand the theory and techniques involved in this process.

The use of the positive double-bind may involve a manipulation and a sales pitch on the part of the therapist. He takes the energy generated from the family's resistance and translates it back to the family in another framework which gives the family no alternative but to respond positively if they want to stay in line with their basic structure. For example, an intellectual family whose operating structure is based on a rigid sense of right and wrong, duty and responsibility, begins to offer all kinds of excuses for discontinuing treatment when the therapist gets close to opening up feelings in family members. Mother suddenly remembers that she has a PTA meeting that evening, and needs to end the session early. Daughter has a class which she doesn't want to miss because there is a special exam. Father has to get back to the office and son who is the identified patient says they're not getting much out of the therapy anyway, so why return?

The therapist may then respond something like this: "Well, I'm sure all these reasons you offer for not continuing are valid, and perhaps you do feel you aren't getting what you came for. However, if we look at the other side, every time we get close to feelings, which we did a moment ago with father and son, an avoidance pattern immediately begins to emerge. Now, since you are a logical, reasonable group committed to learning and growing (the family's already-presented image of how they see themselves), then you must want to take this opportunity to explore whether this avoidance means something more than you are consciously aware of instead of leaving before you exhaust all the possibilities for learning. Wouldn't you agree?" The last comment, "Wouldn't you agree" is very important because it requires the family to acknowledge the therapist's recapitulation of their basic structural stance and accept that what he is asking them to do fits with that stance. The family is thus in a bind, because if they do not go in the direction of further exploration, they have to consider that their previously accepted picture of themselves may be full of holes. The presence of doubt about the validity of their structure is the first step toward opening the system for a rigidly structured family.

We believe there are several factors necessary for the positive double-bind to operate effectively. First of all, the family members must have trust that the therapist is a potential or an already-accepted survival person. In other words, they experience him as someone solid who will be there for them in certain specific ways if they begin to question and perhaps relinquish their rigid survival structure. He will not be intimidated, manipulated, or frightened off by them. He can be trusted to see the positive intent in their attempts to express themselves and will hold them to the growth framework. He will not depreciate or intrude on them by usurping their individual and family decision-making processes even in their most confused or uncertain states. The family sees the therapist as a kind of pseudo-parent who will block their manipulations and support even their faintest attempt toward growth. The therapist is thus a polarization of the schizophrenic double-bind parent who makes it impossible for his family to operate in any but a manipulative way.

A second factor is the therapist's ability to translate what the family offers him in such a way that suddenly they have alternative ways to go without suffering a loss. In the example we discussed earlier in Mrs. Satir's interview, the blind man could choose to add skills to his repertoire without feeling less of a man, via her translation of his resistance to change into a growth framework. In the intellectual family described above, the therapist offered to them that while all they said might be true, there could be other facets to their complex personalities and interaction that they could learn about. Thus, they don't have to give up their previously accepted ideas—they can just add to them. Suddenly, then, growth does not necessarily mean a loss. The therapist, by his translation, makes it possible for the family to see other ways of looking, behaving, and responding as added skills and knowledge rather than an invalidation of their former values. We feel the key to the effective use of the positive double-bind is the therapist's ability to offer alternatives outside of the frameworks of right or wrong, good or bad. Thus, his translations open up the system without directly attacking it. He uses the structure of the current system to make a bridge into a new open system. Again, in the example of the intellectual family, the therapist used their commitment to logic and fairness to maneuver them into a position in which the only logical thing to do in order to be fair was to continue to explore. Wouldn't you agree? (Ha!)

The third factor necessary in the effective use of the positive double-bind is that the family is placed in a position in which their choices become explicit. Most dysfunctional families see themselves as victims buffeted about by the vagaries of chance and the whims of others on whom they are dependent. They pretend they are not making choices by the use of denial, rationalization, or avoidance. With the positive double-bind technique, they are confronted clearly with choices and equally clearly with whatever choice they have made in response to the bind. There is no way to avoid acknowledging that a choice has been made. All the reasons for not making choices are invalidated by the therapist because he removes choice from the area of right or wrong, good or bad, pleasing or not pleasing an authority figure, and he translates the choices into whatever the client or family sees as fitting or enjoyable. When the choice has no strings on it or holds no implication as to the worth of the individual making the choice, it seems absurd not to acknowledge one's choices. However, the very process of owning where one is without judgement, analysis, or self-depreciation will automatically catapult the individual into a growth direction. Thus, in a way, the therapist seduces the client into growth by not only removing all of his previous defenses against growth, but also by presenting his opportunity for choice to him in such a way that it seems absurd not to choose and therefore grow!

The fourth important factor is that the client is forced into an assertive response and therefore has to give up the role of victim. One of the positive double-bind techniques Fritz Perls used to use was to fall asleep on a repressive patient. The individual then had to either wake Fritz up, which required considerable assertion, or he had to face the fact that he was deliberately choosing to allow himself to be invalidated in that way. He could not deny the fact that he did have the choice to awaken Fritz. Again, one of the principles of growth is that assertion, even if bizarre in manner, will promote growth within the individual or family. In response to a positive double-bind, the individual or family is forced to assert anger, desire, need, rebellion, or helplessness. There is no escape.

As you can see, the response of the individual or family to the consistent use of the positive double-bind process requires that old survival structures be shifted or at least challenged. Therefore, the therapist must be prepared for crises generated when old survival frameworks are discarded and families or individuals go into their unstructured, desert phases prior to the establishment of new open systems based on what fits the individual and family rhythms and identities. Thus, the therapist and the client need to be able to provide the conditions which we discuss in detail in the preceding chapters on integration and in Chapter Seventeen on the Survival Shift.

The end result of the therapist's use of the positive double-bind process is that family members will begin to incorporate this process internally and set up situations themselves in which the only direction they can go is to grow. For example, an individual may say, "I'm trying to hang onto my marriage, but since I've returned home following our separation, I've had consistent vague physical complaints for which my doctor can find no cause." The individual may not be aware he is putting himself in a bind until the therapist makes this fact explicit. He may ask him to have a dialogue between his head (what he thinks he wants) and his body (what is it telling him?) as a way of learning how to take responsibility for the bind in which he has placed himself so that he can use it as a conscious growth mechanism. The therapist then teaches him not to make judgements or to try to analyze his problem or force himself into action. He encourages him to simply own his bind as a first step in beginning to understand why he has to force himself into growth rather than make clear assertive steps in the growth direction. The focus on his own internal bind is the beginning basis of integration because the awareness of that bind enables him to differentiate between the parts of himself that want to grow and the parts that are fearful of or antagonistic to growth. The awareness of those different parts lays the base for eventual resolution and formation of a clear identity.

Chapter 19

PSYCHOSIS AS A STATEMENT OF POTENTIAL GROWTH CHANGE

If we consider the human being as a balanced organism, then we must accept that psychosis has no one major cause. It can be the organism's homeostatic adjustment to external stress, historical experiential attrition, nutritional deficiency, deprivation, trauma or shock; and in some circles, may even be considered as demon-possession. In our experience, we have seen psychosis as part of the evolutionary flow in an individual's process of growth. We believe that, too often, professionals in the psychiatric field have reinforced psychotic processes in people by treating the psychosis as an isolated fixed state rather than a process the individual is going through related to where he has been and where he is going in his growth. When an individual is hospitalized, stripped of his identity, and numbed with shock treatment or drugs, it is difficult, if not impossible, to accurately assess what the psychotic behavior really means in terms of the individual's internal process or even if the behavior really expresses psychosis.

In some families, psychotic behavior is the best way to survive in the family unit with the least amount of damage to one's self-esteem. If one is deemed crazy, he doesn't have to take responsibility for coping with impossible demands or double-binds; neither is he subject to the guilt trips of others in the family because they feel so guilty about his illness that they leave him alone. We have seen many supposedly psychotic people who were really expert manipulators using psychosis as an effective defense or form of attack against other family members. Granted it is a self-destructive defense, yet it is often not a state imposed upon a helpless victim, but a matter of the victim's choice. We treated a couple at the Institute who came because of the wife's periodic violent episodes in which she hallucinated, threatened suicide, and attacked her husband physically until she had to be restrained via hospitalization and drugs. The husband would not come for therapy, so we saw the wife.

After two months, she was overdue on paying her bill and began to call the therapist in the middle of the night in hysterics. The therapist offered that if she was that out of control, she would have to go to the hospital since he could not offer twenty-four hour assistance. Obviously, if she could not accept the limits of outpatient treatment, then it was not what she needed, and he would be glad to arrange a referral to the local hospital out-patient service where inpatient care was also readily available when she needed it. She slammed down the phone in fury, but called two days later requesting an appointment. The therapist agreed, but indicated he would see her only if she paid for the appointment at the time she came and arranged some definite plan for paying off what she already owed. Again, she hung up the phone in fury. A week later she called again saying she did want to come in, but she couldn't get the money from her husband and that he used money to manipulate and control her. The therapist indicated he could understand how difficult that must be for her, but that it would not be helpful to her if he (the therapist) allowed either her husband or her to control *him* with money. She then said she would get the money and made an appointment. When she came, she proudly handed the therapist the money even before she started the session and indicated she would pay each time plus ten dollars extra until the old therapy bill was paid off. She stated that she had taken a stand with her husband about the money when she realized that she had allowed herself to go crazy when her resentment of his manipulation of her built to the point where she could not handle it. When she confronted him with this, he admitted great resentment about her hospitalizations, saying he felt she was getting revenge on him in a way he could not fight. He agreed to come into therapy with her when he realized how they were manipulating and destroying each other because of unexpressed feelings and assertions. They were seen for a year in marital therapy and there were no subsequent hospitalizations.

Another family came for treatment at the Institute because the father had been hospitalized twice during the preceding year for severe depression accompanied by delusions, hallucinations, and disassociative behavior. At the time of their first contact with the Institute, the whole family was seen because they were all confused and shattered by this experience, not understanding it or able to cope with it. The father was depressed and discouraged, although not actively psychotic at the time.

The family was seen by a therapist who was in training in our advanced course in family therapy at the Institute because in that setting they would have the support and consultation of eight other therapists who would be observing them from behind a one-way vision mirror.

The family interaction revealed that the mother was in control and that the father related to her as mother and judge, torn between his resentment of her control and his fear of being alone. The children were very subdued, overly affectionate in a cloying way with both parents, and unable to assert even the most minor difference of opinion or rebellious behavior. The wife was torn between sympathy and concern for her husband and her fear and resentment at being unable to depend on him. At the same time, she obviously needed to be in a control position because that is where she felt most comfortable. She grew up in a family in which she got her goodies by being the one who was reliable in an emergency and took over for everyone else. Her father was an alcoholic and her mother worked, so she took over the house and the younger children. She is not happy with her role in this respect but it is all she knows and at least she knows she can survive that way. If she lets go of her controls, how does she know she can relate in any other way, let alone survive?

The husband's father deserted his family when he was three months old and his mother had a nervous breakdown at the time. Later, she mobilized herself, went to work, and pulled the family together. However, he remembers her as stable in terms of providing the physical necessities, but with very little emotional warmth and contact.

In the treatment process, the therapist is very gentle in enabling the family to see and understand their fears and the price they are paying for continuing their survival framework. They are seen by a male-female co-therapy team to give them maximum support and the husband also sees the male therapist individually for assistance with his internal structuring of himself in terms of his male identity.

In about the tenth session, the husband begins to actively confront his wife for the first time with some of his angry feelings and in the process of their interaction, he suddenly shifts into a psychotic state. He begins to make a high whistling sound like a banshee, to flex his arms and legs as though he is going to leap, and to stare wildly at everyone in the room. The male therapist quickly moves in close to him, touching him and explaining where he is in process. He also motions the male therapists who are observing to come into the room, explaining to the man that he wants them to give the man room to express himself without worrying that he will hurt himself or someone else. They will provide external controls. The therapist keeps talking to the client asking him to breathe deeply and feel himself physically, so that he can stay in touch with his physical boundaries. Then he clarifies that in beginning to express his anger, the client suddenly broke his defense structure and got flooded with impulses which he has been sitting on for years. He urges the client to get the feeling under control by measuring his breathing, holding on physically to the other males in the room, and by continuing to make whatever sounds he wished. After a half hour of this, the client began to refocus his eyes and visually come back into a reality framework. At this point, the therapist again explained what was happening and suggested he go into the hospital voluntarily for two to three days to have some external supports until he began to feel more in control of his impulses. He labeled the process as very positive, but proceeding faster than the client's internal structure was able to handle. The client did go to the hospital for three days, was seen by the therapist while he was there and returned to out-patient treatment when he came out. He hospitalized himself two other times during the course of treatment for the same purpose until he began to develop a strong enough sense of his own identity that he could express his more powerful feelings without terrifying himself.

In another situation, a member of a therapy group was expressing deep pain and rage with tears and physical pounding about her father whom she experienced as distant from her. During her expression, the intensity of her feeling triggered a reaction in another group member who had deep repressed rage toward her father, previously not even on a pre-conscious level. This individual reacted by looking as though she was in a state of shock, holding her breath and turning blue. The therapist had her lie down and asked her to begin to breathe deeply and slowly, with other group members slowly massaging her arms and legs. She would break the even breathing with hyperventilation and had to be reminded over and over to breathe rhythmically. As she did so, she experienced herself as out of her body and registered great terror. The therapist asked her to stay in touch with the touch and warmth of the hands on her and to use her own hands to feel the outlines of her body; in addition, he asked her to experience her breath going to different parts of her body, to feel the hardness of the floor, the temperature of the room, and smell the scents around her. In about a half hour, she began to sob. When the therapist asked her what she was experiencing, she began to choke out that the other group member's experience had suddenly triggered a memory of hers about her and her father when she was six years old which she had completely repressed up to this point. She had always retained an image of her father as kind and gentle and of their relationship as close and warm. With that memory came a rush of anger and pain that was unbearable to her, as she realized the extent to which she had blocked other aspects of her relationship with her father.

The therapist urged her to continue breathing, not to be afraid if she felt light-headed, disassociated, or out of control; just to allow herself to stay with her feelings without trying to analyze them or shut them off. Their presence was only an indication of her awakening aliveness and we would gradually go into those feelings slowly with exploration and understanding at a later time. For now, just let herself appreciate the breakthrough. With this, she began to giggle uproariously. The therapist encouraged her to laugh, and began to laugh with her as did the rest of the group. He offered to her that she had a right to feel relieved—a great weight had been lifted. She was then ready to sit up and begin to deal with the therapist about how to take care of herself until he and the group could help her to further explore and integrate the experience she had had in this session.

PART IV

MALE-FEMALE CO-THERAPY

Chapter 20

INGREDIENTS OF MALE-FEMALE CONNECTION AND THEIR EFFECT IN TREATMENT

We have worked together as a co-therapy team since 1965—in therapy with couples, individuals, and groups; in teaching family therapy; and in the administration of the Institute. With the possible exception of Bob and Mary Goulding and Al and Eva Leveton, we don't know of another male-female combination whose experience in team work with each other is as extensive as ours. In addition, we are unique in relation to the other two couples in that we are not married to each other. We feel we have learned much by our experience that we would like to share since we think co-therapy is an extremely effective and powerful treatment tool.

In our experience, co-therapy has effect on the client or clients in geometric ratio far beyond the simple fact that there is one more therapist present in the treatment session. This treatment modality has impact on at least three levels.

PARENTAL TRANSFERENCE

Sometimes, when we see a family for the first time, we can get immediate diagnostic information based on the way they respond to each of us when we walk into the room. In one family, for example, the father will direct all his responses to Marty (Dr. K) and almost totally ignore Shirley (Mrs. L). In addition, he becomes defensive or can't hear when Shirley makes a comment, but can respond when Marty says exactly the same thing. We can then explore, via his reaction to Shirley, what gets in his way to relate to women in general or Shirley in particular. Since he hardly knows her, it is likely that he is responding to some deep distrust of females. This can be explored via his relationship with his wife and with his mother in his origin family.

With individual clients who are beginning to get in touch with early deprivation and pain, we have frequently used the technique of sitting—one of us on either side—and holding the individual. We ask him to close his eyes, experience both of us near him and let himself sink into his internal experience of what that is like. Usually, the client experiences a sense of safety and relief, which enables him to let go more deeply into feelings which are frightening and confusing to him.

The team can produce a growth framework similar to the natural growth system. Marty can affirm and validate the assertion of males in the family as part of their maleness; Shirley can validate the maleness of their assertions from a female point of view as well as model ways of responding to male assertion that are supportive and accepting rather than defensive or depreciative. Thus, family members get both a male and female reaction to every assertion which provides an immediate base for integration.

With one-parent families, the team can be very effective because it prevents the single parent from incorporating a therapist of the opposite sex as the pseudo-parent in the family. At the same time, it gives children in the family both male and female models which they would not have if there was only one therapist who was the same sex as the single parent. Because of this, it is possible for both therapists to give much more to the family without the risk of being seductive. It also makes it possible for the single parent to get a great deal of nurturing from both a male and a female without triggering his or her sexual fantasies to the point of blocking receiving such nurturance. In our experience, the most salient problem in single parent families is the parent's internal experience of being drained and empty. There-fore, the co-therapy approach is much faster because of the double nurturing and the freer framework in which the client can receive it.

MALE-FEMALE INTERACTIONAL MODELS

The co-therapy team models two separate whole people who are in charge of self and yet working together. Each can be strong and confronting and each can be soft, tender, and supportive. At times, one can confront while the other moves into support and structure. For example, Marty may comment to a couple that when they argue they sound like two little kids saying, "Nyah, nyah!" Shirley may then move in to soften that with, "I know it must be frustrating to you to have your attempts to contact each other degenerate into name-calling," and at the same time, provide structure with, "It is easy to fall back into old patterns of communicating, even though they don't work. We tend to rely on what is familiar. However, it is necessary for you to learn what doesn't work about your old ways, so you can begin to develop new processes." Marty will then move in to lay the beginning base for new learning by getting a commitment from them: "Is this something you want to change?" If they agree, then we have a contract with them for experimental exploration.

If the team members are comfortable with each other, they may disagree openly in front of the clients or freely question what the other one is doing or where he is going in his treatment direction. They may then ask the family to comment on what they observed about the therapist's interaction and integrate their response back into the family interaction. For example, Marty may be working with a family around a specific incident that happened the evening before, getting everyone's picture of the event for the purpose of clarifying the negative processes. Shirley intervenes with, "I find myself tuning out while you're doing this—I feel something else is going on in the family right now." Marty asks her to clarify what she is experiencing. Shirley: "I feel a heaviness in the family as though people are holding back a lot of feeling." Marty: "I feel that also, but I think we might get at the feeling easier if we nail down an actual situation. In this family, it's easy for people to wrap everything up fast and lose track of what they experienced on a feeling level." Shirley: "O.K. Let's try it and see what happens; if it doesn't work, I have another avenue I'd like to explore."

The children in the family began to giggle during this exchange between us, so we asked them how they experienced our interaction. One girl said she didn't like it that Shirley "gave in," and this led to an exploration with family members about how each of them experienced giving way to someone else's idea. Family members indicate they would feel a loss if they gave in and would have to pursue the issue more. With exploration, it became evident that such decisions were not based on whether the individual really felt so strongly about something that he could not back down. They were based on a feeling that he could not back down, no matter what, or he would appear wrong or stupid. We then related this process to the family interaction which usually dissolved into a power struggle even over the most unimportant issues.

We then discussed with the family some of our views about disagreement between us. Each of us indicated that if the other felt very strongly about something, we would make room to explore the idea even though we might not understand or agree with it. This was because we respected the other's ability and because we felt we had nothing to lose by experimenting with each other's ideas—there would always be room to try our own ways. Neither of us felt the other had the ultimate word—we just sometimes had different ideas and always felt we could learn from each other. Needless to say, if such a statement were not the truth, we would get nowhere with a family.

We also let a family know, by our words and actions, that there are times when one of us teaches the other something, when one of us takes care of the other, or when one of us takes criticism from the other. Occasionally, in a session, one of us notices the other looking tired or preoccupied and will comment on that observation. The other may say he or she is a little tired, concerned about something at home, or maybe just feeling hungry. The concern and comments are genuine, and by being open about what we are observing we are modeling that it is all right for us to comment on each other, for us to comment on the family, and for family members to comment on us and each other. There are times when one of us will do most of the work in the session because the other is tired and that may be made explicit to the family, giving them room to comment on how they feel about that. We may continue that plan of operation, even if they object, modeling that we have to be in charge of our limitations though others don't like it; but, we hear their responses, modeling that we can hear their feelings without feeling depreciated or guilty.

Occasionally, one of us gets caught in the family system, and the other will comment, "You're convincing the family—they've sucked you in!" Usually, each of us immediately recognizes and accepts this as gift from the other. If we don't immediately catch on, each of us will back down, trusting the other's judgement about our system error.

Each of us models strength and tenderness, giving and receiving, confronting and being confronted, disagreement, and compromise.

None of these processes is male or female—we are each clear about who we are in these areas without using the other to make up for a lack on the part of one of us. The co-therapy relationship, to be effective, must provide the treatment situation with two distinct individuals who have developed processes for mutual sharing, enhancement and added dimensions; not two bodies with one ego.

THE EFFECT OF TWO THERAPISTS

With two therapists in operation, it is almost impossible for a family to manipulate the therapy situation for any appreciable length of time, if at all. Usually, when one is working, the other is observing and can be particularly attuned to the nonverbal behavior in the family. Or, the other can take space to tune into his subjective experience of being with the family and pick up on fantasy or imagery clues. For example, Marty may be working with a dyadic interaction in the family, and Shirley is sitting back, observing him and the family and letting herself experience the meta-message. She may then offer that she experiences deep sadness and wonders if that is coming from someone in the family. At that point, the mother may begin to cry, and the treatment process then shifts from the interaction to the mother's pain which is surfacing and which she has been experiencing all week.

It is possible, with two therapists, to be more confronting with a family because you know your co-therapist will move into support so the family won't feel attacked and can more readily look at what you are offering. For example, one therapist may comment, "I feel very defeated when I work with you—as though I'm plowing through molasses. No matter what I offer you, it doesn't seem to be good enough. I want you to know you can very easily defeat me." The other may then step in with, "Do you understand what Shirley is saying? There is some kind of process going on in the family that defeats change even though you say you want to change. Do you experience that?"

Having two therapists in the session makes it possible for each to validate the other's perceptions. For example, one therapist may say, "You're talking very rationally and reasonably, but I feel a lot of anger inside." The family may deny that anyone is angry; however, if the other therapist has that identical perception, it is difficult for the family to sustain that denial.

Chapter 21

DEVELOPMENT AND MAINTENANCE
OF CO-THERAPY RELATIONSHIP

There are many advantages to the co-therapy relationship for the therapist. It is an extremely effective learning framework. We encourage people in our training courses to try to work out arrangements to do co-therapy with each other so that they can observe other people's styles and add to their own repertory of techniques. In addition, it offers the pleasure of sharing. Doing therapy can be a very lonely business as anyone who has been in private practice alone can verify. The opportunity to work with someone else with whom you can share triumphs and rehash the interview later is very nourishing to the therapist. Also, the opportunity to develop the co-therapy relationship into a powerful treatment mode is exciting and stimulating. However, anyone contemplating the development of such a team approach needs to be aware that the relationship requires almost as much care, time, and feeding as an actual marriage. It is, in reality, a professional marriage with all the relationship depths and nuances that term implies.

We began the development of our relationship in earnest in 1966 when we taught our first course in family therapy. Up until that time, we had worked together more in a consulting capacity, doing some therapy together, some teaching and writing. We taught the class through the Institute on the Family, a branch of the Family Service Agency in San Rafael and had two members of the agency staff—Jay Shinohara and Audrey Dreyfus—act as consultants to observe us work in terms of our teaching, our therapy with families who were in treatment as part of the course, and our relationship with each other. The class ran for four hours once a week for six weeks and we scheduled two hours after each class with Audrey and Jay to get their feedback and try to work out our problems. All went swimmingly until the third session, when we both began to feel somewhat constrained in the teaching period and noticed that we weren't flowing well together. After the class left, the real work began. We (Marty and Shirley) sat facing each other with Audrey and Jay observing. We began to try to communicate what we were experiencing in the class. Shirley commented that she felt Marty was withdrawing from her and that he cut her off several times when she was expostulating to the class. Marty indicated that he experienced Shirley as not making room for him, but operating as though she were alone in the room. At that point, Audrey and Jay suggested that we tell each other how we felt about those perceptions rather than just describing our behavior. That was all we needed to launch us into a fair-sized brawl. We raged at each other for some little time until we cleared the air. We still laugh about the instance, at one point, where Jay supported something Marty said and Audrey (who is all of five feet tall) stood up, stamped her foot, and said, "You damned men!" That stopped the fight for about thirty seconds and we were off again. Later, Audrey and Jay helped us clarify the process between us which was that each of us was holding back, trying to treat the other with kid gloves, rather than coming out with what we wanted to do and letting the other respond. As a result of the holding back, we were building up frustration and resentment because neither of us is the passive type.

We later shared that whole process with the class who had perceived something was going on, but had also held back and not confronted us. We were then able to integrate that process of our withholding and that of the students into the learning experience of the group. We continued to utilize Audrey and Jay's assistance during the rest of that course and, in addition, spent an average of two hours a week on our own dealing with the treatment direction, our goals in the course, our feelings toward each other, and simply brainstorming about treatment dynamics and theory. The amazing thing is that none of this investment of time and energy was too much—it was too little, if anything, and vitally important to the success of the teaching and of the therapy we were doing. We learned very quickly that if a co-therapy team isn't working, it can be as destructive to a family or training group as an actual destructive parental relationship in a family. All of the groups were amazingly sensitive to our process, and as they got to know us, they would frequently pinpoint trouble between us before we were consciously aware of it. Again, we encouraged this both in our classes and therapy situations as a means of keeping our own systems open as well as a useful learning tool for us and the trainees and clients.

In our beginning experience in doing co-therapy with each other, we made it a point to sit where we could readily observe each other. In that way, we could communicate much more clearly and be aware of nuances in the other's expression or behavior. We also spent some time, usually fifteen minutes or so, both before and after therapy sessions to make sure we were in harmony with each other. Over the years of working together, it is no longer necessary to expend that kind of time in order to work together, and we are more apt to just take time as something emerges that we have to deal with rather than scheduling regular conference times. However, we would strongly recommend that beginning co-therapy teams schedule regular times with each other to nourish the relationship and work out the bugs in their relationship.

We find at this point that we no longer even need to sit facing each other. We have developed our communication processes to the point now that we can communicate fairly clearly with our backs turned to each other. Just as in a marriage, a co-therapy relationship, over time, will move into deeper levels of communication—imagery, fantasy, intuitional communication. By that we mean that we are usually aware of each other's feelings even when they aren't evident in words or body behavior. However, we still check out those perceptions because we believe you can never be sure of what another person is feeling until he or she validates it, no matter how deeply you are in tune with each other.

Based on our experience with each other as well as the development and teaching of other co-therapy teams, we think the first level that has to be worked out is the intimacy aspect of the relationship. If either has sexual feelings toward the other, those feelings need to be brought out into the open and shared. We have no rules about whether or not co-therapy teams should get involved sexually with each other, only the knowledge that it would be difficult, if not impossible, to continue the co-therapy relationship if the affair cools or does not work out. That may be possible, but it would take a level of maturity that we haven't observed yet. Therefore, teams probably need to make a decision early about which comes first—the personal or professional aspects of their coupling—and set their boundaries accordingly.

We think it is important that each experience the other as an equal. Neither feels he is one up or that he has to carry or protect the other. Each must be able to feel that he can depend on the other to be there if he gets lost, confused or makes a mistake; that he can depend on the other to be in charge of himself. That doesn't mean that he expects the other to take over when he fails; it just means that he knows the other can readily handle the situation alone; and he doesn't have to feel as though everything will fall apart if he is not in top form.

It is also important that each have genuine respect for the other's ability and know-how—that cannot be faked or the lack of it hidden. If such trust is there, it will be easy to allow the other to have room to go his own way at times when the partner does not understand or follow his process.

There must be an absence of competitiveness or a power struggle. Such a framework is infinitely destructive to a treatment situation and is immediately perceived by clients or trainees as an indication of instability in the relationship and therefore cause for lack of trust. It is possible for people to have trust, respect, and a free give-and-take while operating professionally, and not have it to that degree in their personal relationship. As long as there is a clear differentiation between those two areas, they can function well as a co-therapy team, but eventually their personal process must be resolved or the teamwork will begin to deteriorate. However, for such personal process to be resolved, each person must have a clear, strong internal structure of who he or she is as male or female. That makes it possible for each to continue growing, experimenting, and exploring without threatening the other. With continued work together, the intimacy level deepens and it becomes increasingly important for the individuals involved to have strong, clear boundaries and the willingness to make those boundaries, as well as their wants and limitations in the relationship, explicit. Such explicitness is predicated on a clear, secure internal structure. Without that, the deepening intimacy will trigger fears of being controlled or abandoned. For this reason, many co-therapy teams are short-lived. People work together long enough to learn from each other and get through the superficial levels, but are either not willing or not able to make the investment to go deeper.

Our experience has been that most co-therapy teams, including our own, have not continued beyond a certain point but that each person has branched out into his own exploration or into working with other co-therapists. We are not sure if that is simply the nature of the co-therapy process—to trigger individuals into greater expressions of individual creativity or if there is something about the process itself that is self-defeating.

The second major area of concern in the development of the co-therapy relationship has to do with making room for each other's differentness. In our experience, the best co-therapy relationships are those in which symmetry is equally balanced with complementarity. In other words, both therapists are equally skilled, equally strong, and equally knowledgeable; but have different ways of expressing their skills, their power, and their knowledge. For example, Marty may confront in a more vigorous, sometimes even somewhat assaultive way, whereas Shirley may be just as direct, but more subtle. It's like the difference between a solid blow between the eyes and a sharp jab. In addition, Marty will hang on much longer in trying every conceivable way to penetrate someone's defense, exhibiting superhuman patience, to Shirley's way of thinking. Shirley, on the other hand, will not push as hard against the client's resistance, preferring to acknowledge the resistance and hope that the client's anxiety will eventually push him toward change. Neither of these ways have to do with right or wrong; they have to do with the personality differences between us. We operate according to our own abilities and limitations in terms of what fits us and what we can do comfortably. The important thing is that each of us be able to acknowledge and appreciate these differences between us without having to force the other to change to make for more comfort in the relationship, or forcing ourselves to change because we feel we are less than the other.

The third major area of development has to do with negotiation. Co-therapists must have processes for working out their differentness that do not involve a loss to either of them or reflect into the treatment situation. Such processes are based on a mutual understanding that, in the context of the treatment situation, the treatment focus is more important than the co-therapy relationship itself. Therefore, whatever has to be worked out to facilitate effective treatment takes precedence over any other aspects of the relationship. If the personal relationship becomes more important than the treatment relationship and the therapists are unable to separate the two, then the clients will get used and treatment effectiveness will be destroyed.

With that basic agreement about focus, co-therapists will then begin to focus negotiation around what works with the clients rather than what is right or wrong or what fits the therapists' own value systems. The components necessary for successful negotiation then are:

1. Adequate trust in each other so that each is willing to experiment with techniques and processes unfamiliar to himself.

2. Willingness to live with disagreement and difference so that everything does not have to be understood or brought to a compromise. In other words, one therapist might go along with the other's way of operating in a particular session because it works, even though he doesn't understand it or agree with the procedure.

3. Willingness to be clear about one's own limitations—what one considers intrusive on the part of the other and the areas in which one feels inadequate—without depreciating or defending oneself.

4. Willingness to be clear about one's demands—what one wants from the other in order to function best in the therapy situation.

5. The ability to hear each other's demands and limitations without experiencing them as a personal attack or attempt to control but as honest statements about the uniqueness of each individual.

The final major area in the development of the co-therapy relationship is that of decision-making. This involves a clear understanding on the part of both therapists regarding whether they are operating as equals with equal responsibility or whether one is operating as an assistant therapist or in a trainee position. If the latter is the case, then the therapist in charge usually takes the lead and makes the decisions when there is a conflict about which therapeutic direction to take. Marty has worked successfully with many female co-therapists who were in a training framework with him. Shirley has not worked with other co-therapists, so we don't know from our experience whether therapy would work as successfully with a female in the lead or whether our cultural expectations are such that that would skew the treatment process. In a co-therapy relationship in which both therapists share equal responsibility, they may have to work out an explicit structure in the beginning, spelling out who takes the lead and who supports at different times, who makes the decision when there is a direction conflict and who takes responsibility for phone calls and follow-up in cases. In our experience with each other, we have been able to handle these issues in a relatively easy process flow based on what fit at the time, with relatively little pre-arranged structure. We think this is because our training and conceptual base were so similar from the beginning. We have had a minimum of disagreement about treatment dynamics or direction; however, that may not be the norm in most co-therapy relationships.

Therefore, considerable structuring may be necessary until therapists can evolve a more natural flow based on what evolves in the treatment process. As their views of interaction and process begin to merge, they are more likely to agree on whether the family would respond more quickly to the male or female therapist, what treatment direction the process is pointing to, and to sense each other's moods so as to know when to take over or be able to pull back.

Chapter 22

THEORY AND USE IN VARYING TREATMENT METHODS

We would like to say more here about our observations about the effect of a male-female co-therapy team in different treatment frameworks. These are, of course, subjective judgements, but they are the result of considerable experience in working with each other in a variety of treatment situations over eight years.

Individual. We touched on the effect of the co-therapy team with individual therapy a little earlier. However, we would like to add here that the co-therapy team makes it possible for the client to achieve a regressive state, sometimes instantaneously—always within a matter of three or four sessions. There is a direct parental transference which triggers early infantile conflicts. Now, we don't think that just has to do with having two therapists in the room who happen to be male and female. We think that regressive process is set off by the power of the connection between the male and female co-therapists. If they have a connection which is discrepant with the client's original parental connection in a positive sense, then the client will often open readily, almost in spite of himself.

We think the power of the co-therapy team is generated by their ability to develop a process between them that allows each of them to express his uniqueness totally in the treatment situation, and also cooperate in terms of sharing with each other and supporting the client. Such a connection, in order to generate this kind of power, must be fed with communication in order to clear out the unfinished business of any hurts or resentments and to provide nourishment in the form of checking in with each other to make sure we're in contact.

The co-therapy team provides a particular type of grounding for the client who experiences himself as out of control or in an infantile place. The grounding is the result of the combination of the strong individual uniqueness of each therapist plus the enhancing process between them. That combination projects a meta-message of solidity that we haven't found in any other combination or treatment modality.

As we have already mentioned, the co-therapy team provides the client with the opportunity for simultaneous reintegration, as he has support, affirmation of his maleness or femaleness, and validation of his assertions from both male and female.

The team approach provides the individual with an opportunity for learning assertion that approximates the natural growth process. He can push one pseudo-parent away while he connects with the other and vice-versa. Thus, he is more likely to risk assertion because he is never alone.

The team provides opportunity for model identification and, with a third party always observing, the client always has assistance in differentiating himself or herself from the model, to facilitate later separation and establishment of his own internal identity.

The client develops a sense of trust based on his experience that both of these people will respond to him and to each other clearly and solidly, and they will not intrude on him even in his most helpless state. This enables him to trust them enough to begin experimenting with his own assertions. As he learns to assert and receives support and feedback about his assertions, he learns to trust himself and is then ready to begin to experiment in other arenas.

This experience gives him an experiential knowledge of a kind of intimacy that is not hurtful or intrusive to his own identity, but is enhancing, nurturing and desirable. Thus, he has a base in something other than fantasy for what he wants to look for in terms of a marriage or family.

Married Couple Groups. The co-therapists are models of communication as they share how they deal with each other over concrete issues like money, group process, and responsibility in terms of time and commitment to the group.

They are models for how to handle differences, so that there is room for each of them to be totally unique without the other feeling depreciated, threatened, or competitive.

The power connection that we discussed earlier is vital in that many people get a sense on a meta-message basis for the first time what a connection between two whole, separate people is like. Many have never experienced such a connection with each other, between their parents or with any other couple they have known well. Experiencing it with the therapists, even though they may not be able to put words to it, takes the idea out of fantasy land and makes it a reality—therefore possible to achieve.

The group members get continuous male and female perceptions to events that occur in the group. This makes it difficult for a client to absolve himself from responsibility with the ruse, "You see things that way because you're a man (or a woman)."

The team provides the group with models for identification and assertion of feelings. Both male and female express sadness, anger, power, limitations, demands, warmth, and tenderness. Each has his unique way of expression, but each has avenues for all these parts of himself.

Couples. In addition to all of the aspects above that also apply to work with couples, the team opens up the dimension of sharing when working with another couple. The male therapist can share with the husband some of his experiences in growing up and learning to be a man. He can share with the wife how he responds to her—what turns him off and what he likes. The husband and wife can share with him in the same way. The wife can risk confronting him and as she works something out with him, she can then transfer that process to her husband. The female therapist can let the husband know how she responds to him as a female so that he can compare this with what he hears from his wife. She can confront the wife with her subtle seductive maneuvers that the male therapist might easily miss, and she can at the same time support the wife's more direct assertions both with her husband and the male therapist.

Thus, the team places the couple in a positive double-bind. They get confronted if they manipulate and praised if they assert. Either way they learn something, and the process is usually discrepant in a positive way with the origin family systems in which they each grew up.

Again, the team provides a transference base, an interactive base, and a sibling base. Sometimes people project onto siblings what really belongs to the parent—the process is once-removed. With a team, the projection gets back to the parental core since the client can be confronted with the discrepancy that he is seeing them as siblings, but behaving toward them as though they were in authority.

The therapists themselves feel free to go deeper into the feeling process because each knows the other will catch him if he is in error or misses something.

Families. Again, the aspects are much the same as we've already discussed. In addition to the above, a team is very helpful with a family because one therapist can take care of the children while the other is deeply involved with one or both parents. We have had many sessions in which one of us was working with one of the parents around some deep or explosive feelings, and the process was a little frightening to the children. The other therapist would then explain to the children quietly what was happening, or he might touch or sit next to them. With very young children, either of us might ask the child to sit on his lap while the parent was working, as physical contact with the therapist is often very reassuring to children. We're always careful to ask their permission because it is important not to take liberties and risk intrusion.

The co-therapy team can be a tremendous support to family health in that the children get to see how others respond to their parents' processes. Suddenly, things they had wondered about get brought out into the open and validated. For example, a child may have been aware that he tuned out when father talked, and felt guilty about it. When the therapist comments that he does the same thing and offers this observation to father as something that could be helpful for him to know, the child is suddenly freed. Not only is his perception shared, which means he isn't crazy or bad, but it is presented as positive and not hurtful.

In addition, the children have two more models because they see the ways of responding to intimate feelings that the therapists have that are different from each other and different from the parents in the family.

Individual Groups. The same comments that apply in married couple groups apply here. In addition, it has been our experience that without a co-therapy team, the group will reach a place in treatment where there is a learning gap for those people in the group who are the opposite sex of the therapist. Usually, then one group member takes over the role of co-therapist which we have found can work all right in the group but is detrimental to that individual's learning. It is like the child in the family who cuts into her learning in order to be a substitute mother for the other children. She gains something in experience, but experience she can always get—another childhood she cannot get.

PART V

TRAINING OF FAMILY THERAPISTS

Chapter 23

WHO CAN DO FAMILY THERAPY?

In our experience, not everyone likes to do family therapy; some are not qualified to do family therapy, and others find that the active use of self required by the method does not fit their personalities. We have found that people who come into our training courses in family therapy at the Institute begin to make major personal life changes during the course of their training. This has occurred with such repetition that we have realized that they are not just learning a method of therapy, but they are espousing a major life style.

The family therapy method requires that the therapist use himself actively and aggressively. It is not like individual therapy in which the therapist can often just be non-directive and supportive. In family therapy, if the family system operating in front of you is destructive, the lack of intervention by the therapist is immediately construed as supportive of the destructive system, and the family will leave treatment pronto. It is impossible for the therapist to maintain a distant, god-expert pose and do family therapy successfully. He must be willing to constantly risk himself in exposing his feelings and in trusting his internal perceptions when his head is not clear about where the therapy is going. For example, a therapist may, after a few sessions with a family, find he dreads seeing them and does not want to work with them. It is not uncommon for therapists to occasionally feel this way about some client or family with whom they are working. However, what often happens is that the therapist feels guilty about this and tries to work even harder, or he coasts and lets the family get the message by osmosis that his heart isn't in his work, or he manages to refer them to someone else.

The reality is the therapist's reaction to the family may be very important diagnostically and very useful in terms of the treatment itself. The therapist has to be willing to risk exposing his feelings to the clients without knowing what the feeling really means and how the family will react. That means trusting the process he is teaching— that feelings are not destructive, but can always be used for growth because their expression insures an open system. Therefore, the therapist tells the family, "I don't understand the reasons, but I don't feel comfortable working with you. It's an effort to drag myself to a session. I don't know if that's because we just don't fit and I'm not the best person to help you, or if it's indicative of some problem on my part that I'm not aware of, or if I'm picking up something from you. That's why I'm opening this up because I thought we could explore it together and see what is going on." Family members then begin to admit that they have felt annoyed with he therapist and begin to share with him what they don't like about him. In the process, they own the fact that they frequently behave in this way with each other—they don't like something, but rather than say so, they will drag their heels and go through the motions, but not really share with each other. They admit that is what they have been doing in therapy and the therapist realizes that that was part of the message he had been getting—that they were his problem and he was supposed to do something to make them well. As the annoyance got expressed, the therapist began to feel better with the family and indicated he would like to continue to work with them but with a clearer contract regarding what their mutual responsibilities were in the treatment situation.

We think there are several major areas to consider in determining an individual's qualifications as a potential family therapist.

CONTRACT FOR PERSONAL GROWTH

The individual must be committed to his own personal growth and willing to keep himself open to his own emotional blocks in the treatment and training process. This means that if he encounters a block in himself in working with a particular family, he is willing to look at that block within the context of the training situation. For example, he may be treating a family under the observation of other members of the class. In discussing the interview later, the other trainees indicate that he seemed to have difficulty confronting the father in the family, appeared very protective of him, and worked more extensively with the mother and children. The therapist was not aware of this, so we had class members simulate the family and asked him to begin to deal with the father in this make-believe imitation of the actual family he had been seeing. As he worked in the simulated situation, he became aware that he was finding it difficult to confront the father in the simulated family with the discrepancies in his communication. We asked him to close his eyes at that point and get in touch with what he was feeling. He indicated he experienced an image of his own father who was a very hard-working man who literally killed himself for his family. As he described this image, he began to cry. We then asked him to talk to his father and tell him how he felt. As he did this, it became evident how much he had protected his father from his own needs as a child in order not to burden him. He saw that he was conflicted by his sympathy for his father's pain and his own anger and hurt at not being able to share his feelings with his father. The therapist then saw that he was still protecting his own father by not confronting the father in his treatment situation, based on the same distortion—that his feelings were burdensome and potentially hurtful. When he saw this, he then had the basis for pursuing his own exploration of this block in his own personal therapy.

It is not our intent to make a full-fledged therapy operation out of our classes, but we do deal with any emotional block insofar as it relates to the treatment situation, at least to the extent that the trainee is aware of it and then he is in charge of what he does about it. If the individual's emotional block is so great that it pervasively prevents him from separating himself from the family system with which he is working, we would suggest to him that he discontinue training until he had therapy to get him past that block.

If an individual is unwilling to consider the feedback of the group and to explore emotional blocks that appear in the course of training, then we feel he is not a candidate for continued training or for family therapy. Individuals who are closed in this way do not have success in working with families.

PERSONALITY OF THE THERAPIST

We have found that the people who like doing family therapy and continue with it are those who are more outgoing, aggressive, and extroverted. That is not to say that more introspective types can't do family therapy. It's just that the majority of those people we know who have continued to use and develop the method are the outgoing ones. Many people use the family therapy training and experience more for their own personal development than as a professional tool. We don't think this is a conscious decision, but it seems to work out that way.

We think part of the reason for this is that family therapy can be an exhausting technique for the therapist if it doesn't fit his natural way of operating. It requires more constant activity and intervention from the therapist than any other form of therapy we know. It is the most difficult form of therapy that we know because of the simultaneous levels of operation which we discussed earlier in the book. Please don't confuse "most difficult" with "best". We don't think family therapy is better than any other form of therapy; it is just different and thus has its own unique properties.

THERAPIST'S COMMITMENT TO CHANGE AND EXCITEMENT

The family therapy method does not allow the therapist to proceed in an orderly fashion from A to Z with a slowly evolving treatment plan. The therapist must be prepared to shift gears instantly, perhaps many times in the course of a session. If he likes excitement and change and gets bored easily with more traditional forms of treatment, he will probably do well as a family therapist.

The therapist must be committed to the growth model as a treatment goal as well as his own personal goal if he is to do process family therapy. He must have an understanding and acceptance of the individual's natural rhythm and flow so that he can develop that flow between himself and the family as a way of teaching them how to shift from outcome orientation to the movement of process.

There are therapists who work in a behavioristic fashion around a specific goal for the family such as a job for father, a B average for the son, or the discontinuance of temper tantrums in the youngest daughter. We see that as a behavioristic treatment framework in which the whole family takes part. Also, there are therapists who do individual or marital therapy within the framework of the entire family present. Again, to us that is not family therapy as we are describing it. To us, family therapy is always the treatment of the system as a dynamic, flowing unit with the desired outcome of opening the system so that growth can occur unblocked.

LACK OF STABLE STRUCTURE

Because the therapist is treating a dynamic system always in a state of flux, the structure of therapy is not as stable and predictable as individual therapy, for example. In individual therapy, it is often possible to relax and coast periodically, letting the client do all the work. We know of very few family therapy sessions where it was possible to coast for five minutes without missing something or triggering a reaction on the part of the family.

In addition, although the therapist may have a treatment direction in mind, the direction may shift constantly and the whole treatment plan must be revamped regularly. For this reason, even the physical structure of the therapy sessions is unstable. In individual therapy, the therapist can schedule an hour weekly for a client and expect that he'll be there regularly, with very few exceptions, for six months or a year. In family therapy, that type of regularity is not possible—there are just too many variables. The potential for emergencies, crises, and time shifts because of other factors goes up in geometric ratio. In addition, the nature of the therapy is such that the treatment may shift to other individuals or dyadic units in the family with fewer family sessions and more sessions of other kinds. Also, because each family's growth rhythm is different, some families do better every two weeks or every week for a while and then once a month. We have found it is important for the therapist to have some flexibility in his schedule to allow for such necessary variations in order to treat families most effectively.

Because of the external instabilities in the process and the physical structure of the sessions, it is vital that the therapist have a strong internal structure in order to survive and feel comfortable with this method. Very often he has nothing to guide him except what he feels is fitting, inside of himself. He has to trust his internal experience to determine how often the family needs to be seen, when it is time for a change in the treatment schedule, and whether the family emergencies are real or a manipulation. In working with families, there just are more shifts in time arrangements and more cancellations. Frequently, in the course of treatment, sessions are just not effective unless the whole family is there, so the therapist may cancel the session when one person, who is key to the process, cannot come. Other times he may decide to see whoever is available—again, his choice depends on his internal perception of what the absence means in terms of the family's ongoing growth process.

Some therapists have difficulty living with that kind of uncertainty in their schedules, so they find families very frustrating groups with which to work.

We feel it is important for therapists to accept that they do not enjoy every kind of therapy and should not push themselves to work in a modality that does not fit them. Therefore, we would like to see therapists try family therapy, and learn what they can from it, but also to be able to give it up if they don't enjoy it. In other words, we do not feel that family therapy is any proving ground and that the best therapists can do it. Some therapists do family therapy well and are not so good at other forms of therapy.

We also feel that every therapist cannot work successfully with every family. Sometimes you just don't like a family. There are no blocks, nothing is really wrong with the therapist or the family— they just don't fit well with each other. When people call the Institute for a referral, we always tell them that in addition to checking the therapist's credentials, they also need to take into consideration whether or not they like the therapist. If they don't, we suggest they shop around until they find someone with whom they feel a positive connection.

Chapter 24

THE TEACHING PROGRAM
AT THE FAMILY THERAPY
INSTITUTE OF MARIN

We handle our training program on a process, growth model base—just as we do our therapy. In our experience, the most effective teaching is accomplished when the instructors follow the flow between didactic material, clinical example, experience, and the personal process of the group and of individuals within the group.

For example, we may begin a training session with a lecture on the interactional framework such as outlined earlier in this book. Sometimes trainees rebel a little at the didactic material because most of them got so much intellectual material in their graduate work and also because the process part of family therapy is more dramatic and interesting. However, we feel the conceptual base is vital so we insist on at least laying the basic framework. We will then have a family come in for a treatment session and ask the trainees to use the lecture ideas as their base for observation of the family. We may ask some members of the class to observe the homeostasis of the family, others to look at the coalitions, and specify other observers for the communication patterns, non-verbal behavior, and rules. Then we can discuss the family session later, based on these specific concepts. Without some format which ties the didactic and clinical material together, trainees will get lost in criticising the therapists or expostulating about possible diagnostic implications. It takes considerable effort in the beginning to wean people away from the individual psychoanalytic way of looking to observation from a systems framework.

Also, we have found that the most effective way to educate is to provide people with live data. If they have the clinical example in front of them, the concepts come alive quickly; otherwise, these concepts remain intellectual insights and leave the trainee with a gap between knowing and doing.

Very often, the treatment interview, or the discussion of the treatment interview, will trigger an emotional reaction of the part of one of the class members. Both of us try to keep an eye open in the class, just as we do in a therapy session, for non-verbal behavior or expression that will clue us in on such a reaction when the individual does not immediately make it explicit. If such a reaction does occur, we will deal with the person's feelings right at that point. The theory is that as long as feeling is building anywhere in the group, it will eventually get in the way of the learning process for everyone if not expressed and handled. Trying to push ideas, concepts, and techniques through a layer of heavy feeling is like trying to swim upstream. This process must often be made explicit to all the class as some people feel they aren't learning unless they can take notes. Again, we feel this idea is a carry-over from most graduate school training, where feelings were ignored and the emphasis was on performance and intellectual knowledge. We don't mean to downgrade either of these aspects of learning; we just want to emphasize that learning is often sabotaged when these are the only areas considered, especially to the exclusion of the feeling process.

In another instance, we may be lecturing and one or both of us will begin to feel that the group is not with us—that something is getting in the way. We may stop to explore that possibility and find that many people are feeling overwhelmed with all the material and the newness of the ideas. We then stop to give everyone a chance to ventilate how he or she is experiencing what we are doing—whether we need to slow down, offer more examples, or simply reassure people that it is natural to feel overwhelmed because family therapy is a complex method to learn. After everyone has had a chance to ventilate, we may shift to another form of learning like a simulated family or viewing a video tape. In this way, we give people a chance to assimilate at their own speed rather than having to force themselves into a rote performance. We believe that every group has a rhythm of its own and if we can discern and follow that rhythm, we stand a better chance of getting maximum mileage out of the learning situation.

Sometimes class members will have difficulty grasping certain concepts even with the clinical data. Then, we may have individuals simulate their own original families as a way of experiencing the system concept—what it is like to be locked into a framework with certain set rules and closed areas. We may change the rule structure and have people experiment with different types of family structures. We can then relate the experiential data back into our original lecture on interaction.

The nature of our teaching situation is determined by which of these areas (didactic, feeling process, clinical data) appears salient at any particular point in time. Therefore, while we have a basic amount of material we want to cover in each course, the way we do it is never the same because we constantly fit the material to the group's natural rhythm and flow. We also let people know that this learning situation is unique in that they will not feel complete or finished at the end of the course. Each course is a beginning, and additional learning and integration continues to take place long after they have left the training situation.

Therefore, we ask people to look at the teaching situation on the same basis as they look at process therapy—the proof of the pudding is whether or not they feel they are moving and growing, not whether they have everything all wrapped up and completed.

DESCRIPTION OF THE TRAINING PROGRAM AT THE FAMILY THERAPY INSTITUTE OF MARIN

Our training is divided into three courses, as follows.

The beginning course is called Family Diagnosis. It is devoted to diagnostic methods by which one may systematically recognize, identify, and sort out various patterns of disturbed, intra-familial interaction. There is the opportunity to observe a variety of therapists in the treatment of several types of families through live and simulated family sessions as well as taped family and married couple group sessions. Emphasis is on the analysis of communication, interactional assessment, family diagnostic methods, and analysis of the survival concept as it relates to the symptom and treatment goals.

Because this course is an assessment course to teach people new ways of looking at families, and is not a treatment course, we do not require specific training in therapy for trainees. All that we require is that they be working in a setting in which counseling or therapy is part of the job. On the other hand, many of the people in the course may have extensive therapy training and experience. The course is equally important for them, however, because we are teaching a whole new way of looking in terms of process therapy and the growth model. This course lays the foundation for further training in the treatment aspects of family therapy and for the individual's own personal growth experience.

The Family Diagnosis course runs for five weeks, five hours per week. We have found this is the best arrangement for teaching the course because it allows people adequate time for integration of the material and the experience from week to week. We cover a great deal of conceptual material, and in addition, the concepts of process and growth model learning are usually new and have great impact on people. We do teach the course on a one-week basis in the summer in which the course runs for five straight days, five hours a day. We feel this is a difficult feat for people—to handle the impact of their course in such a short time—but most would not be able to take it any other way since they are not living in the area or cannot get away from work, so must use vacation time.

In this course, we discuss the growth model, define the interactional framework and process therapy, and describe fundamental communication analysis. We have at least three actual family sessions with Marty and Shirley interviewing the families. Now, we usually sit on the floor with the family in the center of the room and have the class members gather closely around us to observe. We used to interview the families in a separate room with the class viewing from behind a one-way vision mirror. However, we found that the families liked to be able to meet and talk with whoever is viewing them, and occasionally want the feedback of the group after the therapy session.

We also have audio tapes of interviews by Virginia Satir, Don Jackson, and Frederick Perls. We feel it helps people to be able to see the different styles of many different therapists to give them a better base for developing their own styles. If they only heard us, it might be too tempting just to imitate.

We make a contract with class members in the beginning of the course that we require a willingness on the part of each of them to explore his own personal process if it is necessary in order to facilitate his or the group's learning. We learned to do this from painful experiences with people who really blocked the movement of the whole group by their refusal to deal openly with processes that were permeating the atmosphere and controlling everyone else. True, there may be some learning from the group's finally having to confront that person and deal with him, but we feel that is too time-consuming a process for this kind of a training situation. Therefore, we make it known early that a contract for exploration is basic to enrolment in the course.

Our focus in this course is on getting people to understand the concept of systems, to develop a beginning understanding of the growth model, and to learn how to observe accurately without analyzing or interpreting. We feel they have learned a great deal if they integrated those three aspects.

The intermediate course is called Family Conjoint Therapy, Theory, Observations, and Techniques.

This is a treatment course open to psychiatrists, social workers, and psychologists who have taken the Family Diagnosis course. We also take some people from other disciplines if they have had didactic and clinical training roughly equivalent to those people who have degrees in the psychiatric field. We consider ourselves a post-graduate training center, and do not have the facilities or the desire to train therapists from the ground up. We teach family therapy, and we have found that we must require people to have a fairly sound base in individual therapy in order for our training to be most effective. Then they have a base for knowing what to do when they get through the interactional blocks of the system and into individual pathology. Adequate training in individual therapy also gives therapists a strong internal structure for assessing the strengths and weaknesses of individual family members. Thus, we have some assurance that they have experienced clinical judgement and will not push people too far or be too afraid to confront them.

There is additional didactic material in this course including a discussion of the basic interactional unit, the therapist's use of himself, and intervention techniques.

Marty and Shirley see two families in ongoing treatment during the extent of this course. This means twelve sessions as the course meets once a week for twelve weeks, five hours per day. Periodically, other members of the course will see families for intake sessions or someone will bring in a family he is treating in his own practice for consultation about his work. The clinical material is used as the basis for learning. In the beginning of the course, the emphasis is on teaching the trainees to observe and diagnose from an interactional base. As they get familiar with the interactional framework, the emphasis shifts to actual treatment experience. We will frequently have the class break up into smaller groups after the family session and take turns simulating family members and acting as therapist with the feedback and consultation of others in the group as well as that of Marty and Shirley.

Again, there is a process orientation to the course, so that feelings are dealt with as they emerge in the interplay between the teachers, the therapy sessions, and the conceptual material. We may: work with group process; do a limited amount of individual therapy to enable the individual to ventilate and determine the direction he wants to go for further work; have the individual simulate his origin family from among the group members and play himself at the age he experienced his block; or open up our own feelings or difficulties between us if they are getting in the way of the group process.

The major focus of this course has to do with solidifying the individual's understanding of the interactional framework, developing his concept of the use of himself, and establishing a beginning understanding in the therapist about how to intervene to facilitate an open system.

The intensive course in family therapy is called Conjoint Family Treatment. It is open to nine people who have completed the first two courses and whom we select as most eligible for intensive training. Each trainee is involved in the treatment of a family for fifteen sessions under the direct supervision of the instructors. This course runs for seventeen weeks, meets one day a week for eight hours.

We have a unique audio-visual system which we feel permits instant integration of training during the treatment sessions. The therapist wears an ear phone and Marty and Shirley can talk to the therapist while he is working to give him direction and feedback about the family's process. The instructor is observing from behind a one-way vision mirror, so that he can talk to the therapist without the family hearing him. The family knows it is being observed and that the instructor is periodically giving feedback to the therapist who is working with them. This process has an extra bonus, we feel, in that it forces the therapist to deal with issues about taking help and still being in charge of himself, as well as learning how to be comfortable going his own way when it doesn't fit with what his instructor is saying to him over the earphone.

We also video-tape every third session, so that the therapist can play back the tape to look at himself and see his errors as well as his positive moves.

Because of the intensity of this course with the wealth of treatment material, we are able to theorize about the growth model and the lethal processes we see operating in all the families being viewed. In addition, the major focus of this course is on an understanding of the integrative structure and how to build it in the individual, couple, and family.

Again, we use the clinical material to facilitate exploration of personal process. Because therapists see their families for fifteen sessions, the depth of the therapy extends our awareness of individual blocks and the process of exploring those blocks becomes a major part of the last half of the course.

We feel these three courses give an individual a solid base in family therapy, but that most people need at least two more years with good consultation in order to feel really comfortable with the simultaneous levels of operation in family therapy.

PART VI

ON-GOING DEVELOPMENT
AND NURTURANCE OF
THE FAMILY THERAPIST

Chapter 25

AWARENESS OF SELF

We have never previously seen anything written about the stress factor involved in doing therapy. For that matter, the subject is seldom discussed among professional therapists. It is as though we assume we should be able to handle other people's pain and problems without any cost to ourselves, or at least any admitted cost.

In our experience, most therapists are rescuers—we come from families in which we took care of the pain of other family members either by being the identified patient in the family and drawing attention away from the pain of others, or by being responsible child-adults who accepted adult roles in the family at an early age. We usually took care of our own feelings as children and became super-givers as a way of not having to deal with our own deprivation and/or pain. Patients then become extensions of ourselves whom we take care of as we would like to be cared for, or they provide us with a focus outside of ourselves to protect us from having to deal with our own anxiety.

The irony is that for the therapist to grow professionally and learn how to be most effective, he has to give up the rescue operation—which was the motivation that got him into the field in the first place. We think that many people unconsciously move into studying family therapy because on a deeper level, they are ready to take a look at that rescue phenomenon, and family therapy certainly does bring that operation into bas relief more clearly than any other form of therapy. The therapist's rescue patterns become very obvious in the more direct and active use of himself that is required in family therapy. In addition, the destructiveness of those patterns to himself and to the family become equally obvious. He can no longer delude himself that he is helping other people by his sacrifice of himself. Family therapy is successful only if the therapist trusts his own limitations, wants, likes, and dislikes. If he tries to operate according to some image of a nice guy who is always kind, considerate, giving, never gets annoyed, and is infinitely patient; he is in trouble if that image doesn't fit his insides. The minute a therapist steps out from behind his facade of the distant, objective observer, he trips over his rescue operation repeatedly.

Therefore, by placing himself in a framework to learn family therapy, the therapist is often putting himself in a positive double-bind. He ends up either having to give up his rescue operation in order to do family therapy successfully, or to face that operation more fully than he has ever owned it before and recognize he is not ready to give it up. Either way he goes, it is a growth step for him.

We think that for the profession to survive, the rescue aspect of therapy has to go. That process infantalizes the client because it puts the therapist in a control position. He is like the calm, cool, collected parent who is patting his teenager on the head when the young person is having a temper tantrum. He reinforces a pattern of rage and dependency on the part of the client by virtue of his superhuman facade. We think that the therapist has to promote growth in others by doing what he teaches—presenting his thoughts, feelings, and behavior in a clear, spontaneous manner congruent with his internal process. He is teaching processes for each person to learn and use to express his own uniqueness, not an image of perfection for someone to strive for and imitate.

In addition, the rescue operation is a death trip for the therapist. It is no accident that suicide is disproportionately high among the psychiatric professions. The rescuer becomes increasingly isolated and because he has to maintain his image of perfect control, he can't go to anyone for help with his pain or express his need to be taken care of at times.

To give up the rescue operation, the therapist must accept that the client is really responsible for himself at all times. The minute he steps over that fine line and takes responsibility for someone else's behavior, happiness, or reason for living, he is in trouble and so is his patient.

Fritz Perls dealt with this issue more clearly than anyone in his gestalt therapy. For that reason, we think gestalt theory and therapy have revolutionized the field. We think that gestalt therapy and family therapy have each made a major contribution to the field by laying the base for the movement of the profession into preventive education rather than just emergency problem-solving which is pathologically oriented. Gestalt has contributed the idea of the individual taking full responsibility for the world he creates; family therapy has given impetus to bringing therapy out from behind closed doors, so we could all be exposed and learn from that exposure. The seemingly simple act of allowing an audience to view a therapy session and letting yourself be criticized automatically destroys the god-image. We exchange the destructive process that says we must know everything to be an expert and be effective for the growth process which says we can afford to make errors and learn from our errors without a loss to ourselves.

Even when the therapist is not operating out of a rescue framework, there is still a particular kind of stress associated with the therapy situation that needs to be appreciated.

The therapist allows himself to be open in order to make maximum use of his subjective resources such as imagery, fantasy, and physical sensation. However, then he is also open to the client's pain and his toxicity. Sometimes rage and pain have been festering so long in an individual that he is like an emotional sewer. We have seen people throw up what looked like green bile in the midst of therapy sessions. In the book *Psychic Discoveries Behind the Iron Curtain*, the authors mention photographing toxic auras from people who could kill plants by laying hands on them. We know some therapists who, after a particularly heavy session with a client, will run around the block or even take a shower as a way of getting rid of toxicity they feel they have absorbed. Other therapists experience themselves as drained even though they may have felt fresh prior to the session.

Whatever the scientific explanation, we think that everyone in the field knows that to hold your ground and stay with someone who is expressing intense pain or pent-up rage and hurt takes something out of you. Therefore, it becomes very important for the therapist to learn how to take care of himself.

One of the most important ways of caring for oneself is to try to establish a therapy schedule based on one's own rhythm. For example, we prefer to work long hours three days a week and have four days off. Some people like fifteen minutes between sessions. Others may prefer to work only mornings or only afternoons doing therapy and plan other activities during the rest of the day. We understand it may be difficult in agency or clinic settings to arrange that kind of flexibility. However, if professionals at least recognize the need to take care of themselves in terms of the realities of what they do, that would at least be a first step toward a solution. Otherwise, what happens is that therapists do therapy for a few years and then move into administration or teaching or some other activity. Therefore, we lose many good therapists not necessarily because they prefer to do those other things, but because they cannot maintain the therapy grind as it is now established in many settings.

Another area of concern is the stimulation of the therapist's intimacy needs. When the therapist is working with a couple in marital or family therapy and that couple has gone beyond the problem area and is developing a growing intimacy; the therapist is confronted with problems of his own in that area. He may be in a marriage in which he feels he does not have the kind of give and take he really wants. Or, he may not be connected to anyone and thus is confronted with his own yearnings.

Therefore, many times, we have had therapists in our courses take a searching look at their marriages for the first time, within the context of the training program. The point is that process—growth model therapy—will force the practitioner to unmask his own deficiencies in the areas of growth and intimacy. If he is not ready to do this, then he had best stick to some other type of therapy or aspect of his field.

To us, there is much greater satisfaction and less strain in working with people in the building and integration of a relationship. It is a pleasure to experience their awakening to a new way of relating and the warmth that generates from a loving connection. However, we have also been painfully aware at times of the longing, memories, and dissatisfactions that that experience has aroused in us. Again, we need not expect that we should be happy just because the clients are happy. We need to be appreciative of our limitations at different points in time and not live with the illusion that we can ever help someone else by hurting ourselves. There is a line in a book, *Seth Speaks*, in which Seth says, "The only reason for suffering is to teach us how to live without suffering." And someone else has said, "God save us from the people who would save us." In other words, we are growing and changing constantly. So, we need to be cognizant that our abilities and limitations change according to what is going on in our lives, separate from our professional skills and knowledge. We need to be clear about those limitations with ourselves and with our clients, so that we don't over-extend ourselves when it doesn't fit us to do so. And we need to be able to do that without guilt or apology. The greatest gift we can give our clients is our own humanity.

The ultimate move in the destruction of the rescue operation is for the therapist to determine what he does based on what is fitting for him and what he can give without hurting himself, rather than on how great the client's need is or how upset he gets. The rescuer responds to the plea of helplessness even if he has to get up out of a sick bed to do it. The individual who operates on the principle that he is helpful by being who he is rather than by doing, will determine his giving and his withholding based on what is fitting for him and not on the type of plea or the strength of the plea. Thus, he is doing what he is teaching. His message is, "I can only be what I am. I will give whatever I can as long as I don't have to hurt myself to do it. If I have to hurt myself to please you, then you and I don't fit and what I have to give isn't sufficient for you or is different from what you want or need." That message frees the other from guilt, gives him a clear choice and prevents the build-up of resentment and unhealthy dependency. The therapist is defining himself—his boundaries, abilities, and limitations—in a clear way and operating out of that framework. As he holds to that, he will force the client to do the same because he cannot be manipulated, seduced into a power struggle, or intimidated from that place.

As we have already mentioned, there is a trigger mechanism in family therapy that forces growth on the part of the therapist. We'd like to reiterate here the factors we see in that.

The need to use oneself spontaneously, directly and actively in the therapy sessions makes evident conflicts on the part of the therapist that were previously concealed by the defense of the therapeutic objectivity and distance.

The power of the family system is such that it triggers familial blocks on the part of the therapist that may never have been touched by any personal individual therapy he has had.

The process of dealing with intimacy on a building, integrational level opens up the therapist's own conflicts and needs in this area.

The requirement in family therapy training that the therapist be under observation in his work by his peers as well as instructors makes it impossible for him to conceal personal blocks behind closed doors and elaborate diagnostic reports.

The concept of the growth model is revolutionary in that it shifts the focus away from pathology and onto the flow between members of the family and between the family and the therapist—a very exciting and seductive idea to many whose life style has been built around handling pain rather than joy.

Chapter 26

EVOLUTION OF THE THERAPIST

As a therapist learns and grows, he will find that he works better with certain types of clients or particular therapy methods at varying points in his career. For example, a therapist may in the beginning prefer doing individual therapy because he can set his own pace and gradually solidify his understanding of individual dynamics and treatment process. He may then begin to get a little bored and see couples because there is a little more action and he has an opportunity to to learn about interaction. As he works with couples and individuals, he begins to realize that there are some people who don't respond to either of these methods of treatment, so he moves into a study of family therapy.

In working with families, he finds he does better with the repressive type of family because they move more slowly and require a great deal of structuring in the therapy process which is easy for him to do. They move slowly into process. As he begins to get comfortable with family process and interaction, he may begin to get a little bored again, so he starts working with family types that are difficult for him, like delinquent families or uproar families. He may work extensively with families for a couple of years and then find that either because of his own growth, or because of new ideas the family work has triggered, he is now interested in working with individuals around primal processes in which the focus is on pre-verbal pain blocks. As he integrates this learning into his internal personal-professional structure, he may find himself moving back into working with marital pairs from a deeper level of integration.

We feel that the various ways of working and the various types of clients with which a therapist works enable him to build an internal, integrated structure about how growth takes place. He then uses this structure as his model to help him recognize and deal with destructive processes more clearly and quickly, and as a model to enable people to build their own internal structures to permit positive growth to take place. In other words, the therapist himself is not a model of how others should be, but his internal structure, which is an integration of positive growth processes, can be a model which he can pass on. The client can incorporate that model, with perhaps slight modifications, and use it to express his own unique identity so that maximum growth and opportunity for intimacy can occur for him.

We have often considered that some kind of vibrational message must go out to the community, because we frequently find ourselves getting calls from people who are particularly suited to where we are in our current growth phase in terms of our work. Also, we have noticed in our intensive course in family therapy that trainees seem to get families whose process tends to point up the trainee's greatest area of concern in his professional development. We don't know what magic is operating here or if there is a simpler explanation; however, whatever is occurring, the process works out very nicely.

We think the important thing is for therapists to be aware that they are not static. Each person is in the dynamic flux of his own evolution and needs to be aware of the changes he is experiencing so that he can relate each change to his past experience and his future direction. In that way, he builds a very solid professional as well as personal structure. It is important not to make judgements about oneself because you suddenly find you don't work as well with a certain method or type of client as you used to. It is also important not to jump to conclusions that you have lost something. There is not a loss, either in ability or knowledge. It is simply a law of evolution that for something new to emerge, something else has to give way. These things are not lost; they are temporarily displaced so that energy can be focused on the new and difficult. It is often far too easy for us to stay with the familiar and easy approach professionally. However, the therapist who has begun the growth trip will find he has created a monster. He no longer has a choice about whether or not he wants to go into new and uncharted territory. Something inside of him gets hooked on the aliveness and excitement of growth as a life style and he will find that he will continue to grow whether he likes it or not. He may go kicking and screaming and dragging his heels at times, but something inside of him will not be denied.

So, the moral of our story is—join us, but approach with caution! You can't know in the beginning what it is you are really getting into!

Another evolutionary step that occurred naturally for both of us and for many of the members of our staff at the Institute was the move into teaching family therapy.

For us, the teaching offered an opportunity to clarify and develop our conceptual framework. Teaching requires an ability to integrate the theory to the clinical data which automatically forced us to think along those lines. We then put our ideas out for our trainees to consider; we learned a great deal from their feedback and we were able to use their reactions to polish and develop our conceptual base even further. The teaching program has therefore offered us a continuing opportunity to test our new ideas and theoretical concepts as well as new techniques in a way we could not do in therapy or just with each other. We develop a process between us and our trainees that is mutually stimulating and enhancing to our professional development in ways particular to the teaching program. For example, we really learned about the rescue operation and its relevance to our field from working with the personal and professional process of so many of our colleagues. Also, the classes keep us on our toes and enable us to maintain an open system because the trainees constantly observe our treatment work as well as our personal process, and are not a bit bashful about commenting on what they see.

The teaching framework also provides an arena for brainstorming. Most professionals get so tied up in actual therapy sessions, consultations and administrative responsibilities that they forget how exhilarating and nourishing those kinds of sessions can be. The teaching program is a natural arena for ideas to flourish and we periodically will take off with our students on flights of fantasy.

It has been our usual experience that when an individual finishes the intensive training course and has about two years of intensive family therapy experience with good consultation, then he feels ready to try his wings at teaching. We have trained teachers at the Institute by having them sit in again on our courses, this time to watch how we work with a view toward teaching rather than being a student. Then, Marty takes one or two teacher-trainees with him into each course and shares some of the teaching responsibility with them for that course but also acts as observer, consultant, and trainer. Then, we feel they are ready to try a course on their own. Usually, most people have had to teach a course two to three times to feel secure and totally competent and to find out whether they really like teaching. Whether an individual continues to teach or not; teaching always provides a tremendous impetus to the development of his conceptual base and expertise.

BIBLIOGRAPHY

BOOKS

Ackerman, N. W., Beatman, F. L., and Sherman, S. N. (Eds). *Exploring The Base For Family Therapy.* New York: Family Service Association, 1961.

Luthman, Shirley G. *Intimacy—The Essence of Male and Female.* Nash, 1972.

Ostrander, Sheila and Schroeder, Lynn. *Psychic Discoveries Behind the Iron Curtain.* Prentice-Hall, 1970.

Perls, Frederick S., M.D., Ph.D. *In and Out of the Garbage Pail.* Real People Press, 1969.

Perls, Frederick S., M.D., Ph.D. *Gestalt Therapy Verbatim.* Real People Press, 1969.

Perls, Frederick, S., M.D., Ph.D., Hefferline, Ralph F., Ph.D., Goodman, Paul, Ph.D., *Gestalt Therapy.* Dell Publishing Co., 1951.

Roberts, Jane. *Seth Speaks.* Prentice-Hall, 1972.

Satir, Virginia. *Conjoint Family Therapy.* Science and Behavior Books, Inc., 1964.

Weakland, John. "The Double-Bind Hypothesis of Schizophrenia and Three-Party Interaction," in *The Etiology of Schizophrenia.*

ARTICLES

Ferreira, A. J. "The 'Double-Bind' and Delinquent Behavior." *Archives of General Psychiatry.* Vol. 3, 1960.

Jackson, D. D. "Family Rules, Marital Quid Pro Quo." *Archives of General Psychiatry.* Vol. 12, June 1965.

Luthman, Shirley G., and Kirschenbaum, Martin. "Survival Patterns in Family Therapy—Myth and Reality." *Family Process,* 1967. In Press.

Bibliography

Riskin, J. "Methodology for Studying Family Interaction." *Archives of General Psychiatry.* Vol. 8, 1963.

Riskin, J. and Faunce, E. E. "An Evaluative Review of Family Interaction Research." *Family Process*, II, 4, December 1972.

CONJOINT FAMILY THERAPY by Virginia Satir

Now in its fourteenth printing, this popular classic remains an excellent introduction to family dynamics. Written in a direct, step-by-step manner, free from psychoanalytic jargon, it presents a challenging theory of family function and dysfunction in clear, readable terms. It is an enlightening book for both the professional and the layman.

$8.95

PEOPLEMAKING by Virginia Satir

The entire book is written in a lively, down-to-earth style, making it useful and readable for the layman as well as the professional. Peoplemaking is not just informative or entertaining. It fills a unique need in that it concerns itself with one of the most neglected yet integrally important parts of life—the family, its health, welfare and survival.

The points she makes about self-worth, communication as she defines it, system, and family rules are, then, the main concerns of the book. They are presented in human terms, relying on the use of simple language, anecdotes, case histories, and perhaps the most effective means of all, a series of "communication games" and other exercises that literally bring her research findings home to the reader in a real and telling way.

$7.95

Science and Behavior Books, Inc.
P. O. Box 11457
Palo Alto, California 94306